Hypnosis

How To
Put A Smile On Your Face
And
Money In Your Pocket

🐃 *The Stockwell System* 🐃

The Stockwell System offers proven and effective tools to make your mind work for you.

This complete learning encyclopedia is guaranteed to put a smile on your face and money in your pocket; in your personal life or as a professional hypnotist.

CREATIVITY UNLIMITED PRESS ®
CREATIVITY UNLIMITED®
30819 Casilina Drive
Rancho Palos Verdes, CA. 90275
(310) 541-4844

© 1998 SHELLEY LESSIN STOCKWELL
ALL RIGHTS RESERVED

ISBN 0912559-17-9
Library of Congress
Catalog Card Number 96-086133
Printed in the United States of America
All rights reserved. No portion of this book may be reproduced in any form or by any mechanical or electronic means without the written permission of the author, except by a reviewer who quotes brief passages in connection with a review for a newspaper, magazine, newsletter, or media. Foreign Rights Available.

PRINTED IN THE USA

"The one thing people are more private about than their sex life is their money. Leave it to Shelley to bring people to a financial orgasm, that is proud and loud."

                  "Dr. Judy" Kuriansky
                  Generation Sex, and
                  The Complete Idiots Guide To
                  A Healthy Relationship.

"Your mind is your greatest asset. It holds the past, experiences the present and creates the future. In this book, Shelley Lessin Stockwell, gives you the tools to heal the past, create your future in peace and prosperity and celebrate the present in harmony and joy."

                  Suzy Prudden, Life Coach,
                  97 Ways To Heal YourLife

"Thank you Shelley, this stuff works! I've doubled my income and my love life perked up too."

                  J.Tessler,
                  Hypnotherapist

"The Stockwell System has everything you need to know about hypnosis as a personal tool or as a career. Hypnosis can help you eliminate fears, quit smoking, lose weight, and find happiness and °success quickly and easily."

                  Lynn Lofthouse, C.Ht.

"Shelley Stockwell's hypnosis course transformed my life. It gave me workable tools to quickly and simply deal with limiting patterns and the gratification of helping others."

                  Beryl Middleton, N.D.

"If you quest for success this book is the best. My only complaint is that it was not sold with a highlighter; There are so many things I want to underscore to share with family, friends and clients."

                  Nica B. Lee,
                  Human Resourses Consultant

"I know but one freedom and it's the freedom of the mind."

                  Antoine De Saint Expugery,
                  The Little Prince

Books by Shelley Stockwell
Automatic Writing & Hieroscripting:
Tap Unlimited Creativity and Guidance
Channeling: You Conduit!
Denial Is Not a River in Egypt:
The Stockwell System To Bust Bazaar Behaviors
Hypnosis: How To Put A Smile On Your Face and Money In Your Pocket
Insides Out
Sex and Other Touchy Subjects
Slim and Sexy
Time Travel: Do-It-Yourself Past Life Journey Handbook

Books by Shelley Stockwell and Ormond McGill
Everything You Ever Wanted To Know About Everything
Out of Your Mind: Hypnosis and Creative Writing

Audio Tapes by Shelley Stockwell
Great Golf
Great Tennis
How My Mind Works (with McGill)
Hypnomeditation (McGill)
I Love To Exercise!
Kundalini Rising (with McGill)
Lose Weight
Master Cosmic Consciousness (with McGill)
Meet Your Angel (with Fitzsimmons)
Mer•Ka•Ba: Ascension To The Forth Dimension (with Perry)
Mommy Bunny's Going To Work
No More Alcohol
No More Sugar Junkie
Peace and Calm
Quit Smoking
Sex And Other Touchy Subjects
Sleep Beautiful Sleep (with McGill)
The Fountain Of Youth (McGill)
The Money Tape (with J. Lessin)
The Violet Flame (McGill)
The Wellness Tape (with Dr. Prado)
Time Travel
Universal Abundance (McGill)
Yes I Can!
Yoga Nidra: Hypno Yoga (McGill)

Video Tapes by Shelley Stockwell and Ormond McGill
Hypnotically Yours, Ormond McGill
Shelley Stockwell's Art Of Channeling
Trance-Formations, Hypnosis, Channeling and Past Lives

ACKNOWLEDGEMENTS

Thank you to my beloved; Jon Nicholas, my sweet brother Alex Lessin, my son Bryce and of course, Nica Lee. What would I have done without your support.

Big kisses to my dear friends, students and support team (teachers all) Barbara McNurlin, Lynn Lofthouse, Joel Gober, Lilia Prado, Elaine Young, Helen Shaw, Beryl Nozedar, Jae Webster, Judy Umansky, Pamela McHenry, Sandra Albright, Dianna Whitley, Rhonda Carpenter, Sandi Medearis, Suzy Prudden, Pamela Parton, Martha Sternberg, Nevada Prewitt, Alexis Upton Knittle, Solange Dunlop, Allison Cook, Lee Berman, Kay Risberg, Sally Wright, Liz Herschland, Scot Alpert, Katia Michelidas and all my many outstanding hypnosis clients and friends.

To my loving mind mentors, Ormond McGill, Diane Zimberoff, Irv Katz and Floyd McGuire, thank you for your support. And to my spirit guide Kendra, you are my shining one.

Thanks to myself for taking time to draw the illustrations, to Jon Nicholas for his wonderful photographs, to Laura Wagg, Bryce Stockwell and Barbara McNurlin for their graphic ideas and input.

Illustrations	Shelley Stockwell Jeff Bucchino
Cover Photo	Jon Nicholas
Cover Design	Laura Wagg Bryce Stockwell
Photography	Jon Nicholas Shelley Stockwell Bryce Stockwell Renee Parenteau Chris Gordon Liane Dyson Janus Welton Jill Searles Carole Powell Gerry Lumian
Editing	Nica Lee Alex Lessin Pamela McHenry Allison Hogan Elaine Young
Formatting by	Shelley Stockwell Nica Lee Wendy Wilsing

FOREWARD

by Ormond McGill

Hypnosis is sometimes known by the verb: CHARMING. Shelley Lessin Stockwell's book *Hypnosis: Smile On Your Face Money In Your Pocket, The Stockwell System* is definitely charming.

The study of hypnosis is a science. The practice of hypnosis an art. Shelley Stockwell's methods presents the subject from both directions *plus* personal applications for the betterment of your life. I am pleased to write the forward to her book on the subject close to my own interest.

The author of this book is a professional hypnotist, instructor, and certified hypnotherapist: Which means she devotes a considerable portion of her practice helping clients master mental disturbances and obtain more peace of mind.

Having written numerous texts related to hypnosis myself, I can truthfully say that the author of this book presents hypnosis in a wonderfully unique way for the helpful use and understanding of the reader. Some write from their head with the intellectual approach. Shelley writes from the heart by telling us how she applies self-hypnosis to her own life and then how to successfully use it in your own. She blends the objective and subjective study of hypnosis into enchanting poetry which lends universal appeal that is charismatic- for which the synonym is....CHARMING.

Dr. Ormond McGill
The Dean Of American Hypnosis

Photo by Jon Nicholas

This complete encyclopedia
is all you need to know
about your brain and using it well
to live and love and grow.

Hypnosis for happiness
hypnosis for career
hypnosis for yourself
and those whom you hold dear.

A portal to abundance
in joy, and love and wealth
peace of mind, living dreams,
success, energy and health.

Learn what hypnosis is
and how you can use it
to harness your mind and talents
any way you choose it.

A secret key opens your mind
so you stay subconsciously aware
unlock potentials, and have fun
for success beyond compare.

TABLE OF CONTENTS

Step One:

STEP UP TO ABUNDANCE

CHAPTER 1	QUESTIONS ANSWERED	1
CHAPTER 2	WHAT CAN HYPNOSIS DO FOR ME	13
CHAPTER 3	THE BRAIN	23
CHAPTER 4	THE MIND	41
CHAPTER 5	TO DEFINE IS DEVINE	63
CHAPTER 6	HYPNOSIS HISTORY	71

Step Two:

TOOL TIME

CHAPTER 7	PREPARE FOR THE JOURNEY	85
CHAPTER 8	HOW TO DO HYPNOSIS	97
CHAPTER 9	AFFIRM AND SUGGEST	117
CHAPTER 10	FEEL TERRIFIC	133
CHAPTER 11	SWEET DREAMS	161
CHAPTER 12	MAKING MONEY	173

Step Three:

HYPNOSIS IN ACTION

CHAPTER 13	LIFE ATTITUDES	199
CHAPTER 14	LIMITS & UNLIMITED SOLUTIONS	219
CHAPTER 15	RECYCLE OLD PATTERNS	243

Step Four:

THE STOCKWELL SYSTEM

CHAPTER 16	HOW TO BE A HYPNOTIST	267
CHAPTER 17	STOCKWELL HYPNOTHERAPY	285
CHAPTER 18	TRANSPERSONAL HYPNOTHERAPY	303
CHAPTER 19	STOCKWELL BREATH TECHNIQUES	333
CHAPTER 20	THE BUSINESS OF HYPNOSIS	357
CHAPTER 21	QUIT SMOKING	385
	ABOUT THE AUTHOR	406
	DEFINITION OF TERMS	407
	REFERENCES	410

hypnosis smile money hypnosis smile money

STEP ONE:

Step Up To Abundance

Give one your wisdom and they might succeed. Give one tools to tap their own wisdom and they most definitely will succeed.

So you want to be abundant! Lots of other people have created abundance, why not you? The book you hold in your hands is your portal to having it all. With it, you'll enlist the power of your conscious, subconscious and higher self to master the secrets of manifesting money, love, wellness, creativity, peace and harmony. And, if you'd like to spin a career of hypnosis into gold, this books tells you how to do that too.

You now embark on a journey that will change your mind and the course of your life. With tools you learn in this book, you'll create abundance on all levels. And, if you like, make money as a highly respected professional on the cutting edge of the most exciting career of the new millennium.

What is hypnosis? How can you use it? How does the brain work? How does your mind interplay with the brain? What are the natural laws that govern your mind? And how does one harness the power of the mind? These and many other questions will be answered in depth.

Follow each of my procedures carefully and then be creative and adapt them to your own unique style and needs. That way, you create your own approach to abundance on all levels, mentally, physically, emotionally and spiritually. Practice my methods on your family, your friends and your clients and watch their dreams come real also.

In the past, hypnosis was cloaked in mystery, Look into my eyes. You are in my power. Today it is embraced as a science. I first wrote this book for my beautiful hypnosis students: friends who are now certified professionals practicing hypnosis in their fields: hypnotherapy, nursing, social work, psychology, dentistry, medicine, teaching, body work, motivational speaking, sports, police sciences, advertising, faith healing, parenting and more.

I offer you the Stockwell System as your own magic carpet, to transport you to the sacred land of abundance, self-satisfaction and the gratification of helping others. It is gleaned from my twenty-five years as a Hypnotherapist and over fifteen thousand hours of holding the mirror for others and myself. Each step-by-step technique, is the result of observations, research, case studies and experimentation. My guides, from the part of my consciousness that goes beyond the reading, theory, brain, mind and personality, expanded my perspective.

The very essence of hypnosis is the elusive butterfly of the brain and mind where we discover unlimited potential, and startling multi-dimensionality. Human consciousness intrigues and challenges. For the mind to understand itself great dexterity is required or we can easily drift into ethereal mists. The entire arena of altered states of awareness is untracked snow and, for some, a blinding white out. Perhaps Santiago Ramon y Cajal, Psychologist, the father of brain science and winner of the Nobel Prize said it best: the mysterious butterflies of the soul, the beating of whose wings may someday clarify the secret of mental life.

So, you begin a journey of change that will enhance and exhilerate you. With tools you learn in this book, you'll create abundance on all levels. And, if you like, make money as a highly respected professional on the cutting edge of the most exciting career of the new millennium.

Now, I'm going to give you an assignment. Your assignment, if you choose to accept it, is to become happy and wealthy: abundant on all levels physically, mentally, spiritually and emotionally. As you read the following words, let their meaning sink into your brain, like earth soaks rain.

I feel so good. I am prosperous, productive, diligent and abundant. More and more opportunities for money manifest in this moment just for me. I am an open channel for money. Money flows easily to me and from me. I am comfortable with more and more money. I know exactly what I need to do to make more money, and I easily do it. I like money. Money likes me. Money comes easily. Money and I have a great relationship.

What you just read is an affirmation that, if taken in by your subconscious or deepest mind, will literally change your life. The power of suggestion is very strong for all of us. You've just taken the first step toward putting a smile on your face and money in your pocket.

There are many other steps waiting in the pages ahead. As you take each one you will come alive inside yourself and recognize your divinity, beauty, freedom, live well, love yourself and prosper.

I Embrace You,

Shelley Stockwell

Chapter 1

☺ Questions Answered

Most have lots of questions about hypnosis. Answering them clears confusion, educates and puts the conscious mind at ease. If you have more questions than these, ask yourself "What is the implied statement behind my question?" and discover how much you already know.

Can Everyone Be Hypnotized?

Yes, of course! Everyone goes in and out of trance, the basic hypnotic state, throughout the day. You, dear reader, have been in trance several times today. You just may not have called it hypnosis.

Daydreaming, runners high, before sleep, upon awakening, reading, watching TV, video game playing, a boring meeting, or a freeway drive, all naturally entrance you. Anytime you move from an outward perception to an inner awareness you enter trance. Words you use induce trance too; "wonder," "amaze," "puzzle," understand," "curious," "mesmerize," and "hypnotize," cause you to go inside to make them make sense.

Hypnosis techniques put you in charge of your natural ability to enter trance. Hypnosis is a skill, like reading or writing, that anyone can easily learn.

Who Can Do Hypnosis?

Anyone who has the mind to, and even those who don't, can and do, do hypnosis. If you can concentrate for a few moments you can easily learn the steps it takes to induce a self-hypnotic trance. You practice hypnotism every day with the things you say to yourself and others. You hypnotize yourself with repetitive actions and thoughts.

This is called autosuggestion.

Mothers and fathers are master hypnotists and their verbal and nonverbal conditioning often stick for life. Advertisers use hypnosis in all their work and so do religions.

Professional hypnotists receive special training in the technique and use of hypnosis before they achieve certification. To choose a professional hypnotist, find out what training and experience they have and if they belong to a hypnosis organization.

Professional groups, like the National Guild of Hypnotists, offer training and opportunities to keep skills updated.

Some psychotherapists may have only attended a lecture or a one day class in hypnosis and then present themselves as hypnotists. If you want psychotherapy, go to a psychotherapist. But if you want hypnosis, go to a professional hypnotist. Hypnosis is the hypnotists' main focus and training.

How Does Hypnosis Feel?

Familiar! The by-product of all hypnosis is relaxation where muscles, nerves and mind relax. Some describe it as feeling passive, placid and mellow, others as filled with light or surprised by new perception: "I saw strange pictures for the first time, felt new feelings, thought new thoughts and understood things I never could before. It's difficult to find the words to describe the hypnotic experience."

When in hypnosis there is often a distinct experience of automatic, spontaneous or involuntary thought or action as compared to the feeling you get with conscious choice. Returning to regular "room awareness" makes everything more peaceful. One friend says that after a hypnosis session, "My heart went around grinning all day."

Hypnosis is definitely a common and varied experience. Each hypnotic trance may be different from what you expect, or from the last one you experienced. This makes sense considering you are not the same person you were the last time! Your experience of trance will differ from another's.

Sometimes part of us can be hypnotized while another part is not. For instance, if you are driving a car and having an animated conversation with your passenger, the part of you driving may be unaware and hypnotized and the part of you talking, fully conscious.

Hypnosis, like sex, looks different than it feels. From the observer's point of view, the subject might appear caved in or passed out and, therefore, we might presume that the subject is unconscious. Actually, subjects are super-conscious and keenly aware of everything going on around them. This keen focus may leave the subject feeling like they aren't doing anything particularly unusual.

Why Do Some People Have Doubts About Hypnosis?

Since hypnosis looks different than it feels, it is often misunderstood. Once you feel it, the apprehension goes away.

The Media cliche "Look into my eyes you are in my power" and the stage performance "Cluck like a chicken" have sometimes misrepresented the value of hypnosis.

Unknown Quantity

Some doubt the value of hypnosis because they themselves have not experienced its benefits. And there is a tendency for the conscious mind to judge new unfamiliar ideas harshly. Once they experience hypnosis for themselves, they know how safe and rewarding it is.

Fears

Some folk's fear that hypnosis will force them to "go out of control" and then they'll reveal some buried truth that they're "not supposed to." Or that they'll lose control. Or, even worse, look foolish.

While in trance your inner wisdom is your guide and that wise part of yourself will tell you the truth. Such truth offers insight and a tremendous relief. And, you needn't worry; your subconscious mind will only reveals what you choose to reveal.

In a trance, any suggestion that violates morals or self preservation is greeted with a natural "cancel, cancel, cancel."

Shelley: A True Hypno-Tale

The first time I was hypnotized I was 21 years old. I went to see Pat Collins (the "Hip hypnotist") at the Celebrity Club in Hollywood. After watching one show I was doubtful: "Where those subjects set-ups?" I thought.

So to prove something to myself, I stayed for the second show and bounded on the stage when Ms. Collins called for volunteers.

During the show I followed her instructions so as "Not to embarrass the nice lady." After all, she was an entertainer. I noticed that every time she exclaimed "Sleep" I felt an irresistible urge to cave in on top of my neighbor and even to the floor!...But I definitely "was not hypnotized."

When the audience chose me to be suspended between two chairs (my neck on the back of one chair and my heels on the back of another); I found myself supine and staring at the ceiling stage lights for many minutes.

"Maybe I'm hypnotized," I said to myself. "Just maybe, because I don't think that I'd normally do this."

Monkey Business

Some put down hypnosis because they think hypnotists take away their business. Evangelists, faith healers and those who make their income using veiled hypnosis techniques sometimes preach against it. These folks use fearful suggestions to keep their flock in their pocket.

It's so much fun to watch a skilled "faith" healer use hypnosis techniques called "rapid inductions." The faithful (literally) fall into a deep trance and the powerful healing suggestions work wonders.

There is, of course, room in this world for all that offer nourishing and positive service to humanity yet, in several states, psychologists have initiated legislation in an attempt to eliminate competition.

A few health professionals say that hypnosis should only be practiced by medical doctors because "lay practitioners" are not qualified to make a medical diagnosis. Certainly, hypnotists are not doctors and doctors are not hypnotists. For most professional hypnotists, hypnosis is their main therapeutic method and they have spent hundreds of hours learning and practicing hypnotic techniques.

Some doctors, dentists and psychotherapists are thoroughly trained as hypnotists too. But most doctors have had little or no instruction in hypnosis and are not qualified to practice hypnosis or make hypnosis diagnosis.

Those not trained in hypnosis, regularly refer their patients to professional hypnotists. Referring doctors understand that hypnosis is complimentary to conventional medicine. They know that a patient who learns relaxation techniques while dialoguing with symptoms relieves pain, reduces stress, alleviates insomnia, changes negative patterns into positive attitudes and stimulates the body's innate ability to heal. Just what the Doctor ordered!

> Over half of all people who seek health care now go to alternative providers.
>
> According to a 1993 study published in the New England School of Medicine Journal, providers of "unconventional" therapies (non medical physicians) had an estimated 425 million patient visits in 1990. This figure exceeds the 388 million visits to primary care physicians.

Can Hypnosis Be Dangerous?

Hypnosis is no more dangerous than natural slumber. Practiced by yourself or a qualified hypnotist, hypnosis is safe, satisfying and self-empowering.

Not learning hypnosis can be dangerous. If you allow all suggestions to accidentally enter your mind during your natural trance states, you may buy things you don't want and act in ways that harm you. Advertisers use hypnosis to sell products. If you are hypnotized to smoke, for example, you could kill yourself smoking. If you are "hypnotized" by parents, teachers, mates or your own self talk to believe you are 'less then,' incompetent or a failure, that harms you too.

Self-hypnosis lets you decide which suggestions to embrace or discard. It puts you in the driver's seat of your behaviors and emotions. When you learn to choose which suggestions you receive or act upon, you take back control of your life. If you don't control your subconscious mind, it will definitely control you.

It's ironic that some folks worry that hypnosis will make them lose control, because hypnosis gives them back control.

There was a young man of the Clyde,
who went to a funeral and cried.
When asked who was dead,
he stammered and said,
"I don't know, I just came for the ride."

Do I Need Hypnosis or Hypnotherapy?

If you want to use your natural resources to your best advantage, get the most out of life, be your full potential, and have great relationships, then hypnosis is perfect for you. There's nothing to lose but tension, depression, fear, fatigue and pain. You gain relaxation, joy, peace of mind, energy and feel great.

If you have hurtful patterns, habits and behaviors or limiting beliefs, hypnosis can change them into helpful habits, peaceful patterns and beneficial beliefs. If you want to improve your golf game or up your libido, hypnosis is the ticket.

Can I Really Resolve Physical Problems With My Mind?

Many physical symptoms are psychosomatic, which means that they have an emotional basis. Come to think of it, it's not really so strange that emotional strain or worry would produce physical symptoms. After all, every organ in your body is connected with your brain by nerve channels. Crisis or conflict upsets your nervous system and therefore your body. When you learn to relax the mind/body, your central nervous system returns to homeostasis and wellness.

If I Can't Solve My Own Problems Without Help Does It mean That I Have A Weak Will?

Of course not. It is sometimes struggle to work out emotional problems yourself because you're too close to see clearly. More and more, even those with a great deal of psychological knowledge, hire someone to "hold the mirror" for them. Hypnotists help people overcome emotional symptoms, increase abundance and creativity, and better personal relationships. Hypnosis strengthens the part of you that chooses growth.

How Does Hypnotherapy Work?
Unresolved inner conflicts cause nervousness and unhappiness. Hypnotherapy helps you understand and constructively resolve these conflicts.

What Happens To The Hypnotherapist's Information About Me?
Records necessary to clarify problems and generate solutions are kept confidential by professional hypnotists. No outsider, not even your closest relative or family physician, is permitted to see your records without written permission from you.

What Happens If I Don't Come Out Of Trance?
Some worry that if they go into trance, they won't come out. Ormond McGill, the Dean of American Hypnosis, says, "Where would you go?"

You have been going in and out of trance since you were born. It is the most natural thing in the world to dream, relax, sleep and return to critical thinking. Your body naturally cycles in and out of trance. You easily terminate any trance when *you* choose.

If, when you were sleepy, you put yourself into trance, without a "come on back" suggestion, you might drift into sleep and naturally awaken as you would after any nap. If there's an important reason to return to room awareness during the trance (like someone calling your name or a baby crying), you would easily detach from trance state and attend to any business that needs attention.

It's easy to forget linear time when you relax deeply. If you have time restraints, it's a good idea to set an alarm clock before you enter trance and to give yourself a timely suggestion, "I choose to relax for half an hour." or "At 2:30 I will come back to my regular awareness."

Affirmations For A Perfect Life

present

Where I am today, is perfect. I have been on a journey arriving right here, right now, in this moment in time. I am welcome in the world. I'm part of the whole. I'm here to make a new beginning on my spiritual journey and to experience and accept joy in my life.

I'm in a perfect place for growth and change. Everything I have done in my life has brought me to this very moment. Today, I am open to be touched by love, joy, and nature. I am free to experience fully the joy of this very moment. As I breathe, my dreams come true.

It's up to me to bring out the best of myself. I have a boundless capacity for joy and pleasure. I am keenly aware of all self-talk and I quickly and easily turn any negatives into positives. I listen to the still, small, inner voice within, for I know that my senses tell me the truth. I trust my deepest inner wisdom. My inner self knows the truth about everything in my life, so I listen, hear and act from its wisdom.

social past

I remember every minute of my life. Any pain I may feel by remembering hurts less than the pain of knowing and not remembering. I accept the truth. The truth sets me free. I don't need to cover up past hurt with self-destructive thinking, behavior, food, drink, drugs, or sex.

My parents and their relationship are separate from me. I am not a reflection of my parents or children and they are not a reflection of me. I am whole and perfect in my singularity. I forgive my parents and others for any mistakes they made. They did the best they could, given the way they were.

I forgive myself fully for mistakes I made; I did the best I could and I do better and better every day. I understand that my behaviors in the past were learning experiences. Everything in my life teaches me valuable lessons. When I know what doesn't work I can choose what does work.

My life is now, at this moment in time. The past is over and is but a memory. The future is only the confirmation of what I dream or create in this moment in time. Right now is my life and I enjoy the experience of being 100% alive in this moment in time.

love

I am lovable and capable. It is easy to love me. A unique and priceless person, I love myself fully, just the way I am. I'm enough, and perfect just the way I am. I'm kind, gentle, and compassionate with myself. I grow and learn every day. Everyday I learn new ways to celebrate myself.

My honest, loving spirit draws other honest, loving spirits into my world. I am enriched every day through my loving. The more I love, the more I receive love. I deserve to be loved for myself, just as I am. I easily receive and give my loving.

I give myself permission to be myself and express myself. I express my ideas easily. I'm worthy of the respect of others. Others respect my point of view, just as I respect theirs. I am a good listener. I listen well to myself and others. People respond when I reach out. It's safe and rewarding to love others. I am my true self with others and I am loved just for being me.

I accept compliments easily. I am proud to be me. No matter what others say to me, I know, in the deepest level, that I am a worthwhile and special person. I enjoy complimenting others.

positive emotions

I breathe light into any real or imagined fears or limits I may have had in the past and they leave easily. I am filled with true serenity. I feel worthy, safe and secure.

My emotions flow freely. I learn from my emotions. My emotions are messages from within. I stand tall in my emotional magnificence, crying or laughing freely. My emotions easily flow through me and I always return to joy. My inner brightness shines

through and others are attracted to my light.
I hold myself in high esteem, I am self-confident and can easily express and assert my own ideas.

physical well being

I breathe fully and freely. I am a sensuous being, able to allow myself pleasure, fun, and spontaneity. I approve of my sensuality and sexuality and the gifts they bring me. My body pleases me. I enjoy my sensuous self.

I am healthy. My positive thoughts create my healthy body. My body is my perfect friend. I feel my body. I love my body. I am my body. I do good, kind and nourishing things for my body. I am fully in tune with my body. If my body is uncomfortable, it's communicating with me that something needs my attention. I listen to my body and I take whatever actions are necessary to bring myself back radiant wellness, natural balance and homeostasis.

I love moving my body; stretching, flowing, dynamic movement makes me look and feel terrific. I feel so glad to be alive and moving.

success

I am a growing and maturing personality, and the changes I make nurture me. I accept change easily. I easily transform any limiting behaviors, those that no longer serve me well, into ones that bring me joy and inner harmony. I approve of actions and myself. It is O.K. that I am sometimes unpredictable, after all, I'm human.

I am powerful. I enjoy taking and accepting responsibility for myself. I am responsible for own happiness and fulfillment. Life's most challenging and important task is to grow up and take responsibility for my own joy. I love being responsible for my joy. I love the joy I bring to myself. I choose to be happy.

I deserve to have whatever I want. I follow through easily and harmoniously in things I start. I live my dreams. Life is good to me. I am abundant.

Professional Hypnosis Schools

California
Creativity Learning Institute
Instructor: Shelley Stockwell, Ph.D. author of this book with guest instructors.
Curriculum: The Stockwell System learning intensives offer Certification Courses for Hypnosis, Hypnotherapy and Transpersonal Hypnotherapy. Special emphasis on creativity, addiction and compulsion release, time travel, and spiritual development.
Location: 30819 Casilina, Rancho Palos Verdes, CA 90275
Phone (310) 541-4844 or FAX (310) 377-7946
e-mail:http://www.palosverdes.com/shelleystockwell/hypnosis

Wisconsin and Illinois
Hypnosis Wellness & Training Center
Instructor: Charlene Ackerman, C.Ht., A.C.I. Special workshops by well-known leaders in the field.
Curriculum: Basic and advanced Certification courses in Hypnotherapy in Wisconsin and Northern Illinois. Advanced classes have a special emphasis on regression therapy
Location: 20 South Main Street, Suite #24, Janesville, WI 53545
Phone (800) 757-8226 or (608) 757-0716
FAX (608) 757-0945

Institute Of Medical Intuitive Studies
Curriculum: Emphasis on wellness, and the balance of mind, body and spirit. Techniques enhance other hypnosis approaches and evoke rapid change.
Location: Offered throughout the U.S and other countries.
Phone (800) 757-8226 or (608) 757-0716

Australia
Infinity College Of Hypnotherapy
College Of Advanced Hypnotherapy
Instructors: Frank Garfield, Executive Director
Curriculum: Diploma course in Basic Hypnotherapy. Certificates in Advanced, Medical and Hypnoanalysis. The instructors in this institute are experts in the field of hypnosis, wellness and the explorations of the dream state. Well worth a trip down under. Endorsed by the International Medical and Dental Hypnotherapy Association.
Location: 136 Moore Street, Leichhardt, NSW 2040 Australia
Phone (02) 9550-9673 FAX (02) 9568-5935
E-mail: aaap@fl.net.au

Hypnosis Organizations
The National Guild Of Hypnotists
The "NGH" is the oldest and perhaps the friendliest group. Offers a dynamite yearly convention every August in New Hampshire and a fine referral service. I am a Guild recognized trainer and offer certifications courses for them in California.

International Medical and Dental Hypnotherapy Assoc.
Provides excellently trained and Certified Hypnotherapists through an International Referral Service. Has been featured in Prevention and McCall's Magazine as a source for qualified hypnotists. Associate and certified memberships are available.
Edgeland, Suite 800, Royal Oak, MI 48073
257-5467 FAX (810) 549-5421
Email: aspencer @infinityinst.com http://www.infiniteinst.com

Photo by Bryce Stockwell

Chapter 2
What Can Hypnosis Do For Me?

"If you think you can or you can't you are correct"
-Henry Ford

My mind is a garden
I reap what I sow
I affirm goals and dreams
and watch how they grow.
My higher self's here
to make me my best
As I fulfill my life purpose
with perfect success.   *-Shelley Stockwell*

Though not a magic act, hypnosis seems that way because it evokes permanent and profound results. Hypnotic relaxation allows you easy access to the past and a future where you re-member, re-frame, re-enforce and re-cycle any attitude or behavior you choose.

If you want to be more abundant, hypnosis helps you replace limiting attitudes with positive ones and motivates you to succeed.

Affirmations For Having It All
Every day in every way, I am getting better and better.

I am my own best friend. I am enough. I am perfect just the way I am. I love myself completely, just the way I am. I love and accept myself just the way I've been. I love myself the way I am becoming. I am kind, gentle and compassionate with myself. I forgive myself for any time I may have hurt myself with insensitivity. I forgive myself or anyone else I might have hurt with insensitivity.

I give myself permission to be myself and express myself. I express my ideas easily. I deserve to have whatever I want. I ask for what I want.

I am worthy of self-respect. I am worthy of the respect of others. Others respect my point of view. I accept and give compliments. No matter what you say to me, I know, on all levels of my being that I am a worthwhile and special person.
It's easy to love me. I deserve to be loved for myself, just as I am. I easily receive and give love. The more I love, the more I am loved. Loving and being loved is as easy as breathing in and breathing out.

Inner Awareness

Hypnosis goes where you direct it. Like an inner flashlight that beams upon whatever you'd like to see. Focus your beam upon positive and you reinforce and strengthen them.

Positive Change

Your inner focus identifies behavior patterns that aren't working and replaces them with behaviors that do work. These changes bring happiness, health, self-empowerment, abundance and a satisfying love life, as you master the ultimate of self-control.

Pizazz

Hypnosis puts positive pizzazz into life. With the unlimited the unlimited power of your mind healing and renewal are miraculous!

Goal And Dreams

The powerful motivation of positive thinking lets you manifest abundance on all levels: money, love, peace and joy. Here you employ your natural resources and creativity and real-eyes dreams.

Self Exploration

As you learn to simultaneously tune into conscious and subconscious thoughts and actions, you become your own observer. This helps you understand the reasons for patterns, behaviors, gifts and style. This also allows you to accept and empathize with yourself. Familiarity brings content (ment) as the purpose of your life is revealed to you.

≋Relaxation

Hypnosis relaxes parts of the body or mind that causes pain. That's why surgery, while performed with hypnosis, requires little or no anesthesia. The by-product of all hypnosis is relaxation, and that alone helps you feel terrific. Hypnosis is the perfect antidote for chronic stress, pain and anxiety.

♪ Personal Expression and Creativity

Your higher self makes you high. Here you discover creative ways to be yourself in the world, and that makes you feel out of this world! Hypnosis spontaneously opens the door to all creative expression such as writing, music, art, invention, problem solving and fun.

☻☻Better Relationships

Hypnosis puts you in touch with your sub-personalities and various ways to look at life. It helps resolve inner conflicts and integrate multi-dimensionally. As you learn to love and accept your selves, it's easier to love and accept others.

⚢ Better Sex: Up Your Libido

Hypnosis uncovers the culprits of sexual frustration: performance anxiety, guilt, shame, and embarrassment. Limiting myths or socially unacceptable behaviors are reframed. Vitality replaces numbness. A good hypnotist educates and motivates passion, play and sexually wellness.

▦Behavior Modification

Negative behaviors and attitudes shift into positive ones that heal underlying emotional stress. Millions have released limiting behaviors, like overeating and smoking, by readjusting behavior patterns imprinted in the subconscious mind.

With hypnosis you can de-hypnotize or de-program painful past patterns and imprints. This holistic tool helps you rise above difficult times so you create new procedures to cope, clear and get back on track.

> **The Relative Success Of Smoking Cessation Programs**
>
> Hypnosis RULED in the largest-ever scientific comparison of ways to quit smoking. Results showed that a visit to a hypnotist beat out a psychologist, social worker, psychiatrist and other physicians by a margin of 19% (or one to five).
>
> This meta-analysis of more than 600 studies of quit smoking programs covered more than 72,000 people in America and Europe and was conducted by the University of Iowa.

Hypnotic Time Travel

Past, life regressions, future life progressions and between lifetime journeys serve as an overlay for issues in the here and now. Time travel clarifies and resolves current problems. Discovering the source of problems (past trauma, decisions and reinforcing actions), releasing stagnant emotions and reprogramming limiting attitudes and behaviors makes life dynamic.

Trance-personal, Trance-formational, Transcendental Hypnosis

The Balinese people call trance kerohan that means "God coming." Trance opens the door to profound "ah ha" experiences and bigger pictures. When you connect with the part of you that knows itself to be infinite and eternal, you experience unconditional love.

Encounters with the divine make us whole and holy. Shamen, priests and healers throughout time have used soul retrieval, healing hands and altered states for enlightenment and wellness. Hypnosis is the quickest way to develop intuitive or psychic abilities.

Sports Hypnosis

Sports hypnosis can be used to improve concentration and "stay in the zone." Studies prove that mental rehearsal enhances performance way beyond simple physical practice. Body builders influence body contours with visualization techniques, so can you.

?Memory

"I've got water on the brain and in the winter it freezes and everything slips my mind."　　　　　　　　-Irv Lessin

Everything you experience is permanently recorded in your brain; yet, most experiences quickly slip below conscious awareness. That's because much information seems unimportant. Painful or traumatic moments are tucked away so you return to homeostasis. Memory techniques allow you to re-member the past, re-lease pain and to positively re-frame it (put a new frame around a renovated picture) in the present. Hypnosis increases the storing and retrieving of data. With it you recall; names, faces and things you read.

"Nothing's really lost, it's just where it doesn't belong."
　　　　　　　　　　　　　　- Suzanne Mueller

♀Learning and Test Taking

Hypnosis helps you think about knowing and know about thinking. Highlighting hypnotically allows you to vividly think, focus, absorb and re-member what you learn and perceive. During hypnosis you actually stimulate and create synapses (connections between one brain cell and another) and "oligodendroglia" (helper cells that make you smarter!). People with doctoral degrees have a lot more oligondendroglia than high school dropouts on the average. And in the genius category, Albert Einstein's brain had four times more than any others studied.

> Dr. Peter Mutke of Monterey Peninsula College, California, conducted a study of two groups of 95 children being taught to read. He wanted to see if hypnosis enhanced learning. It did! It took the control group of children twenty-two sessions to learn as much as kids learned after only five hypnosis sessions!

▊Wellness

Psychosomatic illness reminds us that the mind does affect the body. Hypnosis teaches psychosomatic wellness.

　　You stimulate your body's natural self-renewal via the

subconscious mind. Thoughts create changes in your body. If you make an idea vivid enough in the mind, it creates physical responses. This influence of mental focus and consciousness on the body is real, yet how this happens is a mystery. The placebo effect, the power of prayer, false pregnancy, and hysterical stigmatic (bleeding from palms, feet, crown) are examples of thought effecting form.

Because of its positive physical results, hypnosis is considered a science by doctors, dentists, those in the healing arts and professional hypnotists. The American Medical Association has recognized hypnosis as a science since 1955.

Hypnosis reduces tension, pain, and rehabilitation time. It supports the body's innate ability to heal cuts, bruises and broken bones. By stimulating your natural gift of self-renewal, hypnosis speeds up recovery time after surgery and others enjoy painless childbirth.

Hypnosis can help you "turn off" asthma, pain, skin rashes, warts and stuttering. Dentists and surgeons use hypnoanesthesia (hypnosis in lieu of anesthesia) and orthodontists use hypnosis to straighten teeth. Breast enhancement and hip reduction resulting from "hip-nosis" are well-documented successes.

HYPNODONTICS
Get This Straight
"I was exposed to the use of hypnosis as a type of anesthesia when I was an Orthodontics student.

Now when I work with someone who has really difficult handicapping facial and dental abnormalities, I help them clearly visualize and use hypnosis and self-hypnosis. I find that they are able to achieve results that they would not be able to obtain any other way."

-Dr John Goode, Orthodontist
Trance-formations video

❦ Career Hypnosis

Hypnotherapists, hypnotists, hypnoanalysts and hypno-counselors reframe limiting patterns of body and mind into positive changes. A hypnosis career is personally and financially rewarding and is listed as a legal profession by the U.S. Department of Labor.

➡ *Hypnotherapy*
One-on-one counseling helps people reach goals while eliminating self-destructive habits and counterproductive beliefs.

➡ *Educational Hypnosis*
Motivates students for power-learning and easy test taking.

➡ *Investigative and Forensic Hypnosis*
Used in criminal and civil investigations for over 100 years, this powerful tool enhances recall of both victims and eye witnesses, and offers valuable leads that help law enforcement investigations.

Hypnosis is usually used to help witnesses or victims recall details of a crime. In the Chowchilla kidnapping case, hypnosis helped the driver recall a "forgotten" license plate number.

➡ *Medical Hypnosis and Hypnodontics*
Uses hypnosis, relaxation, visualization, and suggestion for medical and dental procedures. Hypnotism is a wonderful tool for the ill. It helps dental professional's sooth phobic clients, enhance procedures, eliminate pain and stimulate self-healing.

Hypnosis benefits the immune (and other body) systems and reduces real and psychosomatic problems, anxiety, and depression.

Rashes, warts and other skin problems respond well to hypnosis. Hypnosis easily "turns off" an asthma attack.

➡ *Hypno-anasthesia*
Hypnosis soothes chronic pain without drugs by stimulating the body's natural ability to numb. It druglessly assists patients undergoing medical and dental procedures.

➡ *Midwifery Hypnosis*
Hypnosis shortens labor, eliminates pain. Studies show that some 56% fewer cesareans are needed for moms trained in hypnosis.

➡ *Sports Hypnosis*
Sports hypnotists work with individuals and teams to enhance the

psychological aspects of playing their best. When we learn to stay in the zone, avoid distractions, and relax, we are better athletes. Mental imaging becomes a self-fulfilling prophesy.

Weight lifters who visualize body sculpting get better results then those who don't. Basketball players who mentally rehearse scoring freeshots actually make more freeshots. Golfers who play the shot mentally score better. A positive mental attitude evokes peak performance.

➡ *Stress Management Hypnosis*
About one-third of us feel overloaded with stress. Hypnosis unloads overload and chronic fatigue. Hypnosis to the rescue for profound crisis intervention.

➡ *Motivational Hypnosis*
Motivational hypnotherapists sometimes call themselves motivational speakers. Their seminars and workshops offer hands on tools for success at home, in relationships and at work and make deep permanent and lasting impressions on participants.

Corporate seminars are big business. Business owners and managers know that hypnosis holds the key to keep employees productive and positive. The fiscal consequences of job stress in the United States is estimated at some $200 billion dollars a year lost to workers compensation claims, low morale and poor performance. Corporate hypnotist trainers are in much demand.

➡ *Stage Hypnosis*
Hypnosis in front of an audience is entertaining and enlightening. The hypnotist most do two things at once: keep the audience's attention, while carefully controlling the subjects (who *are* the show).

Fire walking and other sensational demonstrations of mind power fascinate and amaze us.

➡ *De-Programming*
De-hypnotizing breaks the hypnotic seals of hurtful and destructive imprints. It is often used for surviving prisoners of war and others

who have been brain washed by stress, circumstances or radical belief systems. Patti Hurst was deprogrammed after her stressful abduction.

As a cure for the common cult, de-hypnotizing is a powerful and effective tool to break free from the dogma of Moonies, Jim Jones, Heavens Gate or the like.

➡ *Special Needs Hypnosis*
Stutterers and those with other speech difficulties, ADD (attention deficit disorder), hearing and visually impaired (tinnitus, blindness), brain injured, dyslexics, and aphasics (those with word understanding difficulties) have all benefited from hypnotic techniques.

➡ *Transpersonal Hypnosis*
Transformational and spiritual hypnotherapy enhances meditation and prayer. Here we contact the profound higher self and discover our life path and future. Spiritual guidance and emergence bring life changing perspectives. Trance channeling, automatic writing, spirit guidance, and intuitive awareness offer powerful tools for self-discovery.

Soul retrievals and rebirthing techniques reintegrate us. So do auric cleansing and energy balancing.

➡ *Time Travel Hypnotherapy*
Past life regression, future life progression and between life journeys offer profound personal exploration.

➡ *Creative Arts Hypnotherapy*
Harnesses the creative genius within each of us. Eliminates limiting mindsets like writer's block and stage fright. Gives actors, dancers, comics and speakers the winning edge. Hypnosis makes memorizing scripts: auditions, performances and staying centered, easy.

Creativity coaching gifts a unique opportunity to transcend linear time and conscious limits to explore your creative mastery.

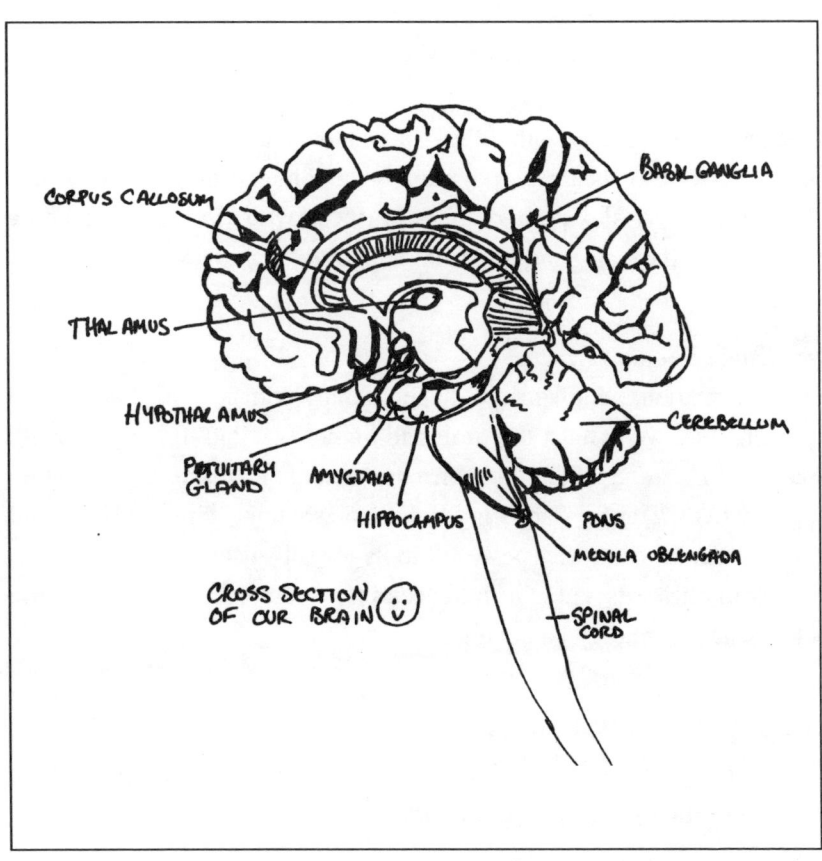

illustration by Shelley Stockwell

Chapter 3
THE BRAIN

"I Think Therefore I Am."   -Descartes

"I Think Therefore I Am, I Think."   -Shelley Stockwell

☺ How Does My Brain Work

♂♀ Do Male and Female Brains Differ?

☞ Laws Of The Brain

☺ How Does My Brain Work?

"..the mysterious butterflies of the soul, the beating of whose wings may someday clarify the secret of mental life"
            -Santiago Ramon y Cajal, Psychologist
            Father of brain science and
            winner of the Nobel Prize

Affirmations For A Dazzling Mind
My brain and mind work perfectly. I have unlimited mental potential. In this moment, I 'up' my mental metabolism and think more clearly than ever before in my life.

I am ready to use my mind in a new way. I am keenly aware of all self talk and I quickly and easily turn any negatives into positives.

I listen to the still voice within, it always tells me the truth. I trust my senses, they tell me the truth. I know the truth about everything in my life. I easily listen to my inner wisdom. I am a good listener. I listen well to myself and others.

I grow and learn every day and right this moment. I am a growing and maturing personality and the changes I make in my behaviors and attitudes nurture me. I have the ability to change any behavior that no longer serves me well. I accept change easily. I enjoy growing up. I hang loose and don't sweat the small stuff.

Wherever I am today is perfect. I have been on a journey arriving right here, right now in this moment in time and space. I am here to make a new beginning on my spiritual journey and to experience and accept joy in my life. I am in a perfect place for growth and change. Everything I have done in my life has brought me to this very moment. Today, I am open to be touched by love, joy and nature. I am free to experience my joy this instant.

The Brain Think about it. This amazing convoluted structure within your skull knows how to create a three dimensional landscape from light that touches your two dimensional retina. It knows how to encode, utter and understand sounds (words) that create meaning. Your brain is mysterious enough to let you read this right now. It controls your mental processes and the mystery of imagination, memory, mood, consciousness and spirit. Your brain is infinitely creative and receptive to learning.

The brain is actually a continuation and enlargement of the spinal cord.

Am I Of Two Minds?
"Because the brain is a physical structure, it exists in space. But the mind operates in time alone.."   -Marcus Raichle
                                        St. Louis University
                                        School of Medicine

The difference between the mind and the brain is challenging to distinguish and differentiate. Brain and mind are two sides of the same coin. You might call the brain the structure and mind the function.

Think about thinking. If you do that right now, your brain changes. As these changes happen, your thoughts change too. When you change your brain function (mind), you effect the very structure of your brain. As a result of these changes in your structure, you change the function. Going round and round and round in a circle game.

Even the location of the mind is controversial. Cells within every part of the body appear to hold memory and make decisions giving us a kind of thinking body.

Many paradigms try and explain this complexly amazing processor of impulses resulting in thoughts. Scientists correlate the connection of mental events and nerve impulse patterns. How do nerves (neurons) interrelate with each other and change with experience? ask scientists.

PAIR•O•DIMES

Science also attempts to "map" hemispheres and territories of the brain by location and job to correlate function with structure.

Historical Brain Mapping

"Not only our pleasure, our joy and our laughter; but also our sorrow, pain, grief and tears arise from the brain, and the brain alone..."   -Hypocrites
                    Ancient Greek Physician
                    and Philosopher

Grey matter is the neurons,
the cells within my brain.
White matter is the bridges
that connect this grey terrain.

Spine, medulla, pons
amygdala, mid-tissue
glands, lobes and hemispheres
work together when I kiss you.

                    -Shelley Stockwell

The Stockwell System

The brain is organized and works as a whole; yet, various parts specialize in the job they do. These separate yet parallel processes are still little understood and offer quite a brain teaser. To date this is how the brain is viewed by researchers:

REPTILIAN
or Instinctive Brain (automatic functioning)

These marvelous structures keep us alive and functioning. The instinctive brain is straight forward, illiterate and lets us live, protect territory, and fight for survival. It's often called the "primitive" brain because it has evolved from a common ancestry over millions of years. This instinctive structure constantly interacts with the rest of our brain. It keeps the heart beating, lungs inflating, regulates wake and sleep and determines which thought will remain buried in the unconscious and which will be revealed to conscious awareness.

Medulla

The medulla is the first part of the brain structure that comes up from the spinal cord. The medulla oblengata regulates breath, circulation (blood pressure and heart rate), and to some degree, digestion.

Cerebellum

The Cerebellum controls balance and coordination movement.

Pons

Latin for "bridge," the pons connects the hindbrain to the cerebellum on the opposite side. Here signals cross over from the right brain to the left side of the body and from the left brain to the right side of the body. The place where this crossover takes place is called the "pyramids" or the "pyramidal deccusations."

The cranial nerves (5-12) is found here. Together with the medulla oblengada, impulses we feel for sensations in our face, facial movement, outward movement of the eyes, taste, hearing and tongue movement enter the central nervous system via the pons and or the midbrain.

Midbrain

Our midbrain houses the third and forth cranial nerves which control reflexes of eye movement and the size of our pupil (3rd cranial nerve only).

LIMBIC
or Emotional Brain

As the size of our brain grew, a second structure, the limbic brain (Latin for border or seam) is said to have formed. It's now the center of our brain and directs energy to the outer portions of the brain or the cortex. The limbic brain stimulates the biochemical impulses that produce all our feelings, emotions and long-term memory. Lust comes from the limbic system, so does aggression. The actual seat (or heart) of our emotional life is found in the limbic systems. Malfunctions of the limbic system have been linked to panic attacks and rage.

Amygdala

This almond shaped knot of nerve cells close to our brain stem specializes in memory, delight, disgust, fear and anger. A concentrated collection of cell bodies, the amygdala imbues mental stimulation with positive or negative emotions.

Hippocampus

Next to the amygdala is a crescent shaped collection of nuerons that coordinates and sorts memory retrieval. Millions of years later, the Limbic Brain evolved into the larger:

NEOCORTEX
or Ordered Brain

The word "Cortex" comes from the Latin word bark. Here abstract thinking, language, calculations, spatial relations, instinctive love, and creativity reside. This larger neocortex houses the two hemispheres and each of these is divided into 4 lobes:

Frontal

Curiosity, foresight, and understanding consequences for our actions, make this part of the mind our social awareness. The prefrontal circuitry, determines how we act upon how we feel. According to Harvard Psychologist Dr. Daniel Coleman the frontal lobe is not fully developed until about mid-adolescence.

Temporal

The temporal lobe is located near the temple. Hearing and memory are its specialty.

Parietal
The parietal lobe is involved to some degree with all sensory awareness except smell.

Occipital Lobes
Deep folds separate the occipital lobes by deep folds. Its highly convoluted surface is concerned with vision and also allows us to plan, learn and remember.

Neural pathways and connections between the emotional limbic and ordered neocortex seem to determine emotional self-awareness, empathy and impulse control (the ingredients for a sense of well being in life).

RIGHT and LEFT HEMISPHERES
The forebrain or Cerebrum is made up of the right and left hemispheres. The outer layer of called the cerebral cortex or neo cortex ("new bark"). Nobel Laureate, Roger Sperry (California Institute of Technology) discovered that the neocortex accesses information separately and uniquely with the right and left hemispheres.

Left handed? You are most likely dominantly "right brained," Each hemisphere directs the movement of the arm and leg on the opposite side of the body. The hand you prefer determines whether you are "right " or "left brained."

> *The left brain maps from point A to B*
> *It's the speaker and the "lister."*
> *It can't be bothered with overviews*
> *like its right brained little sister.*
>
> *The right brain sees the map as a whole*
> *She decides and doesn't explain,*
> *"Of all my relations I like spatial the best"*
> *intuits the right side of the brain.*
>
> *Together they work in harmony*
> *so I don't have two left feet*
> *connected by the corpus collosum*
> *they make myself complete.*
>
> -Shelley Stockwell

The Left Side Knows, The Right Side Understands.

Right Side The non-verbal right side makes order out of chaos as it synthesizes details into unity. The right brain is a "jack of all trades." It functions in pictures and symbols and perceives how parts fit together to form wholes. The right brain controls the left side of the body, as well as spatial, musical, and aesthetic perception and creativity. It's excellent at coping with the novel and unfamiliar.

Left Side The left side is analytical and thinks in sequences. This hemisphere selects relevant details for point-to-point focus. The left brain controls the right side of the body and communication skills.

CONNECTING LINKS

The right and left hemispheres are joined together by mental bridges that transmit information and coordinate activities between the two sides. One of these bridges, the **Corpus Collosum,** is made up of some eight million bundled neurons. These nerve fibers are shaped like chubby curved worms.

THE MIND

Collectively, all regions of the brain create the mind.

Think About Thinking

To understand the mind it helps to understand how the brain processes thoughts. My awesome brain, weighs approximately three pounds and holds billions or perhaps trillions of cells. Anywhere from thirty to one hundred billion of them are **neurons** or "nerve" cells. There are also an unknown number of **glial** (Greek for glue) cells which support the neurons. The brain is a dynamic organ, and at every moment it alters the connections of millions of neurons. This makes counting the numbers of cells a seeming impossible.

The neurons transmit billions of messages each second that acquire and store data, and enhance and inhibit my thoughts, feelings and behaviors. Information travels as an electrical impulse down an axon within a nerve cell and a chemical messenger between nerve cells via 'synapses.' Think of a synapse as a sort of telephone line that also stores information.

Everything you create in life starts as a conscious or subconscious thought that manifests in your brain as a result of these electrochemical responses.

Everything that you see, hear, smell, taste, feel, and intuit is received in patterned connections within a millisecond, and placed into your memory.

Your brain is constantly changing and modifying itself. Some fifty-thousand to one hundred thousand (50,000 to 100,000) brain cells die off each day and approximately ten thousand synapses bite the dust. If you eat MSG, take drugs or drink alcohol we lose even more "grey matter."

Neuron
"The number of possible nerve cell interactions exceeds the number of particles of matter in the universe!" -Richard M. Restak,
Neurologist

A neuron is a brain or nerve cell, composed of a central cell body and long tendrils called axons. Axons transmit information in the form of electrical impulses over long distances and form complex networks.

Synapse
Chemical communication link from one brain cell to another.

Oigodendroglia
Also known as glial cells, these helper cells speed communication among neurons. They network, structure and support the neurons. The more we learn, the more oligodendroglia cells we manufacture.

Neural Transmitters
The brain's bio chemical sending and receiving messengers that determine our mood tone. The brain chemicals that work with the synapse are serotonin, norepinephrine, dopamine, and endorphines.

Neural Web
A network of brain cells and synapses associated with intelligence, creativity, emotion, consciousness and memory.

The Chemical Brain
Q "Who is the largest drug manufacturer in the world?"
A "My brain."

The brain holds the key to joy, pain, pleasure, wellness and addiction. It always searches out ways to feel high.

It has its own pharmacy and offers its own prescriptions. Every thought and substance effects the delicate chemical interplay of brain and resulting behaviors.

Behind my skull are "billions and billions" of brain cells (also called neurons or nerve cells). These act as neuro-transmitters (the keys in my brain) and receptors (the locks). When a neuro transmitter binds to a receptor, it "turns on" brain activity and creates a natural high. That's why thinking, learning and creativity are so rewarding and turn us on. Physical activity, sex, emotions, laughter and hypnosis also get your mental "mo-jo workin." Depression and boredom, on the other hand, are associated with low neuron activity.

Affirmations For A Natural High
From this point forward, I only do kind, considerate, nurturing things for myself. My higher self uplifts me. My higher self makes me naturally high. I no longer do anything that harms me in any way. I only do things that bring my precious body to radiant health and my mind to clear and positive thinking. I am now a full-fledged pleasure seeker. I create a positive and happy life for myself.

I put my hand on my heart and affirm that it is so: I choose joy. I choose wellness. I choose peace. I choose success.

The world has now entered into a conspiracy to do me good. And, even if I try to sabotage it, the world prevails in bringing me pleasure, joy and abundance. I choose to flow with this glorious world that brings only good into my life. And so it is.

Natural Highs
Natural or andogenous opiates are the chemical stimulants in your brain that catalyze pleasure. Endorphins, dopamine and seratonin are such opiates. When you laugh, experience a peak experience, an "Ah ha" or

have "runners high" you've treated yourself to a natural opiate rush. When the septum pellusidum, in the center of the brain is stimulated, it feels so good!

Sexual Chemistry

According to neurochemists, the "chemistry" between two people who are sexually attracted is stimulated by phenylethylamine, norepinephrine and dopamine. With these chemical go the sudden rush you get when you're in love. Which supports the theory that the brain is your most highly developed sex organ.

Your sympathetic nervous system then triggers a rise in pulse, perspiration, shakiness, excitement, and aggressiveness to overcome shyness. Some say that pheromones, the trace "odors" that trigger attraction, result as well. Scientific research has not proven the existence of human pheromones but there is much anecdotal evidence to their existence. Pheromones have been discovered in plants and mammals.

Strangely, fear causes the brain to release the exact chemicals as passion. Maybe that's why sexual attraction can be colored by insecurity and anxiety.

Artificial Highs

Brain function causes all behavior. And behavior influence brain function. Addiction, and its twin sister obsession, take place inside the brain, on a cellular level, because each cell desires stimulation and opening.

Addictions and compulsions stimulate the emotional and motivational centers of the brain by creating brain opiates like dopamine, which in turn causes psycho-active effects and drug dependency. This is what motivates us to take more of the same drug.

Think of drugs and compulsions as burglars with a set of skeleton keys. Drugs do not contain highs. They trigger the brain's natural ability to be high. They bind to the same receptors as the endogenous opiates. Psychoactive drugs have a similar 3D structure as endogenous neurotransmitters. We start to associate this natural brain rush with the substance that stimulates it. We then get hooked on our "brain rush."

Laboratory animals choose stimulants rather than food or water. In a stunning study on human brain cell activity, Dr. Belluzzi determined that single brain cells exhibit addictive behavior. On the cellular level we can be seduced into addiction.

There appears to be a strong correlation between boredom and addictive and compulsive behaviors. Easily bored folks generally show low neuron activity, and the presence of MAO (mono-amine-oxydase, the biochemical marker of "lows.") If you have a low metabolic rate, or idle neurons not being opened, your cells choose excitement anywhere they can get it.

Hypnosis and suggestion can "up" mental metabolism and stimulate natural highs and, at the same time, positively reprogram and reframe behavior patterns. With suggestion we can stimulate the our cells to offer a natural high without harmful side effects.

Obsessions

"Positive thoughts are prophylactic. Though it is yet to be proven, as you embark on the process of structural and bio chemical change, you protect yourself from upsetting or depressing reactions."
-Joel Gober, Ph.D.,
brain researcher

Some dictionaries define obsessions as being "besieged" or "taken over" by demonic influences outside of self. But obsessions are patterned, learned responses within the brain. The power of these thoughts and the way it effects our chemical self can be dramatic. A placebo can cure a disease and a false pregnancy can evoke the same hormonal changes as an actual pregnancy causing milk secretion and change face pigmentation.

A positive mind set dispels obsessions and compulsions. As you teach your brain to learn how to be in a certain mood, the structure on the molecular and macro level changes. These changes might manifest as shifts in the number of synapses between two nerve cells, neural network changes, the creation of more axons and neural transmitters, and our threshold of receptivity.

Inquiring Minds What To Know

Do Male and Female Brains Differ?

"Why can't a woman think more like a man?" -Prof. Henry Higgins,
by George Bernard Shaw

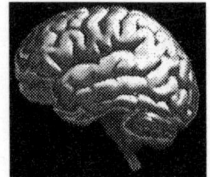 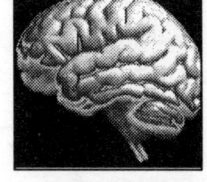

Female Brain   Male Brain

Magnetic residence imaging (MRI's) developed by Bennett and Sally Shaywitz of Yale University allows us to take colorful photographs of the male and female brain. When comparing the blood action of brains stimulated by abstract thought (brain teasers), the larger male brain usually focuses energy on its front corner and the smaller female brain sparks up both hemispheres.

Testy

DNA (Dioxy ribonucleic acid, the blueprint of life) is different between males and females. Male DNA has a special propellant, and female DNA is richer in protein. When a sperm and an egg meet, they perform a kind of genetic swap meet.

Chemically and structurally, the first nuerons in the human brain are female. And the fetus remains female for the first seven weeks. At that time, half of us get an extra blast of the hormone testosterone that transforms our genitals and brains to the male persuasion. The story of Adam and Eve is perhaps backwards!

After that, there are often several distinct differences between the male and female brain. Testosterone makes males more aggressive than females. Women's normally low testosterone levels rises during mid-menstrual cycles.

Viva La Difference

Nineteenth century French Anthropologist Paul Broca collected 432 brains made available to him by the guillotine of the French Revolution. After weighing and measuring them, he concluded that men's brains are 10% bigger and heavier than women's brains.

Female intuition is said to live in the corpus collosum. Scientists, studying the corpus collosum (the part of the brain that links hemispheres), found that the female corpus is bigger, thicker and more complicated than the male. A woman's corpus collosum keeps an ever-going communication between the right and left brain. That's why when a woman tackles a logical problem, she also engages her intuition. Conversely, if she is dealing with an intuitive issue, she pulls in her logic. A woman's left brain knows what its right brain is thinking. A man's brain won't do that as readily without training.

For most men, verbal and spatial mental activity are divided between the right and left brain- left for verbal, right for spatial. Female brains usually process verbal and spatial in the left hemisphere. Because of these structural differences, males keep intuition and logic separate, giving them the edge in spatial talent. That's why men find their way more easily from A to B.

Women are superior in verbal skills and can express and grasp emotional content more easily, and their brain compensates more easily to brain damage than males. Herbert Landsell, in his 1960's study, noted that damage to the left "verbal skills" portion of the brain disabled men's speech, while women usually recovered speech; and damaged right hemispheres, where male spatial intelligence is centered was, of course, more disabling to men than women.

You're Talking Out Of Both Sides Of Your Brain

According to Linguistics Professor Deborah Tannen, men and women don't have a clue what the other is talking about. Men's hidden agenda is to be respected, women's is to be liked. To be respected, guys give reports, information, correct errors and are Mr. Fix It. Women go for rapport and empathy. In Men Are From Mars, Women Are From Venus, John Gray says men and women need to learn each others language to communicate. For example, a wife should avoid saying "could you take out the garbage?" For the word "could" implies, to the man, challenge and doubt. To a man it means "are you strong enough to take out the garbage?" or "Why didn't you take out the garbage before I asked you to?" "Would you take out the garbage?" is less threatening to a man.

If you ask a man "What do you think about that?," he'll give you a terrific answer. Ask the same soul "what do you feel about that and he'll look at you like, "What are you asking. I don't get it?"

Ask a women what she feels about something and, no problem. Ask the same dear what she thinks about it and...Well, don't take my word for it, try it yourself and then let me know what you think or feel about it.

☞ Laws Of The Brain
The brain does its job "without even thinking about it" -Alan Watts

> ☞ Use Or Lose
> ☞ Snooze Or Lose
> ☞ Inspire To Inspire
> ☞ To Think Drink

Use or Lose
Education: Comes from the Latin "educat"- to draw from within

The brain needs exercise. Learning most likely takes place in the synapses, protein or DNA of the brain. The more you stimulate your thoughts and learn, the more you stimulate your brain tissue. More thought creates more neural webs and high speed oligodendroglia helper cells.

Learning reduces the risk of Alzhiemers (old timers) disease, makes life more interesting, and puts our focus away from obsessions and compulsions (unless I become a knowledgeaholic).

Illustration by Shelley Stockwell

Big Brains

The smarter we are the more elaborate the network between cells and the more the brain weighs. The average brain of a person of average weight is your weight multiplied by .01. Wisdom weighs slightly heavier on the mind. In a study of eleven gifted people's brains at the University of California, Albert Einstein was found to have four times more oligodendroglia (glial cells) than any other!

The visual cortex in the brain of someone with a photographic mind is twice the thickness of a "normal" brain.

Snooze or Lose

Our brain requires sleep as a much needed time to solve problems and generate new ideas. That's why listening to hypnosis tapes while sleeping can be amazingly beneficial. Theta sleep which is the brain wave pattern or frequency during the twilight zone between wake and sleep is a fabulous time to give ourselves auto-suggestions and receive powerful in-formation.

Inspire to Inspire

The brain requires oxygen to do its job best. Full breaths and physical activity improve mental metabolism, stimulate neurotransmitters and produce endorphines that kill pain, boosts the immune system and makes us high.

💡 Hypnogogic Gadgets

Thomas Edison, used his brain's natural problem solving capability to "sleep on" a challenging idea and create a solution. He prided himself in sleeping no more than three hours nightly, but made up for it in cat naps. He'd rest in a chair, his arms draped over the side and his hand holding two ball bearings. When he snoozed and dropped the ball, the noise would awaken him, and he'd immediately write down what he was thinking. A light bulb went on when Edison dropped the ball. It is said that some of his most brilliant inventions came this way.

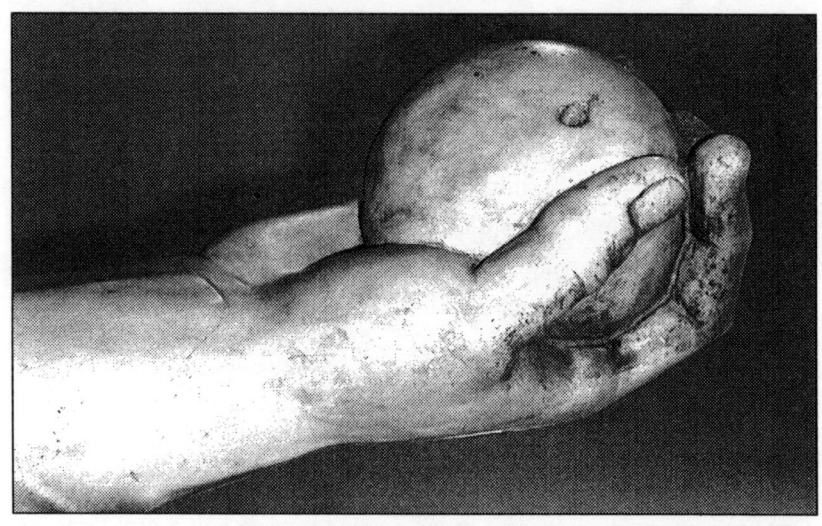

Photo by Janus Welton

To Think, Drink

"I have water on the brain and in winter it freezes and everything slips my mind"   -*Irv Lessin*

75% of the brain is water. Without it we can't concentrate or think clearly. Sugar, salt and caffeine pull water from the cells and they dry up full thought.

Brain Drains

Nicotine lowers the level of brain chemicals necessary for short term memory. MSG, alcohol and cocaine kill brain cells. Over the counter drugs like antidiarrheal agents, cough suppressants, analgesics (like ibuprofen) and sleeping concoctions fatigue the mind. So does overeating because it takes much needed blood from the brain and sends it to the stomach. Salt dehydrates the body and, therefore, the brain. Water is the solution. To think, drink.

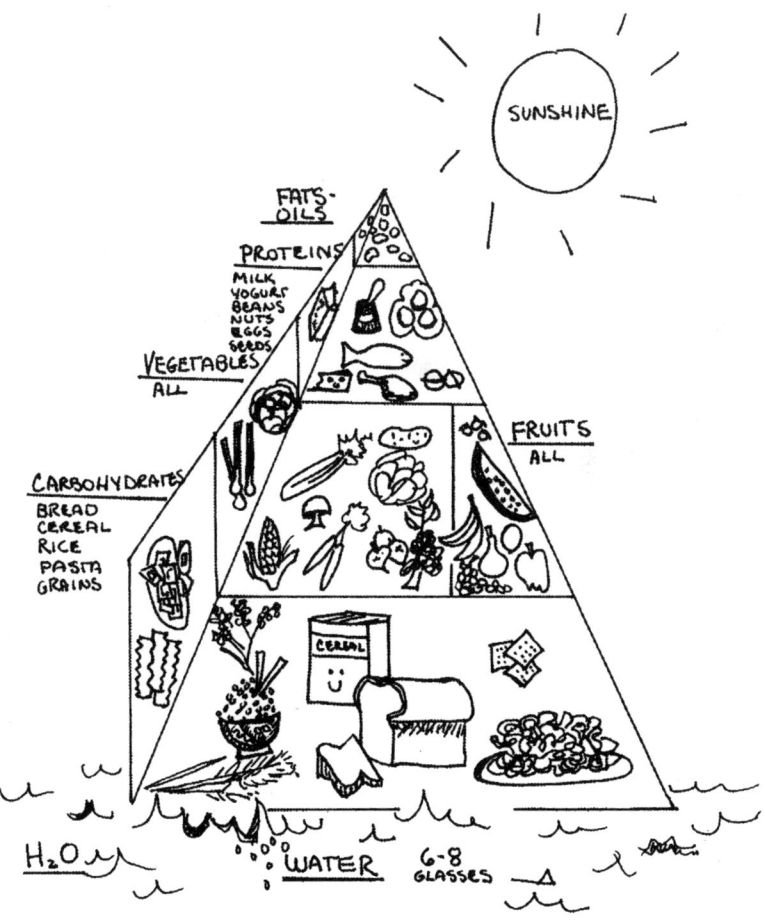

Illustration by Shelley Stockwell

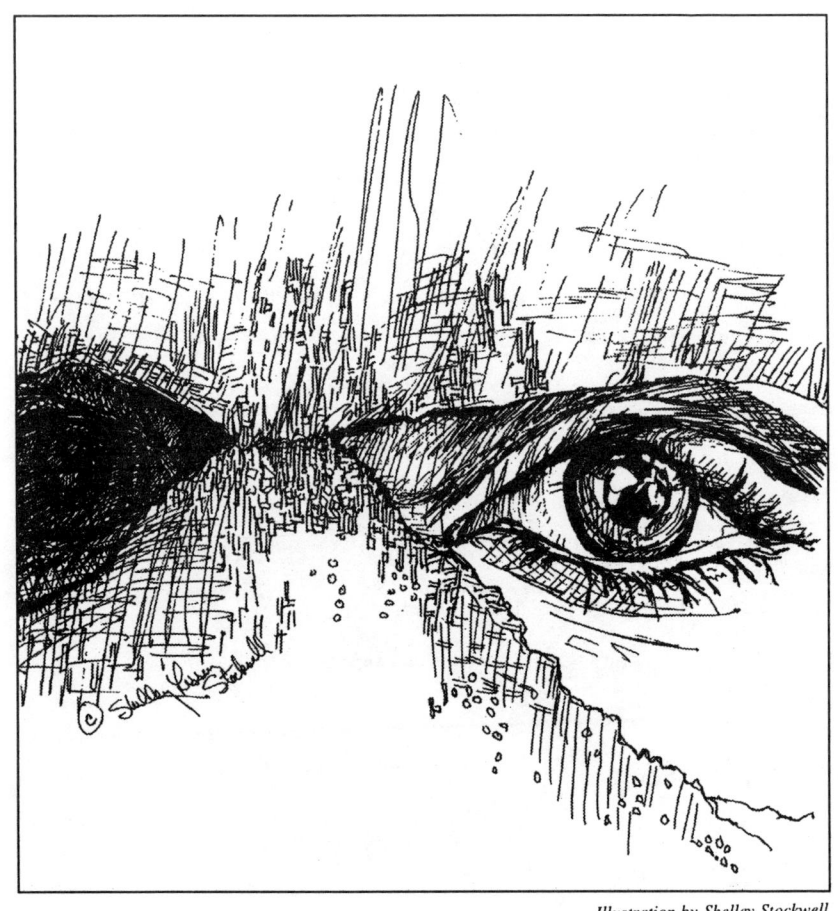

Illustration by Shelley Stockwell

Chapter 4

THE MIND

Imprints///Patterns of Thought

Laws Of The Mind

Historical Mind Mapping

by Shelley Stockwell

Plato : "Mind must live in the spherical head. Mind your head." is what he said.

Aristotle: "Of course the mind is in the heart; the warmest and most vital part.

17th century Frenchman Descartes:
"Forget the head. Forget the heart.
From these opinions I take issue.
Mind is separate from physical tissue.
Cognito, ergo sum;
without a thought your life is done
If I think therefore, I am is true,
you only exist if I think of you.

The Stockwell Mind Map 🏠

Conscious	Subconscious	Super Conscious
Outer Self *Physical* Awareness	**Inner Self** Internal Awareness	**Higher Self** Expanded Awareness
Stories we tell ourselves	Attitudes, beliefs, habits	Inspiration, creative imagination
Concrete analytical Logical, critical, protective, defensive	**Emotional** literal Bio-chemical, autonomic response, body function, survival instinct.	**Ephemeral**
Co-creates with the subconscious and super conscious	Co-creates with the conscious and super conscious	Brings inner and outer harmony and balance to all parts of self
Some short term memory	Most memory: uncritically accepts, records and stores data from the outside world. Combines stored data into hunches and answers, language	Remembers connection to all, universal wisdom, life purpose, spiritual guidance, God, inner knower, silent witness
Honors linear time, aware of now analyzes past might project future	Honors non-linear time, aware of past	Transcends linear time and space know the "future"
Personality	Most sub-personalities	Beyond personality Metaphors, archetypes, symbols
Practical	Emotional	Soulful
Waking states	Hypnotic states	Dream states
Body	Mind	Spirit
Son	Father	Holy ghost
Ego	Id	Super Ego
Earth	Sky	Cosmos
Play a record	Record a record	Invent a record
Eros	Shadow	Spirit
Basic self-child	conscious self-adult	higher self-parent

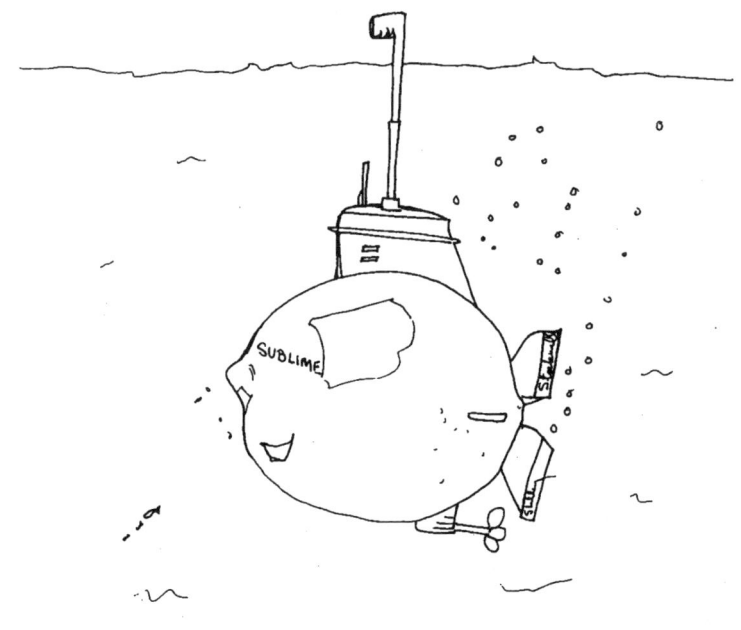

SUB•LIME

Illustration by Shelley Stockwell

📺 HOW DOES THE MIND WORK?

"The mind is not a tangible thing; it is a process of producing thoughts. And thoughts are things: they form energy and manifest powerfully in the physical world   ."
Ormond McGill,
*How To Become A Mastermind
and Operate The World*

I Affirm Success

I am expanding my awareness in every way. I am able to think my thoughts, feel my feelings, and know the bigger picture of my thoughts and feelings more and more each day. I am consciously aware of all self talk and I easily change any negatives to positives. I am well adjusted in everything I think, say and do. I love solving

any challenges in positive ways that benefit others as well as myself.

Conscious, Subconscious and Superconscious Thought

The mind has many levels of focus: the regular awareness (or conscious mind), individual awareness (or subconscious mind), and expanded awareness (or super-conscious mind). When you resonate with these notes on the scale of consciousness, you make beautiful music together. That's how you into-great yourself.

The greatest gift you can give yourself is to be conscious of your own consciousness.

Think of the conscious and subconscious as the receiver of energy and the superconscious as the transmitter. When they work together, you stay tuned in.

♥ MIND AS WELL
Good Things Come In Threes

"As a man thinks in his heart, so is his life."
-Solomon, in the Bible

Your Conscious Mind
Earth Body Outer Self, Room Awareness

'Personality' comes from the Latin word 'persona' meaning coming through a mask.

Think of the conscious mind as the mask you use to interface with the world. The conscious mind controls your personality and the stories you tell yourself. This concrete waking state keeps you physically aware.

Your conscious mind represents only about 10% of your brain-power. A master of logic and analytical thinking, it formed when you were about five years old. You use this part of your mind in daily activity as you shift your attention from one thing to another. Your conscious mind has short-term memory only.

Conscious thinking will try to protect you from danger by critically judging and weighing information. The conscious mind makes decisions based upon information it receives from the sub and superconscious mind, and it impresses the subconscious with its sensory observations.

Your Subconscious Mind
Inner Self Internal Awareness

The subconscious self conducts the majority of your brain functions. Where are thoughts when we are not thinking them? In the little understood mental archives of the subconscious, which remembers all information about yourself and your life. And from these memories, it draws conclusions. Memories and tidbits of information are uncritically accepted by the subconscious.

The subconscious is the home of your individual personality, emotions, feelings, expression, behaviors, survival instinct, and human potential.

The part of your subconscious that controls your bio-chemical self and is sometimes referred to as the unconscious. It's your mind that keeps your heart beating and lungs inflating. It controls every muscle, nerve, ligament, and autonomic response. It fights disease and keeps you alive. It's been doing an excellent job or you wouldn't be reading this right now.

Habits and attitude live here too. What you choose on this level strongly influences your success in money, love and joy. Addictions, compulsions, and obsessions are the result of patterns imprinted into this part of consciousness that no longer serve you well.

Your Super-Conscious Mind
Higher Self, Expanded Consciousness

"The perfect pattern, a divine design. A place you are to fill and no one else can fill, something you are to do, which no one else can do."
                                                            -Plato

Your super conscious mind encompasses and permeates all levels of consciousness. It oversees the conscious and subconscious and it remembers all experiences within and beyond your individual personality. It's the big picture.

Your super-conscious mind knows your true destiny and life purpose. Here, you discover and connect with your life force energy and all living things. Here, you enjoy your intuitive and spiritual gifts and have "peak experiences."

Your higher self blesses you with its profound wisdom. This part of your awareness knows your truth, dreams, and the steps you need to take to make life work perfectly. Your higher self makes you high. All personal transformation, healing, and bliss tap this consciousness. This realm of transcendental joy bypasses the time-space continuum and you easily explore past, future, and between-life memory.

Your super-conscious mind can master the history and mystery of all humankind, past, present and future. Sometimes called the Collective Unconscious, the Akashic Records, the Great Book or The Book Of Remembrance.

❄IMPRINTS:
Mental Patterns Determine My Behavior.
"Answers come from the only place real answers ever come. They come from deep inside me... My negative thoughts and emotions caused me a kind of emotional pollution that kept happiness hidden from me."
—Lester Levenson

Ever notice how sometimes you seem to be on "automatic pilot?" That's because the mind (in particular the subconscious mind) is a pattern-making and pattern-repeating device. The patterns it makes and repeats are designed to keep you active and return you to balance (homeostasis).

You created most mental and behavioral patterns as a child by modeling your caretakers. You did this instinctively to enjoy pleasure, contact and love; and to avoid rejection, abandonment, or worse. The way big people view you influences how you view yourself. Their teachings become your life lessons. So does everything you hear, see, smell, taste, touch and perceive.

Golden Aches
As an experiment, ask yourself: "What are the golden arches?" Did you imagine a McDonald's sign or a hamburger? Does the thought of a big juicy hamburger make you salivate? Are you salivating right now? If so, the words golden arches activated a mental pattern in your mind causing an almost involuntarily response.

To observe this phenomenon with others, whistle a jingle from a popular commercial and notice how others chime in. Or sit in a classroom or business meeting and yawn. Others will join right in and yawn too.

Thought patterns are called "imprints." Once established, you do them automatically, and the initial reason you embraced them may be buried in your memory.

Obsolete patterns continue to influence the way you behave. The shoe you put on first, the way you tie laces, the phrases you use when you speak, and the way you talk to yourself all began as a learned pattern. Now, they are automatic behaviors, or imprints.

Obsolete cultural patterns have also become part of our life, and we don't even notice them. Men's suit jackets have buttons on the sleeve because Napoleon Bonaparte wanted to keep his soldiers from wiping their noses there. Yet today, all men's suits have buttons on their sleeves, and no one wonders why.

A TRUE STORY

I asked my mother why I had to cut off both ends of the roast before cooking it.
She said: "That's what Mom taught me."
So I asked grandma: "Why do you cut off both ends of the roast before baking it?"
She said: " Because my mom taught me to do it that way."
So I asked great grandma:
"Why do you cut off both ends of the roast before baking it?"
"The pan was too small." she answered.

Once a pattern is established, it takes extra effort to change it. And change can be uncomfortable because it thrusts us into the unknown. That's why we sometimes ignore the damage we inflict upon ourselves with self-destructive habits; at least they're familiar we rationalize.

Your behaviors and thoughts reinforce imprints. So does the way you talk to yourself. Some imprints are nice to reinforce. For example, you have an imprint that says you can learn; otherwise, you wouldn't be reading this right now. As you read and learn, you re-affirm that you can read and learn. If you tell yourself: "I'm terrific at making money," "I deserve to be happy," or I love to exercise," these become self-fulfilling and you reinforce them with each affirmation.

Money, Money, Money

We all have imprints about money. Do you deserve to have money? Do you hold a belief that you're a failure when it comes to money? Or do you believe that you can and will create all the money you want and need? What you believe about money you will reinforce.

To change a limiting attitude or behavior that no longer serves you, all you need to do is reprogram your subconscious mind. When you know how to do that, you easily replace negative imprints or patterns with positive ones.

WAS THIS ME?

A little voice whispers in my inner ear:
"Enjoy life and be healthy, happy, and peacefull, loving and loved."
"Yes, that's what I want for myself."

Yet, nothing changes and I continue to feel stressed, unhappy, unworthy, afraid, numb, or lonely.

Again, the little voice whispers:
"Life isn't working. You feel awful. Everything will be better if you'd just stop (drinking, smoking, drugs, bingeing, being compulsive, flying off the handle, obsessing about ...)_____."

"OK, I'll stop: drinking, smoking, drugs, bingeing, being compulsive, flying off the handle, obsessing about _____.

Later, I _____ (throw one down, light one up, eat the whole thing, scream at my child, leave a frantic message on his machine, or ....). I'm a failure. I have no will power. I have no won't power," I bemoan.

SWEET REFRAME
Play It Again, Sam!

A little voice whispers in my inner ear:
"Enjoy life and be healthy, happy, and peacefull, loving and loved."
"Yes, that's what I want for myself."
"OK, I'll stop: drinking, smoking, drugs, bingeing, being compulsive, flying off the handle, obsessing about _____.
I vow. Suddenly I am healthy, happy, peaceful, loving, and loved."

How did I change?
I chose to feel relaxed, happy, confident, alert, and connected on the deepest level. I stopped _____ (drinking, smoking, doing drugs, bingeing, being out of control, raging, obsessing about...), because I enlisted my subconscious and super-conscious awareness to make it happen. I learned the simple tools that let me easily take back control of my life.

Now, I get pleasure out of my many hobbies, interests, and talents. Each day, I find new ways to love myself and to better my relationships with others. I'm a winner. I am in positive action.
What a relief!

Patterns of thought.
"Think big thoughts and cherish small pleasures"

If you're in pain, your brain searches for a familiar pattern of thinking to help you feel better. Like a jukebox, the mind punches "Pain 1" and the imprint, like a record, plays the patterns you use to cope. If you have healthy coping patterns, the record is a positive tune, and that's great. You release pain and return to homeostasis, or pleasure.

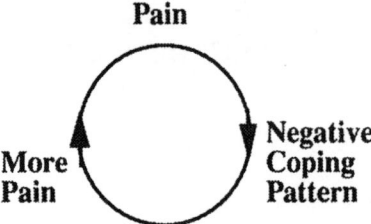

If your coping mechanism is self-destructive, you, in fact, add to your pain.

When you become aware of subconscious patterns (bring them to your conscious awareness) you can more easily revise or replace them. Let's say you want to lose weight and you notice that you eat junk food when you feel stressed.

Ask yourself; "Where did I learn that?"

Maybe you remember mommy giving you, the five-year-old, a candy bar when you skinned your knee. Recognizing this pattern and its origins allows you to reevaluate the pattern in the present.

So, what is your truth in the here and now about eating junk food?

Was junk food eating a family tradition that comforted you then? Is it now the way you felt nurtured by mom? If so, t's probably not working very well now. Junk food amplifies pain. You get mad at yourself for eating trash, putting on too much weight and the sugar in junk food causes stress, foggy thinking and depression. Junk food makes you sickness.

When you enlist self-destructive patterns like compulsions or toxins like junk food, alcohol, tobacco, caffeine and other drugs to numb or resolve pain, you amplify pain. The buzz you may get for a few minutes, eventually makes you feel yucky.

Home Plate

If the grownups told you to "finish everything on your plate to help the starving children in _____ (Fill in the blank)," you most likely have an imprint that says; "I always finish everything on my plate."

You don't think about it consciously, you just eat everything on your plate. If you are getting rolley-polley, this imprint hurts you. That thought, planted in the garden of your mind when you were young and your mind was fertile, has grown into an horrendous weed.

☞ THE EIGHTEEN LAWS OF THE MIND

To be successful with hypnosis it's important to know the laws of the mind.

- ☞ Everything is hypnosis
- ☞ Monkey see; monkey do
- ☞ Learning and change take place in the subconscious mind
- ☞ Change takes place in the present
- ☞ Suggestions work best when the subject has a readiness for change.
- ☞ We are single minded
- ☞ What you affirm you create
- ☞ What you try to ignore or resist, persists
- ☞ Anticipating anxiety causes more anxiety
- ☞ Energy goes where attention flows:

  Attention goes to the subject of a sentence.
- ☞ We seek pleasure and avoid or ignore pain
- ☞ We receive suggestions best via our dominant senses.
- ☞ The harder you try the more difficult it becomes
- ☞ Strong words work best
- ☞ Keep it simple: The mind is emotional and literal
- ☞ Repetition works, repetition works
- ☞ Creativity begets creativity
- ☞ Connecting with your profound wisdom is fun and easy

The Stockwell System

Everything Is Hypnosis

Every sensory perception you experience is taken in by your computer mind that incorporates data as part of the big hologram. Everything you create in your life starts as a conscious or subconscious thought. When you really think about it, whatever you have or don't have, do or don't do, is the result of suggestions you give yourself. Life has an element of fate, yet, how you talk to yourself about things that happen "out of the blue" has direct impact on the course of your life too.

Photo by Jon Nicholas

Monkey See; Monkey Do

Though everyone has different dominant senses, we all tend to imitate what we see. We model what we see around us. Children model their "big people's" behavior. Teen's dress and talk like their peers. Adults model their "mentors" behavior. Advertisers set up vivid depictions of behavior so that we imitate it.

As an experiment, the next time you're with a group of people, yawn boldly. Notice how everyone joins you.

If you want to calm someone, try a typical NLP (neuro linguistic programming) technique and synchronize your breath to his or her rhythm, and then, slow your breath down. They will unconsciously join you.

"Do as I say, not as I do," just doesn't work in parenting. Actions speak louder than words.

Learning And Change Takes Place In The Subconscious Mind

Your subconscious mind initiates and carries out change. If you ask your conscious mind to change behaviors that live in the subconscious, it is like calling in a plumber to fix your electricity. Changing a light bulb with a pipe wrench just doesn't work. You can't change underlying mental patterns with the conscious, analytical mind. That's why you may have tried to change behaviors through conscious will—and it was difficult or impossible. Real change only takes place when a decision is made and carried out on the deepest level.

Change Takes Place In The Present
"I literally program myself"
The subconscious mind is a literal mind; it literally delivers what we ask of it, and it only responds to the present. If we say, "next week I will make more money" or "tomorrow I'll stop smoking," that future time never comes. The subconscious will wait for next week or tomorrow before it begins to carry out your instructions. When you phrase your suggestions in the future you make it impossible to carry out the message in the present.

Winning Suggestion	Losing Suggestion
I make $2000 a week	Next week I'll make money
I have a wonderful full time job	I want a full time job
My lungs are clear and healthy	Tomorrow my lungs will be clear

Define what you want as a positive accomplished fact, speak or think as if it has already happened, take a deep breath, release it and watch it happen. Make it an accomplished fact. No need to analyze or judge your affirmations. Simply focus upon it, repeat and reinforce it and then just let it go, release it.

Sometimes in psychotherapy we're told that if we can uncover the childhood source of our problem and understand it, it will be resolved. To really be effective we have to do more than just understand, we must extinguish any strong reactions, forgive, release and most importantly, return to the present. Real change occurs in the here and now.

Hypnotic Suggestions Work Best When The Subject Has A Readiness and Expectation For Change

Perhaps the most important element for successful hypnosis is the subjects' readiness for change. Many of us think about change for years, almost preparing for that moment of truth, the turning point, the instant when we shift from one point of view to another.

When the student is ready the teacher appears. If you've been toying with changing something in your life, it starts with a decision. What are you ready to change now? How would you rather it be? Give yourself that suggestion now and viola, results!

Most people, who make an appointment with a hypnotist, have the perfect readiness and expectation to accept positive suggestions, they are ready.

We Are Single Minded

If, while test taking, you say to yourself "I can't think of the answer," or "I can't think of the answer," that is exactly what you think about. These thoughts take up the time and energy that you could use to just think of the answer. Mothers understand this when they kiss Juniors hurt and say "all better." Juniors skinned knee doesn't hurt as much when he is diverted by a loving act or new toy.

As an example, focus your attention on the part of your body that, at this moment, is the most comfortable. Is it your hand or foot? Whatever you decide, notice how good it feels. Now focus your attention on the part of your body that is the least comfortable. Pay full attention. When you focus on pain, do you remember the pleasure place? All right, deep breath and focus your attention again on the part of you that feel most comfortable. Deep breath and relax.

What You Affirm, You Create
I positively change.
Keep Affirmations in the affirmative. "I love money, it's good for me." "My lungs are clear. I choose to live. I do good kind and loving things for my precious body. It's now okay to eat healthy food." works wonders. Stating your goal positively and clearly works wonders.

"I don't smoke anymore" will motivate you to light up a white scorpion much faster than a positive affirmation of outcome: "I choose to feel great," "I won't be late for my appointments anymore," won't work as well as "I am always early for every appointment. I enjoy being on time."

The deepest mind grasps only the subject of a sentence. Make sure that you state the results you want. "I enjoy breathing well. It clears away any toxins. My lungs are born again in this moment." Positive focus also serves to override the conscious tendency to judge or resist new ideas.

What You Try To Ignore, Or Resist; Persists
If you say to yourself, "I'm not going to notice the funny way he moves his mouth," makes the funny way he moves his mouth your focal point.

Try this; don't think about a pink elephant. Don't think of an elephant. A huge Pink elephant. Pink, pink, pink ELEPHANT. What do you think about? Of course, an elephant...a very pink elephant.

The mind embraces the subject of a sentence. "Elephant, not" translates into just plain "Elephant." (schwing).

Many a new hypnotist makes the mistake of giving suggestions in the negative. "I am a non-smoker" usually backfires. It suggests the very behavior you want to eliminate. The word not is an ignored orphan to the subconscious. Avoid words that are intrinsically negative. If you say "My headache is gone." The word headache is negative and reinforces a negative outcome. Instead say "My head is clear and I feel great."

Anticipating Anxiety, Causes More Anxiety.
Let's say you can't sleep, so you worry about not sleeping. Your

worry becomes a self-fulfilling prophecy, making sleep more difficult. You may know how debilitating this can be if you experience impotence or lack of orgasm and self perpetuate it with worry. You can solve these dilemmas by using the principle of paradoxical thinking and wish for exactly what you fear. Wish you can't sleep, and watch yourself drift off. This is called the "Law of Reverse Effect" by hypnotists.

This paradoxical phenomenon is used cleverly in hypnotic suggestions like, "I affirm now I will not go to sleep. I will not go to sleep." To eliminate cookie bingeing try: "Instead of eating a bag of cookies tonight. I'm going to eat six bags. If I can eat one, I can eat six." With such an absurd suggestion and the inner mind says; "This is ridiculous. I don't want six. As a matter of fact I don't want one either." The result is that you eat far less than you did before and this takes the anxiety away.

A famous story is told about Milton Erikson.

A hopelessly obese woman came to him. "I have to lose 150 pounds," she said.

"I will help you only if you promise to do exactly what I tell you. Do I have your word?"

"Yes, whatever you say"

"Very good. Come back and see me when you have gained another 35 pounds."

It's said that she forced herself to follow his instructions and was so disgusted with eating that she easily lost all 185 pounds and then some.

The Law Of Reverse Effect (LORE) works by causing us to detach and muse. When we exaggerate a problem, we let it go.

Energy Goes Where Attention Flows:
Attention Goes To The Subject Of A Sentence
Many folks mistakenly give themselves poor suggestions, i.e.; "I'm NOT going to eat this bag of cookies. I'm NOT even going to think about these cookies." And, of course, they eat the whole thing. The subconscious mind wraps itself around the subject of the sentence, NOT (..just kidding). Behavior follows thought.

We Seek Pleasure And Avoid Or Ignore Pain
The idea that we only seek pleasure and avoid pain works best as we seek the meaning in our life and enjoy the ebb and flow of our life experiences. Our pain sometimes shows up so we learn. The trick is to return to pleasure and joy in short order. If we vehemently deny pain, we can count on winding up with pain for a bedfellow. If we stubbornly choose joy, we can count on laughing ourselves to sleep.

To change any behavior, all you have to do is attach more pleasure to the positive results that you want. We often stay in painful behaviors because we focus our energy on pain. When the pain gets too great, we reach our pain threshold and "bottom out." That's when we suffer emotional emergencies or illness. This usually grabs our attention and we decide to refocus (I call that "hocus-focus."). We get the consequences of our limiting pattern and give up the idea that if we repeat the same pattern long enough the results will change. We go for new results by changing to a new pattern.

Most people who read self-help books like this one, or visit a hypnotist, are seeking pleasure and an escape from painful patterns or limits.

Suggestions for Pleasure Seeking
I'm going to give you an assignment today. Your assignment: if you choose to accept it, is to become a pleasure seeker, a full-fledged 100% pleasure seeker. From this point forward, you do kind, considerate, nurturing things for yourself. You only do things that bring your precious body to radiant health that uplifts you to your higher self. Your higher self makes you naturally high. You no

longer do anything that harms you in any way.
You are, in this instant, a full-fledged pleasure seeker. Because this is so, put your hand on your heart and affirm that it is so: "I choose joy. I choose wellness. I choose peace. I choose life."

The world has now entered into a conspiracy to do you good; and no matter how much you try to sabotage it, the world will prevail to bring you pleasure and joy, and only bring good to your life.

You Receive Suggestions Best Via Your Dominant Senses.

We learn best when we employ our dominant senses. To impress a message deeply into the subconscious's, use your dominant sense, or senses. Such suggestions and inductions let you smell, taste, feel, see, hear or intuit. As you come to your senses, you get results. To communicate or hypnotize with another, always talk to them using their dominant mode.

What is my dominant mode or sense?

You can discover your dominant senses by closing your eyes and going back in your memory to a moment when you felt personal satisfaction. Staying in that memory, notice it from each of your senses. What stands out for you? Was it the way things looked? Smelled? Tasted? Sounds you heard? Words spoken? The way your body felt? Something to do with touch? Or something beyond the physical senses all together? As you journey through each of your senses, notice which one stands out dominantly.

Words are also clues to ones dominant senses. For example, if one describes sights and say phrases like "If you see what I mean," you know that they are visually dominant. If their talk describes words spoken and they use phrases like, "that doesn't sound right to me," they are sound dominant.

The Harder You Try, The More Difficult It Becomes
"Avid pursuit of a goal thwarts it."　　　　　　　-Victor Frankl

Don't try hard, try soft. Go with the flow. Hang loose and don't sweat the small stuff.

Then you don't demand solutions, but let solutions unfold, your mind has a way of resolving conflicts and solving puzzles.

Make what you want (your goals and dreams) a byproduct of everything and ever situation. Let's say you want more love in your life; make everything, your work, the drive to work, your sleep, even your trip to the grocery store an act of loving. If you want to be happy, let happiness be the by product of all you do and all that happens to you.

Strong Words Work Best.

Weak words don't work. Words like maybe and try, don't fly. Make words and phrases BIG and get results!

Pick up a pen between your thumb and forefinger. Now think to yourself "I am going to drop this pen." Fully concentrate as you repeat to yourself "I am going to drop this pen." Because you are concentrating on the future nothing happens. Now change the message to "Drop the pen," and notice how you easily release it.

As you look at the pen you just dropped, think to yourself "Try to pick up the pen." "Go ahead and try," Now send the message from your brain to your hand "Pick up the pen" and it's a done deal.

Keep It Simple

The subconscious mind is a literal mind. If you say "you make me sick;" you may be correct. A "pain in the neck" will manifest as a pain in your neck. And if someone "gets on my nerves" they will. The subconscious understands sentences like a five-year-old might. Don't overload or confuse the mind with high fallutin' phrases or long drawn out, confusing, overloaded never-ending sentences that seem to go on and on and on and on and on forever.

Creativity Begets Creativity

Photo by Jon Nicholas

Repetition Works. Repetition Works. Repetition Works.

You can say that again! Repetition works. Keep asking for what you want. Repetition conditions the subconscious mind and lets the universe assist.

Ask! Ask! Ask! Ask! Ask! Ask yourself and others until you get what you want. Keep asking. The more that you affirm, the deeper the message thinks-in. While in trance, repeat your positive suggestions over and over and over again. Rephrase them, enlarge them, write them, visualize and imagine them. Saturate subconsciously the results you truly desire and override limits.

Paste up words or symbols to reinforce your suggestions in your waking world. If you want to remember to slow down for example, paste a heart sticker next to the clock on your car's dash (slow) board. It will serve as a memory peg and reinforce similar suggestions. Other people are not mind readers so you must ask them for what you want to make it easy for them to give it to you.

Connecting With My Profound Power And Wisdom Is Fun And Easy.

Self-hypnosis, affirmations, guided imagery, and positive self-talk are simple tools that allow me to explore my subconscious mind, discover and replace imprints that no longer serve me well, and listen to my higher self.

Illustration by Shelley Stockwell

Chapter 5
TO DEFINE IS

What is Hypnosis?

Hypnosis
From the Greek "hyp" meaning "behind" and "gnosis" meaning knowledge.

When we use it we are "hip" and we "knows" more.

Hypnosis teaches you to *intentionally* enter trance to control information and behaviors you want to enforce or change. Hypnosis done by a hypnotist is a guided trance state.

Hypnosis is a natural state of heightened awareness where you easily take on suggestions, listen to inner wisdom, and replace limiting imprints with those that serve you better.

"..natural state.."
Any time you focus attention from outer to inner awareness, you enter the sacred chambers of the deepest mind.

Whenever your attention shifts from actual events around you to the events of thought, you enter into trance. Fantasy is another word for trance. Hypnosis occurs when a suspenseful book or movie takes you from conscious thought into the "action" on the screen of the mind. If you weren't in-tranced, your conscious mind would say, "These are only actors and fictionalized characters."

When your mind drifts as you drive a car and you don't notice the freeway exits, you enter into hypnosis. Your critical, analytical mind (the same mind that may be reading this right now) takes a vacation as your deepest mind drives. If the vehicle in front of you stops, you automatically hit the brakes because your "hypnotic" mind is 100% committed to your survival. This deeper mind keeps your heart beating and your lungs inflating and deflating.

When do you experience spontaneous trance?

Zone During sleep
Twilight Zone Upon awakening and just before sleep, when not asleep, nor yet wide awake
Oh! Zone When making love
Speed Zone Driving on a freeway and not noticing how you got from there to here
Tone Zone "Runner's high"
Zoned Out Spacing during a boring business meeting or lecture
Fire Zone Staring at a fire or watching ripples on the water
Ohm Zone Chanting, Praying
Baritione Zone Deep Meditation
Gramophone Zone Listening to music
Couch Potato Zone TV and movie watching
Tome Zone Absorbed in reading
Danger Zone During traumatic experience
Dis-zone Arguing and shouting
Monotone Zone Bored out of your mind
Comb Zone At the hairdressers or barbers, eyes closed, relaxing
Stone Zone While under anesthesia
Rub Her Zone During a massage
Chroma-Zone Polishing your car
Obsess Zone During compulsive behaviors
Personal Inner View Daydreaming, fantasizing

"..of heightened awareness.."

Hypnosis makes you keenly aware. Wherever you focus your energy becomes clear and detailed.

Hypnosis harnesses memory and energy. Witnesses to crime, under hypnosis, recall with vivid accuracy license plate numbers and other details.

Subjects of stage hypnosis may appear unaware; yet if you are that subject, you're fully aware.

"..where you easily accept suggestions.."

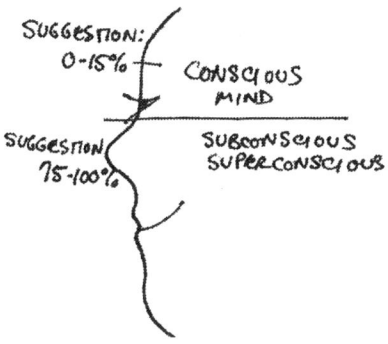

Illustration by Shelley Stockwell

You're suggestible in your normal awareness and even more suggestible when entranced. Suggestions are pieces of information that you receive and incorporate into your attitudes, behaviors, and internal data bank.

As an example of conscious suggestibility, if someone says to us that your clothes look peculiar, you may never wear those clothes again. If you watch someone bite into a lemon, or eat salty popcorn, you salivate. Yawn, yawn, yawn. Think about yawning and (yawn)...and you just might. In trance you're over five times more suggestible than in your regular awareness!

Your conscious mind accepts, receives, and incorporates less than fifteen percent of suggestion it receives. When you enter a trance your receptivity to suggestion jumps to eighty five percent or more. This morning, between wakefulness and sleep, in your natural trance, what did you say to yourself? Was it positive? Did you awaken to depressing news on the clock radio? Did you go to sleep with uncensored TV input? Eighty five percent or more, of what you say to yourself, makes a deep impression on the subconscious mind. The power of these suggestions can effect your attitude for the rest of the day.

All hypnosis is in fact, self-hypnosis; a hypnotist simply guides you into self-hypnosis. Hypnotists carefully phrase suggestions so that your subconscious mind accepts them easily. This "science of words" uses positive colorful phrases to make a deep impression on your mind. You, of course, are always in charge of your mental state.

"..listen to inner wisdom.."

Part of you that knows exactly what you need to do to make life work in every way—physically, mentally, spiritually, and emotionally. Hypnosis lets you access this wisdom. Mother, father, brother, sister, mate or friends don't know your answers, yet you do. Your deepest mind knows and intuits what is best.

Hypnosis lets you focus upon your truth. You identify and communicate with your needs so you may satisfy them. You remember experiences and repressed emotions that heal the past, and celebrate your gifts of wellness, clarity and joy.

Additionally, in trance, you discover bigger pictures and psychic abilities.

"..and replace limiting imprints with those that serve you better.."

An imprint is a piece of information that becomes imbedded in the subconscious mind. These imprints, or buried thoughts and attitudes, strongly influence behavior and success.

Messages given you from age zero to five make powerful imprints (or impressions) upon you because at those ages you are in trance most of the time. These "imprints" may have served you well then, but now as an adult, these imprints may not serve you so well.

As a child, were you taught to "finish everything on your plate?" This message may have been perfect then and encouraged you to eat well and grow. Today, it may not be so perfect. Especially if you are eating mountains of food, are overweight, your joints ache, your blood pressure soars and your energy is depleted.

Imprints evoke unconscious behavior. Think of them as records in a juke box. Mom's words, "finish everything on your plate" is such a record. Facing food mountains you may not think of her word but the jukebox of the mind automatically plays that tune as you eat the whole thing!

> **Automatic Pilot**
>
> How come when I bake cookies I never make enough?
> I follow the directions and stir in all the stuff.
> The recipe keeps saying "I'll yield 36 or more."
> But when the bowl is empty, I've made less than twenty-four!
>
> Do you suppose those little tastes of sweetness on my tongue
> the samples bites, the well licked spoons, each doughy little crumb
> has off set the equation written in the recipe book
> and I ate a bakers dozen before I even looked?
>
> -Evie Streight and Shelley Stockwell

Childhood messages about money often influence adult attitudes. What were you taught about money? How do these scripts color your attitude today? If you were taught: I deserve money. Money is good for me. I'm great with money; these imprints serve you well. If, on the other hand, you were told "You're hopeless with money. Money is the root of all evil or the like; these messages undermine success and abundance.

In trance, you easily identify imprints that obstruct abundance and joy. And plant new, positive imprints that work better for you. Harnessing the mind let's you create what you want for yourself. When you're entranced, you can access information for review and understanding, and reframe your reactions.

The mind is a perfect computer that stores every instant of your life. In trance, the mind becomes an open book for self-enlightenment. You can go way back and vividly recall details like being in your mother's womb, birth, infancy childhood...every minute of your life.

So There You Have It!

Hypnosis is a natural state of heightened awareness in which you easily relax, take on suggestion, and listen to your profound inner wisdom. You naturally enter hypnosis just before going to sleep, upon awakening and many other times throughout the day. Any time you suspend critical thinking, you enter into hypnosis or the subconscious mind. Once you enter this sacred territory of your inner wisdom, you achieve your dreams and goals. Once again, here is the definition of hypnosis:

Hypnosis is a natural state of heightened awareness where you easily take on suggestions, listen to inner wisdom, and replace limiting imprints with those that serve you better.

Hypnosis By Definition

Over the past several years, I've asked my hypnosis students and clients "What is hypnosis?" Here are some of their replies while in their regular awareness and while in trance:

Hypnosis is..

"A tool for a sit down chat with self, a sort of summit conference where you agree on a new way of thinking or behaving that betters your life."
-Sandi Medearis

"A loving dream state where you know, accept and use everything that helps you most."   (trance state)

"A reality check. A direct path and connection to knowing that puts you where you want to be with your life."
-Laurel Birch

"The study of life from an internal point of view."   (trance state)

"The most direct way to facilitate change through positive manipulation and the power of suggestion."
-Meredith Ferguson

"In-to-me-see (intimacy)"   (trance state)

"Lets you go inside, heal, and create new patterns. Here, you know what you need to function in the world and build trust."
-Suzy Prudden

"A tool for change and healing."   (trance state)

" Taps our universal, vast and unlimited resource to help ourselves and humanity."
- Rhonda Carpenter

"A vehicle of change."   (trance state)

"The revelation of the subconscious...Communication with the very limits of imagination and the unknown world"
          -16 year old
          (trance state)

"Living in a new conceptual universe. New power of emotions...new sense of strength."   -Dr. John Goode
          (trance state)

"I call Hypnosis the XYZ technique; X to x-out the past, unpleasant experiences, Y because we like you and Z because everyone likes their zzz's."   -Phill Wells, Hypnotherapist

"I was aware of everything around me and knew that any time I chose I could open my eyes and walk out, but I sure didn't want to do that. The process was too interesting. My chair felt like it was rising and my eyes seemed to make a space between me and my eyelids."
          (regular awareness)

Illustration Compliments of Sandi Medearis

CHAPTER 6
Hypnosis History

The History of Hypnosis
Every culture has used the art of hypnosis in one form or another. Native American medicine men and women use the magic of the trance state to restore the ill to wellness. Shamans, witch doctors, and healers know the power of suggestion and the trance state, so do advertising agencies and PR firms.

TV evangelists often use what hypnotists call rapid induction techniques and auto suggestion to create quite a dramatic show as those "taken with spirit" collapse in trance, "speak in tongues" or throw off their crutches.

♀⚊The Cradle of Relaxation.
Hypnosis has been celebrated as a tool for healing and spiritual enlightenment since earliest recorded history. Ancient Egyptians honored the relationship of body and mind by using altered states in their "sleep temples." Here, during a one-month stay, folks would renew and regenerate themselves by use of trance. Engravings from these times show entranced worshipers performing religious rites and surgical procedures.

Ancient Greeks called their version of sleep temples "healing shrines" and the trance states used there were dubbed "hypnosis" from the root word hypnos meaning "sleep." Chiron and other well-known Greek physicians used hypnosis to prepare their clients for surgery. Hypnosis was used alone or in combination with narcotic herbs and volcanic fumes. Pre-Christian Jews used professional "exorcists" to release negativity or "evil spirits" from folks much like the Catholic exorcists do today.

In 350 BC, Hypocrites, known as "the father of modern medicine," wrote 70 volumes of the Hippocratic Corpus underscoring that "all feelings and emotions originate in the brain and are the source of any disease of the body." Medical doctors honor him to this day by taking the "Hippocratic Oath" when becoming licensed.

⌘ 1700's
Father Grassner and Father Hell (1760's)
These two Catholic priests used magnets and release therapy as exorcism tools and to treat illness.

Franz Mesmer (1734-1815)
In 1770, Viennese physician, Friedrich "Franz" Anton Mesmer perpetuated a theory he called "animal magnetism," in which he used magnets, healing hands and suggestions. "Planetary magnetic-pull influences us through an invisible fluid (gravity?)," he said, and people were mesmerized.

The sick, he reasoned, had less or unequal distribution of this "joy juice" and magnets restored the balance of these fluids. Modern day quantum physics has since shown that electromagnetism does effect body chemistry.

Mesmer invented the baquet, a large round oak cask with metal rods sticking out that was an early version of the California hot tub. Thirty people entered at a time. Each, either directly touching a rod, or connected by a cord to a rod.

Mirrors and music enhanced the experience. The patients sat silently as Mesmer hypnotized them with an eye fixation method or by touching them with a magnetized rod. Eventually, one would "crisis" by coughing, laughing, crying, screaming, perspiring or showing some kind of agitation. When this happened, they were removed to a "crisis room" where they were free to emote freely. Their catharsis was followed by deep relaxation.

He presented his thesis, The Influence Of The Stars And Planets On Curative Powers to the faculty at the University Of Vienna. Prior to Mesmer, it had been believed that human behavior was predicated upon the balance of "humors." "It is not 'humors' Mesmer said, "that changes our behaviors, it is magnetism."

Later, Father Hell claimed that Mesmer stole his work with magnets. Perhaps that's where the expression "mad as Hell" comes from. Following Father Hell's objections, Mesmer took the position that the magnets where ineffective and that it was the magnetism within himself, Anton Mesmer, that cured patients.

In 1784, The King of France set up a commission of inquiry, chaired by Benjamin Franklin, who was then the American Ambassador to France, to decide if animal magnetism was a scam. Ben said that the baquet had no electrical properties and that magnetism did not exist. His findings didn't seem to stop the multitudes from coming and their raving reviews of miraculous results.

Amand-Marie-Jacques de Chastenet, Marquis de Puysegur (1781-1825) (How's that for a handle?)

De Puysegur expanded on Mesmer's approach by inducing the trance state while communing with trees. He called his technique "artificial somnambulism." He was fascinated with the influence and control the "operator" had on the subjects' thoughts and actions, and noted that the subject was "startlingly alert and intelligent."

De Puysegur focused on his patient's "spontaneous amnesia" when they would diagnose their own ailment and prescribe their own treatment.

Francoise Deleuze (1753-1835)

Using Puysegur's techniques, Deleuze observed that suggestions, given when in trance, remained during the waking state. Today this is called post-hypnotic suggestion.

☦ 1800's
Abbe Jose Custodio (Curtudio) de Faria (1755-1819)

In 1815, Portuguese priest, Jose Custodio de Faria, said hypnosis, or "lucid sleep," was only successful with willing subjects and the actual experience of hypnosis was determined by the internal psychology of the one being hypnotized. The better your concentration, the more easily you are hypnotized, he said.

Faria Induction
Have the subject sit in a chair, close their eyes and focus their attention on the word "sleep." The hypnotist now says, "sleep," "sleep," "sleep," until they enter into the hypnotic state.

Jules Cleznet
On April 12, 1829, Jules Cleznet, a French surgeon, reported the first use of hypnosis as an anesthesia. He used it while performing breast surgery.

John Elliotson (1791-1868)
In the mid 1800's, a London physician, John Elliotson, performed 1,834 painless surgeries using hypnosis. Dr. Elliotson is also famous for inventing the stethoscope. He published one of the first hypnosis journals, Zoist, to report his and other's successes.

James Esdaile
"Mesmerism" was also used by Scottish doctor, James Esdaile. As chief surgeon of a hospital in Calcutta, India, he used it in over three thousand operations and noted that it produced "insensitivity to pain." This was a terrific fete, as chemical anesthesia had not yet been discovered.

Esdaile was thrilled that the mortality rate for his surgery dropped from 25-50% to a "mere" 5%. When he returned to England, the British Medical Community tried him for charlatanism and one physician who testified against him said that hypnotic anesthesia was "blasphemous" because God "intended people to suffer" and all pain should be borne with "Christian fortitude."

A report read to the Royal Medical and Churugical Society in 1842 demonstrated the amputation of a leg while a patient was in hypnosis. It was decided that all records of the presentation be stricken from the minutes because as one member said: "...The person whose leg was amputated had obviously pretended to feel no pain."

James Braid (1795-1860)
In 1842, Dr. James Braid from Scotland, dubbed "hypnotism" or "neuro-hypnosis," as a "new science." His book, *Neurypnology,* meant "nervous sleep."

"Suggestions become permanent during the sleep of the nervous system" was his theme. He was right, during hypnosis, brain waves do slow similarly to sleep; yet, unlike most sleep, hypnosis offers heightened inner focus.

Braid had subjects stare at an object for long periods of time to fatigue the central nervous system into sleep. Later in his career, he used little or no ritual or formality. Braid also dispelled the belief that the hypnotist held the power to bestow a trance state to the subject. The subjects "attitude and willingness" determined trance, he said. Perhaps that's why James Braid is sometimes called the "father" of today's hypnosis.

The Bramwells

Dr. Esdaile lived in Perth, Australia for a time and strongly influenced a physician named Bramwell. The son of this gentleman, Milne Bramwell, grew up to become a physician as well, and he wrote the classic book Hypnotism, Its History, Practice and Theory.

On March 28, 1890, Milne Bramwell demonstrated the power of hypnostic anesthesia to a gathering of medical doctors at

Leeds, England. It was then reported in the British Medical Journal and the Lancet. He received so many referrals that he dropped his medical practice to devote himself full time to hypnosis. Milne Bramwell is best known for his work with medical hypnosis, but he also wrote about hypnosis with animals and the phenomenon of clairvoyance and telepathy.

Moll

Around this same time a man named Moll wrote the book Legal Aspects of Hypnosis where he distinguished hypnosis from mysticism.

Leibeault and Bernheim (1837-1919)

Auguste Ambroise Leibeault and Hippolyte Bernheim of France are also credited with taking the mysticism away from hypnosis and understanding it as the normal state it truly is.

Hypnosis they said was not caused by mechanical means but by suggestion. Together they formed the Nancy School of Hypnosis and hypnotized over 12,000 patients. Bernheim published his book *De La Suggestion* that offered "suggestion" as a cure for the body and mind.

Freud (May 6, 1856-1939)

Sigmond Freud, studied under Leibeault and Bernheim and translated their book into German, adding his own preface. In 1895, Freud co-authored his famous book Studien uber Hysterie with a master hypnotist named Breuer.

Freud himself was a skilled hypnotist who often used the power of suggestion to release the emotions of patients in trance. Freud called his process "hypnotic catharsis." He used the nonverbal induction of "touching the patients forehead" and verbally suggested that the patient use "concentration of the mind," "use of imagination," and "the relaxation of the body upon the couch." Later he abandoned hypnosis in favor of sitting behind his clients as they free-associated on a couch.

Rumor has it that Freud rejected "hypnotic techniques" for "psychoanalysis" because his hypnosis clients, mainly wives and daughters of well-known physicians, revealed too much incriminating information about his colleagues. Additionally, Freud narrowly defined hypnosis as a deep trance state with direct suggestion only. So when his patient "Lucie" recalled past memories in both waking and hypnotic states, he put aside hypnosis. The excuse he gave publicly was that hypnosis "led to symptom removal and hindered a 'permanent' cure."

Instead, Siggy tapped the repressed mind by having patients voice their thoughts as they popped up and by analyzing dreams. This approach added two years to the hypnotic approach.

Others

"Neurologists" (mental doctors) Pierre Janet of France, Pavlov of Russia and Doane, Dugas and McDougall of the United States kept the practice of hypnosis alive and flourishing.

Twentieth Century

In the more recent past, hypnosis has moved in and out of public favor. Visions of Svengali's "look into my eyes, you are in my power" dotted the media. Trance-elvania was a place for chills and thrills. Despite efforts of scientific writers and researchers, hypnosis was sometimes cloaked with mysticism. Victorian novelists like Hawthorne, Dickens, du Maurier, Melville, and Poe, all wrote about hypnosis as though it were a mysterious and occult force.

Today, hypnosis is considered a science and is used as a powerful tool by college professors, people in the healing arts, and of course, hypnotherapists.

Dr. Milton Erickson, Ph.D. and M.D. wove true and fantastic stories to serve as metaphor and trance induction. His style of hypnosis did much for our present appreciation and acceptance of this powerful tool. Hypnosis was approved by the British Medical Association in 1955 and more than 40 years ago (in 1958) by the American Medical Association.

For Edgar Cayce, Jane Roberts and many others, transpersonal hypnosis opened the door to trance channeling and personal well being. Psychiatrist Dr. Brian Weiss popularized past life hypnosis in his book Many Lives, Many Masters.

Many redub hypnosis with new names. Napoleon Hill taught us to Think and Grow Rich. In 1936, Dale Carnegie taught How to Win Friends And Influence People and memory building formulas that tapped the subconscious.

John Grinder and Richard Bandler explore the body-mind connection with a style of hypnosis called NLP (neurolinguistic programming or neurolinguistic Psychology). The term Neuro-linguistic was coined by A. Korzybski in 1931. NLP reprograms the mind by reconditioning the patterned responses of body and eye movement, breath, language and vocal pacing. Tony Robbins transformed NLP techniques into a fortune with motivational tapes, books and seminars.

Shakti Gawain popularized "creative visualization." Religions call hypnosis "the power of prayer," "meditation," or "chanting." Therapist and motivational speakers call it guided imagery, visualizations, relaxation, trance therapy and clearing, to name a few.

Call it what you will, the ability to tap the resources of the deepest mind and inner wisdom empowers us to be our best right now, today! Hypnosis is no mystery. It is a learned skill. So let's learn what hypnosis is and how you can use this powerful tool for yourself, your family, and your friends. Master your own mind. You are the "Master of your fate and the captain of your soul."

Actual Letter From Professor L.A. Harranden, Hypnotist
March 22, 1900

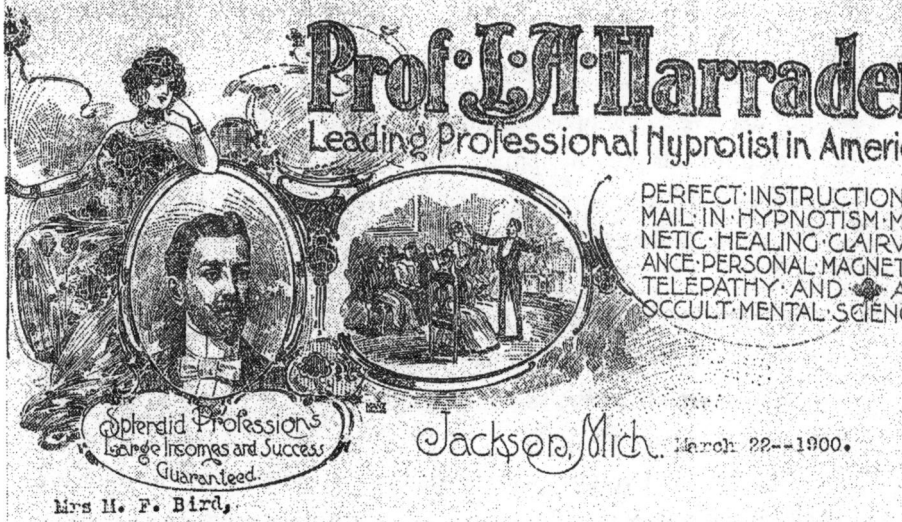

Prof. L. A. Harranden
Leading Professional Hypnotist in America

PERFECT INSTRUCTION [BY]
MAIL IN HYPNOTISM, MA[G]-
NETIC HEALING, CLAIRVO[Y]-
ANCE, PERSONAL MAGNETIS[M],
TELEPATHY AND AL[L]
OCCULT MENTAL SCIENCE[S]

Splendid Professions, Large Incomes and Success Guaranteed.

Jackson, Mich. March 22--1900.

Mrs H. F. Bird,

    Natural Dam, Ark.

My dear Madam---

    Your favor of recent date at hand. I am glad to know of the success you are having with my course, and I wish for you the very best of results.

    In placing a patient in the hypnotic condition for curing the Asthma, it is best to give possible and forciable suggestions for remedying the suffocation. You will find this in many instances of nervous diseases, and as soon as the patient begins to breathe hard you must give suggestions for controlling this. There are no dangerous results whatever, and you need have no hesitation whatever in hypnotizing anyone.

                                    Very sincerely yours

Illustration Compliments of Sandi Medearis

A Channeled Conversation With Professor Harrandon

On January 26th, 1997 my hypnosis students asked me to channel a practicing hypnotist from the turn of the century (1900's) Professor Harrandon. Harrandon was well known for his mail order hypnosis courses and stage shows. This was a closed eye channeling, though the professor seemed to see everything .

"Hypnotism is a spiritual energy experience that is done with magnetism. Magnetic power must be presented only with great authority. Great authority is required for the subject to understand suggestion."
"What is that vibration please?"
(Student: It is the tape recorder.)
"It is magnetism. It is pulling my magnetism as I am transmitting magnetism. It is a very peculiar item may I have it please? It is an item of magnetism. It pulls just as I am speaking but it is in a machine. It is very peculiar indeed."
(Student: It records your words so we can write down what you teach us today.)
"My words are sticking like magnets upon a machine? This sticks you to it. It is perhaps like hypnosis, yes ? It pulls like the voice of the hypnotist. Magnetic it is. I do not wish to hold it more. I have not seen such a thing."

"Hypnosis is the ability to take the strength of the operator, the hypnotist, through magnetic pull, to separate resistance, to separate defenses and to go directly to the place where we take suggestion.
 Hypnotism must be done with power and authority or the person will not yield or succumb to your energy."
(Pamela: I have a pain in my side in my hip)
"The pain requires that you stand up young woman. Reveal your hip. And do not fidget about so."

"You others, hold your fingers like this and let the power of your magnetism emanate and radiate out like this, sending energy through the fingertips to her hip. Make your hands like this." (Hands flat with rigid fingers straight and separated. Tips of the fingers in the direction of Pamela's hip).

"It is the same in the mind as the muscle. You part away any tight musculature. Part the musculature with fluid motion so that you are literally combing the musculature into smooth patterns."

"Now with your breath and your mind, breathe to this place between your hands. You send her magnetic attraction. You part her resistance by smoothing her musculature . Now you are to give her a suggestion verbally to tell her she is well. Begin."

(Lily: "All is well.")
"More power."
(Lily: "All is well.")
"YOU ARE WELL!"
(Lily: "ALL IS PERFECT. THE MUSCLE IS RELAXED.")
"Breathe. Release. Smooth the muscle. Young lady how are you feeling?"
(Pamela: "Wonderful!")
"Excellent! You may be seated."
"It is submission that the mind understands. You must take a posture of being in authority and the body and the mind yield to the power and wisdom of those in charge, you see."

"The subject is putty in the hand of the operator. The hands of the operator hold power and electricity and are able to forcibly shift the energy of the subject. There are invisible strands of light that come from fingers. There are invisible pulls, like pulleys that pull you forth."

"This machine is quite peculiar. What other machines do you have?"
(Judy: "Ones to make the room warm.")
"Like coal?"
(Judy: "Yes.")
(Judy: "We have television where an image comes through a box.")
"I have seen a picture wheel."

(Judy: "It is the same but everybody can see the same thing at the same time from the box.")

"My, my, my, this is exciting! What else do you have?"

(Pamela: "Movies that talk on a machine in your home.")

(Lily: "We have microwaves. Like electricity. They have ∿∿ short waves that go into the food.")

"That is not good. It will hurt the food."

(Lily: "It cooks it.")

"Food in the hearth is cooked quietly; in the manner of nature. The machine could disrupt the tissue not in a natural way. It may deteriorate the structure of the food itself."

(Pamela: "Can we heal the food?")

"You can hypnotize food to be balanced. But it is better to hypnotize the receiving body to receive it with balance. That is why prayer is used. It is a magnetic stranding from the space being."

(Judy: "Do you believe in the space being?")

"They are all around you. They have big eyes."

("Are they here now?")

"It is hard to say, there is much disruption coming in this room from the machines (a computer, lights, a heater and, of course, the tape recorder). When I walked the earth plane, they were everywhere. They would sit on the street corners and say 'hello' to the people who passed by. They would sit in the churches."

("Are they friendly beings?")

"They are all friendly beings. They are part of your world. They are in the dimension of electro-magnetic pull through the hands. They are part of the influence of electricity. They are part of the invisible fluid from the sky and planets. They are part of magnetism."

"Hold hands rigid, send energy to another. Feel the bolts of lightening coming from the fingertips. That is electro magnetic pull as you call it. Magnetism as I call it."

("Do you pull energy from people?")

"You part resistance and then you give a powerful very authoritative suggestion. You are the vehicle of energy."

STEP TWO:

TOOL TIME

Give one your wisdom and they might succeed. Give one tools to tap their own wisdom and they most definitely will succeed.

    The following tools are the nuts and bolts for harnessing your natural gift for success.
    Think of your mind as an out-of-this-world computer system able to categorize, assemble and create limitless possibilities. You've explored how this amazing mind of yours works and how your mind interplays with the brain. Taking control of your thinking and behavior is fun and easy. And when you do, you manifest everything you want.

                                        Let's Go!
                                        Love,

                                        Shelley

Photo by Bryce Stockwell

CHAPTER 7

Prepare For The Journey

☞ **Signposts of Relaxation**

❢ **Rules of the Road**

☼ **Entrancing Guidelines**

🚂 **Ways of Trance**

☞ Signposts of Relaxation

Signposts or observable signs of a trance state are like cobblestones on the road to the subconscious mind. Often they blend into one another in a gentle continuum. As you leave the "here and now" frame of mind, your body naturally relaxes. Each hypnotic journey takes on it's own unique qualities.

Behavior	Brain Wave	HZ	State
active	beta	13-26	conscious
relaxed	alpha	7-13	hypnosis
dreamlike sleep	theta	4-7	deep hypnosis
dreamless sleep	delta	.05-4	sleep

There's no proven correlation between the depth of a trance and the success of suggestion. Yet it's fascinating to notice characteristics of the various trance states; they range from alertness to deep slumber. Your brain wave activity (cycles per second) during trance, is would most likely alpha (7-13 HZ) or theta (4-7 HZ).

Altered states are sensational. When you enter your inner mind, your senses are evoked, heightened and stimulated; so is your creativity.

If someone were to observe you during hypnotic trance, they would notice that you appear to be sleeping or very relaxed. The by-product of altered consciousness is relaxation. The hypnotist also would appear in an altered state of consciousness too, especially during trance induction.

If you're lying down, your feet may fall outward, your arms and limbs become limp, and your breathing deepens. Sometimes, in trance, you release energy as a sigh, yawn, laugh or cry.

The Outward Signs Of Hypnosis:
"What did the grape say when he was squished?"
"Nothing he just let out a little wine"   -Jon Nicholas

The Hypnotic Sigh
Entering or deepening trance may evoke a deep sigh, yawn, laugh or even cry. This energy release heralds the opening to the door of deep relaxation.

Deep Breathing
In trance, breathing tends to be deep and shallow, much like regular sleep. Notice subtle changes in breathing.

Relaxation
The by-product of all hypnosis shows in the relaxed muscle tone of the limbs and face. You can lift up a subject's hand, and it dangles loose and limp and lazy like a loose rag doll. Feet splay apart if the subject is resting on their back.

Rapid Eye Movement
The eyes have it when it comes to trance. With closed lids, the eyes often go back and forth or flicker as they do in dream or REM (rapid

eye movement) sleep. Some folks experience extra tearing and most have a temporary redness in the whites of the eyes or a glazed look for a few minutes after opening the eyes following trance.

Changes In Body Temperature
If you touch the palm of the hand, you'll discover that the temperature, while in trance, is either hot or cold and sometimes very moist.

The Inward Signs Of Hypnosis:
The inward signs of hypnosis include those listed as outward signs, the hypnotic sigh, deep breathing, relaxation, rapid eye movement and changes in body temperature, plus the following:

Feeling of total well being
Relaxation
Peace and calm and well being are the most often reported feelings of the trance state.

Tingling sensation
Tingling in the fingers, toes or the limbs
Often those entering or deepening trance experience a goose bump (pilomotor response) of the extremities or chills down the spin.

Light pattern
With closed eyes many see flashing lights, patterns or vivid colors.

Lightness or heaviness of limbs
Sensational awareness of floating or rising up. Others feel heavy and unable to budge.

Detachment
Some say they feel like they leave their body.

Passivity
Feeling like you just don't want to move or exert any effort.

Relief
Feeling happier, brighter, with fewer problems.

Real time distortions
Time seems to slow down or speed up. An hour session usually feels like ten minutes. Yet the moment of now can seem to last forever.

Increased body awareness
In trance, your senses become finely perceptive and you become more aware of these senses. Some swallow more or are more attuned to body processes.

 **Five Signposts**
On Relaxation Road
Doing it
Thinking about it
Imagining it
Experiencing it
Dreaming it

Relaxation Level	Tell tale signs	Examples
Do it: Here and Now	Logical, analytical, left brain thinking, familiar muscle tone.	I deposit $50,000 into my savings account
Think About Doing It: Gentle Space Out	Breathing and pulse slow. Relax and drift nto a conversation or iactivity not in the here and now.	I think about handing the bank teller $50,000.
Imagine it: Major Space Out	Enter the world of imagination. Detached from surroundings, more aware of senses. Taking suggestion more fully.	I imagine myself handing bank teller
Experience it: Tranced Attention	Inner focus. Relaxed, & detached from surroundings. Easily listening to the voice of inner wisdom and truth. Enjoy feelings and sensations and take suggestion easily. Breath slow, hands warm, loose and limp or stiff and rigid.	I experience handing to the bank teller
Dream it: Good Night	I drift into sleep, unaware of conscious thought.	I dream I deposit $50,000 into the bank.

🗝 Rules Of The Road

The Best Cause:
Be. Cause

To take yourself on a sightseeing trip in a car you'd be sure you knew how to drive the car. When you travel the precious inroads of your mind, you need to be sure that you know how to move yourself through the byways.

Four basic rules keep you moving and joyous:
> **I Trust My Journey**
> **I Use Everything to My Best Advantage**
> **I Trust My Senses**
> **I Trust My Emotions**

Trust The Journey
Whatever information is revealed, it presents you with an opportunity to improve the condition of your life right now. Your very nature, God or inner wisdom (as you envision him, her, it) at all times moves you toward joy and harmony. Each new awareness fills you with light. You become enlightened (in lightened). New awareness leaves you feeling full (full-filled), whole and satisfied. You fall in love with your life. You are aware of your personal destiny and your place in the universe. As you evolve and grow and become aware of this feeling of wholeness, you experience a profound sense of personal satisfaction.

All information enhances each individual's self-love and happiness in the here and now.

Use Everything For Your Best Advantage
This experience is for you to expand your awareness. The more you learn, the more direction and clarity you bring to your life. Take advantage of knowing everything you can. You deserve to know it all and to have it all!

Trust Your Senses
There is a part of you that knows that if you trust your senses, they will never lie. Your senses offer you health on all levels: physical, mental, spiritual, emotional, and psychic. Your body tells you of any problem

areas and offers you the cure. This information is always there if you choose to listen. Occasionally, people experience psychic awareness during a journey. Enjoy the experience if it occurs!

Russell Targ and Harold Puthoff at Stanford's Research Institute proved that everyone is psychic if they simply trust the impressions they receive. Subjects told that they had "permission" to be psychic were.

Trust Your Emotions

Photo by Shelley Stockwell

Deeply emotional experiences when expressed give a tremendous feeling of relief. Laughter, as well as crying, are powerful ways to discharge stored tension, and that heals us. If any emotion comes up invite its release. Held back feelings dams up the nervous system, clogs clarity and blocks self love.

> *Say these four affirmations out loud:*
> **I Trust My Journey**
> **I Use Everything to My Best Advantage**
> **I Trust My Senses**
> **I Trust My Emotions**

Entrancing Guidelines
Expect To Feel Relaxed And Comfortable
The journey is the destination.

Find and ye shall seek.
Expect to feel relaxed and comfortable. All of these processes bring inner peace. The form the journey takes varies each time you depart and explore. Just let it be. Avoid expectations. Be open and see, hear, taste, and touch what you find.

If you are afraid that you will lose control and feel helpless, understand that you take control of your control when you make a choice to relinquish control. You are always in control. Anytime you want, you can open your eyes and return to your present awareness.

"In the center of every fear is a desire." -Carl Jung

Set Time Limits
"I choose to return to full room awareness in _____(so many minutes). When I return, *I will be refreshed, invigorated and clear minded."*

Before you enter the trance state, set the length of time for your journey. If your very tired, set an alarm clock in case you drift off into a nap after trance.

Go Now, Judge Later
"I'm learning to use my mind in a new way and whatever happens is perfect. Every time I enter hypnosis I learn more and more about myself."

The feelings of hypnosis are subtle and it's important for you not to expect your experience to be really BIG. Most folks aren't sure if they were hypnotized at all the first few times. Hypnosis becomes more recognizable with practice. The best thing to do is to suspend any questioning of hypnosis until after the journey, with a little blessing and these preliminary suggestions.

The Stockwell System

 **Ways of Trance**

Self Hypnosis
By a Professional Hypnotist
By a Friend
By Hypnosis Tapes
Spontaneous Trances
(Dreams, TV, Movies, Radio, News, Government and Religions)

All hypnosis, even trance guided by another, is self-hypnosis. You can give yourself powerful, and rewarding self hypnosis journeys. Called autosuggestion, self hypnosis is easy to learn and fun to use.

Hypnosis tapes are another tool for self-hypnosis. All that is required is quiet moments when you won't be disturbed. You close your eyes, turn on your cassette player and enjoy the trip. You can make your own hypnosis tape by using the sample hypnosis script in chapter nine "suggestions" or you can order a professionally recorded hypnosis tape from the back of this book.

Choose A Friend To Guide You

Remember, regardless of whether you are hypnotized by another or you induce your own trance, **You are always the one in control of your mental state.** Having another, guide, share and support you on your journey, can be very rewarding. Choose a sensitive friend or a professional who specializes in hypnosis.

Choose A Friend Quiz

I like this person.	T	F
This person likes and respects me.	T	F
This person acts kindly towards me.	T	F
I feel safe with this person.	T	F
I feel safe to discuss my thoughts & feelings with them.	T	F
"True" to all these questions, means you picked a winner.		

What to Tell Your Chosen Friend

Ask your friend if they are willing to put aside time to be your hypnosis guide. Some friends like to trade jobs. You might serve as support and hypnotist for the first hour, then switch and take the journey yourself while your friend becomes your hypnotist.

It is important that you both:
- Read the chapter on how to hypnotize yourself and others
- Agree to a time and place for the journey where you won't be disturbed
- Communicate how you would like to be supported.
- Are there responses you want to hear or don't want to hear?
- Do you want someone to ask questions, give suggestions or someone to just listen?
    - Do you want to be held or touched or not touched at all?
    - Do you want them to keep your experiences confidential?
    - Do you want them to write down what you say or tape your session?

Talk to your friend first. Tell them what you'd like them to do for you. You may want to give them permission to intuit what to do or you may want to be very specific. Remember that supportive people want to help, yet, often don't know how and, even more often, don't ask. Friends welcome your guidance.

If You Are the Chosen Friend

If you are the chosen hypnotist, read the "How To Do Hypnosis" chapter before you begin. Your job is to be your partner's loving friend. At all times "active listen" and do not play mind reader or God. The profound wisdom of your partner is fully present even if they are not speaking.

Remember that, regardless of what your partner is doing, whether it is laughing, crying or moving, it is simply an outward expression of an inward awareness. Make sure to support them in that expression and not stifle.

If something emerges verbally, scribe for them; write it down. If something seems unresolved, suggest that they forgive, love and reframe limiting attitudes into expansive ones. This way you facilitate them to learn lessons and enhance their life. Make *all* suggestions positive, simple statements.

Choose A Professional Hypnotist
"If you are not in my power raise your hand."

The title of the professional you choose may be varied: hypnotherapists, hypnotist, transpersonal hypnotist, past life therapist, hypnocounseler, stress management consultant, sports hypnotherapist or NLP practitioner.

The title is not as important as the mind set. Be sure this person seems healthy, sensitive, clean, sober, and respectful. Psychologists and psychotherapist may have little or no training in hypnosis. Look for hypnotists who have been specifically certified as a hypnotist. Members of the National Guild of Hypnotists are a good bet.

Choose a Professional Quiz

I feel safe with this person.	T	F
I like this person.	T	F
This person likes and respects me.	T	F
This person acts kindly towards me.	T	F
This person respects the value of hypnosis	T	F
They practice what they teach	T	F
This person is in my price range.	T	F

If you answered "true" to all these questions, you will be choosing someone who most likely will do the job well.

Hypnosis Tapes
Audio tapes are terrific because they repeatedly re-enforce the positive suggestions you want for yourself. You can use them anytime that is convenient for you. And you can rewind them to repeat areas you want to emphasize.

Making your own tape is fun and powerful because you hear the information from your own sweet lips. You can use the self-hypnosis guidelines and script in chapter nine "suggestions" for such a rewarding project.

Hypnosis tapes made by professionals are terrific, inexpensive and save you a trip to the hypnotist. They condition you so, when you do visit the hypnotist, your trance is deeper and more effective. If you don't have time to do your own tape you can order studio recorded tapes from the back of this book.

Use your tape once a day until you have the results you want. Usually three weeks does the trick. Listen as you drift off to sleep, take a midday break, or first thing in the morning. If you play your tape at bedtime, within the first or second time the results will be apparent. And you'll drift into more refreshing sleep as your inner mind accepts and responds to beneficial suggestions.

The more you listen to a tape, the better your results. Fourteen to thirty days really makes a great impression on the subconscious. The positive lessons learned enlist your own wisdom to teach you more positive lessons while you rest or sleep.

If you use a tape to improve your performance, or build confidence before an activity like test taking or sports, plan to complete your "session" about half an hour before so you can get your circulation going again.

Warning: Do not use hypnosis tapes while driving a car or using machinery. Most tapes are meant to put you into a deeply relaxed state that is not conducive to great driving and if you override suggestions so you drive well, you miss out on the benefits of hypnosis.

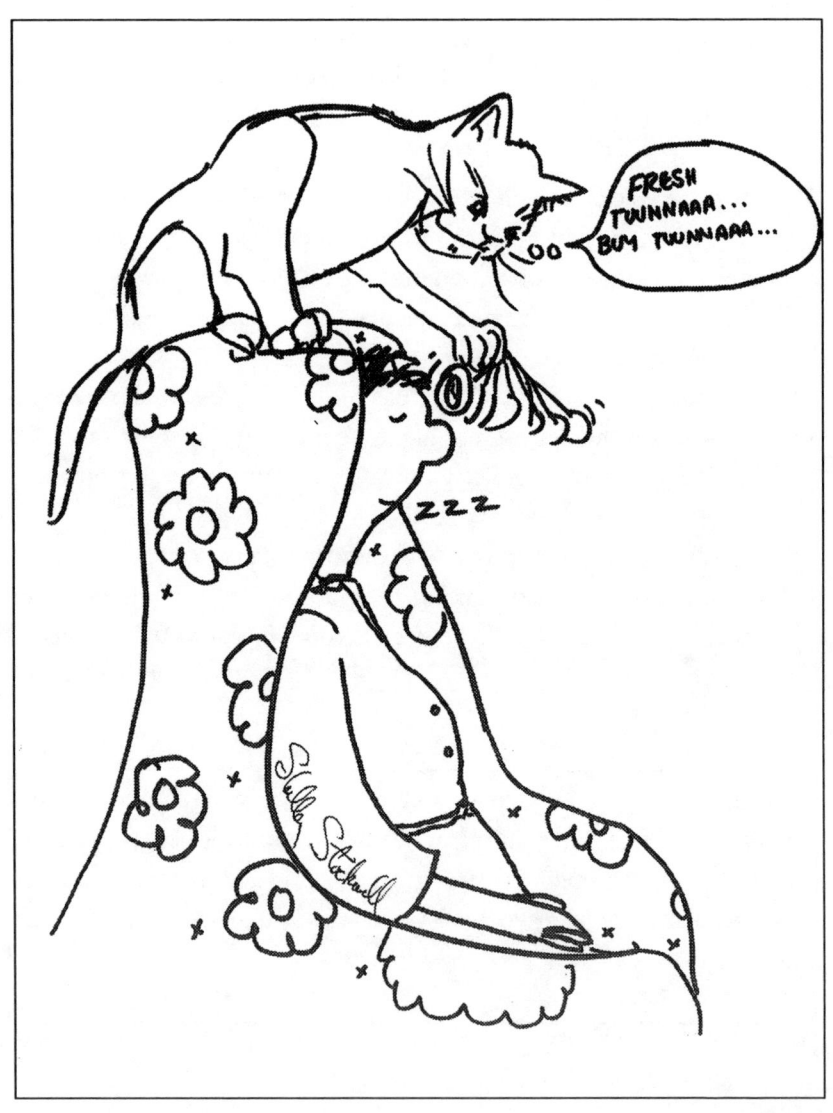

Illustration by Shelley Stockwell

CHAPTER 8
How To Do Hypnosis

- **Structure Of A Trance**
- **Induction**
- **How To Deepen Trance**

Structure Of A Trance

Trance states are best divided into six phases:

Blessing
Induction
Deepening
Suggestions
Conversations with the sub and super conscious mind
Return to room awareness

Trance lets you experience the subtle and refined art of shifting awareness and the innate "ah ha" that comes when you resonate with truth.

The following methodology for trance induction, deepening, suggestion and processing information are the ones I find most effective. Many of the processes were created from my own sub and super conscious data banks, my own deeper creative source.

Experiment with each technique and see how you like them. Then, tap your own inner wisdom and create new approaches to consciousness. You are a creative wonder!

Blessings

A blessing is a gorgeous induction and can be said by the hypnotist silently or out loud. Its purpose is to put you in a loving and centered place, and to calm the subject and induce trance. You needn't worry about the persons spiritual affiliations if you call it a blessing rather than a prayer, stay non-denominational and avoid specific religious references or beliefs. This is mine:

"Bless me on all levels
Mentally, Physically,
Emotionally and Spiritually.
Let all of these experiences be for my highest good
so that I may achieve my goals and dreams
and fulfill my life's purpose
amen, awomen, ah life"

You might like to lace a few suggestions in with the blessing. Like:

Bless (their name) on all levels. She/he has come here today to quit smoking It is my heartfelt desire that she/be be given the guidance and strength to help her/him do just that. Help me to hold the mirror so that (name) can reflect upon their natural ability to be in radiant health...

♥Induction

"Every time I enter into a trance state I go deeper than I've ever gone before."

We are, of course, naturally responsive to suggestion. Suggestions to induce trance may be given verbally as well as non-verbally.

An induction bring on relaxation and open the door to the trance state. Coupled with affirmations and positive suggestions, they move us toward abundance on all levels: self love, success and money in the pocket.

All inductions are ridiculously easy to learn. And they work! There are more inductions than you or I could possibly imagine. Some occur spontaneously throughout the day and others are purposeful performed.

All inductions rely on one or more of the seven principles of relaxation, startling command, loss of equilibrium, misdirection, fatigue or mental confusion. Each effects our brain functioning so we alter awareness. Used singularly or in combinations, the possibilities are endless. Here's how they work:

Relaxation or Progressive Relaxation

Yawn, yawn, yawn. Monotonous repetition bores the conscious mind to distraction. This is usually delivered in a slow sing song or monotone voice. Mantras work on this principle. And a repeated "Pick up your socks" chanted by a mother can send a youngster into the zone.

Energy Transference

As in the magnetic attraction of Mesmer, energy is a powerful tool. Even the thoughts of the hypnotist can influence trance states.

Startling Commands or Shock

These types of commands make the conscious mind say "adios." Usually the subject is given suggestions that they are about to be hypnotized and then suddenly a surprising command results in instant hypnosis.

Loss of Equilibrium

(Magnetic Attraction) offsets balance causing the conscious mind to leave. Rocking puts babies and grown subjects to sleep. So does falling backwards into the waiting arms of the hypnotist.

Fatigue

Anything that fatigues the eyes and the mind resulting in trance. Eye fixation, staring at a spinning disc, a flashlight, a metronome, a pendulum, or an hourglass.

> **Follow the pendulum with your eyes.** (Swing the pendulum slightly above eye level and at least eight inches from the forehead.) **Your eyelids begin to become heavy, droopy, drowsy and sleepy. You'll want to blink. As soon as you notice that you want to blink, that's the feeling of hypnosis coming on. So just let them close and you go deeper and deeper into hypnotic slumber.**

Misdirection

The mind can only grasp one idea at a time. As you move on one mental track you are surprised by another. Usually the hypnotist engages the imagination and once the subject has bypassed their critical thinking, they easily drop into trance.

> **Hocus Focus Headache Remedy**
> **Focus on the unpleasant sensation in your head. What color is it? How much does it weigh? How big is it? Where is it located? Is it transparent, translucent or opaque?**
>
> **It's moving. Where is it now? What color is it? How much does it weigh now? Is it transparent, translucent or opaque?**
>
> **Keep going asking more and more detailed questions as you interject suggestions like: "It's getting smaller. What size is it now?" And, finally as it shifts, say, "I'll take it now" and sweep hands upward from the crown of the subject.**

Mental Confusion

Riding one horse in two directions at the same time. What? Illogic makes it so much work for the conscious mind to keep track that it says "this is too much work" and just lets go. Sometimes involves counted numbers skipping from the mind. Or eyes opening and closing at various intervals. It's all just easier to go into trance and relax. Suggestions using mental confusion can be very powerful:

> **"I wish I knew ahead of time that my wishes, hopes and dreams would all become real.**
> **I wish I knew ahead of time that my wishes, hopes and dreams would all become real.**
> **I wish I knew ahead of time that my wishes, hopes and dreams would all become real."**

Every Day Trance-Formations

Simple spontaneous trances expand your personal limits. You may use one, a combination of several, or all of them. They are exciting ways to help you receive positive suggestion. Everyday trances include:

Twilight Zone
Conscious self-talk
Imagination
Treasure maps
Meditation
Prayer
Friendly persuasion

Any nearly spontaneous induction puts you into an hypnotic trance so you may enforce and reinforce simple positive statements or affirmations. Try each yourself and decide how you like that approach. Follow any positive suggestion with the thought; "Each of these ideas and concepts make a lasting impression on my deepest mind." Then take a deep breath and stretch.

Natural Trance States
"I do good kind and nourishing things for myself."

Twilight Zone
The easiest way to practice self-hypnosis is to take advantage of natural spontaneous trances. Just before getting out of bed in the morning and just before drifting to sleep at night are good ones. Known as vigilia in Portuguese, vigilance in positive self-talk, while in the mists of morning, can reframe even the most limiting patterns.

At this time your imaginative and suggestible theta waves are present as you enjoy a sort of twilight zone between reality and dreams. Some 75%- 100% of what you say to yourself, or hear, in this hypnagogic trance state is received and absorbed by your subconscious mind.

What suggestions did you gave yourself this morning? Were they negative? Did you say, "Oh my God, I can't believe I have to get up," or "I'm so tired, today's going to be a crummy day." Did you awake to depressing news on the radio? If so, you probably feel low. Tomorrow, before you awaken, if you say positive, nourishing things to yourself "I feel terrific. Today, wonderful things will happen to me," you begin the practice of self-hypnosis.

If your goal is to have more money, picture and imagine yourself closing the deal and receiving money. "Money comes easily to me." If your goal is to release weight, visualize, feel, and fanaticize yourself at your ideal weight, put a picture of a slim person on your refrigerator and say, "I eat when I'm physically hungry and stop eating when I'm physically full. I eat for fuel. I listen well to my inner voice. It tells me when I've had enough. I eat good, healthy, nourishing food, fresh fruits and vegetables, and avoid anything that harms my perfect body."

Conscious Control of Self Talk
"I am keenly aware of any and all self talk and I quickly and easily change any negative to positive"

Since you enter trance throughout your day, it is important that you become aware of your self-talk. Some things you say (in those quiet moments when alone in thought), you would never say to another living soul. So in those quiet times, notice what you say to yourself. If you catch yourself saying something negative, immediately stop and change it to something positive. Even if you think it's a lie. For example, if you hear yourself say, "That was a stupid thing to do," stop and say, "I am extremely intelligent. What I just did isn't working as well as I would like. Next time, I will do it differently. Because I am bright, I easily learn, shift, and adjust to strategies and changes that work better for me."

Most self-talk is a result of childhood imprints. If you catch yourself using them you can easily change them into a positive sentence and literally change your life. For example:

"That is the devils work and you are full of the devil"
reframes to:
"My work is full of light and I am pleased to be a light worker"

Imagination
"My power to imagine a dream in the present is the identical power that makes it real"

In your mind's eye, picture and imagine the exact results you desire as if it's all ready happened. Use the power of your imagination. How do you want the outcome of a particular situation? For example, if you want to become the top earner in your office, imagine being presented with a plaque. Imagine your name on the plaque and the clothes you wear as you accept the plaque. Imagine putting all that money in the bank. How much money? Make that clear. Be generous. Imagine all the smiling people who give you money. Imagine the rewards that come your way in this moment. Do you buy a new car? If so, decide what it looks like. You notice how you feel driving it and where you go in it.

The more detailed your fantasy, the more likely you are to lock your mind around it, and the more likely that it will become a reality. The power to imagine a dream is the identical power that makes that dream become real.

Treasure Map or Wheel Of Fortune

Another way to imprint and manifest goals is to make a "treasure map" or "wheel of fortune." Glue pictures and write words that detail the results you want. For example, if you want to lose weight, write down how much you want to weigh. Glue pictures of yourself at your ideal weight, on a piece of construction paper. Pictures of you smiling, pictures of fresh fruits and vegetables, photographs of slim, happy, abundant people, "role models; just like me." Make these images vivid, detailed, and clear. Keep your treasure map in a place where you will see it. They work!

If you want to map abundance you can make a money map. Paste up specific numbers (i.e.: $7 million) and all the material goodies desired (what will you do with all that money?). Be sure to include happiness (ie: smiling faces) and God or Spirit (whatever that means to you) in the collage.

Meditate "In-Chanting Rituals"

Meditation is the most popular hypnosis in the world. Sogyal Rinpoch, the Buddhist Monk and Author says: "The basis of the practice of meditation is relaxation."

Meditation, like it's twin, hypnosis, brings joy and peace, coupled with suggestion, positive goal achievement.

Meditation is easy. Be comfortable and allow thought and feelings to calm down. There is nothing to attain or achieve, so let go. Even let go of the idea that you are meditating. Let the body be as it is, and breathe naturally.

As for the mind, don't suppress, follow or manipulate them. Just let them be without being seduced or distracted by them. "If I am dreaming or thinking; I just dream or think. If I don't add fuel, my thoughts play themselves out. I let thoughts come and go. I don't invite thoughts to tea unless they are thoughts that bring me glee...hee, hee, hee."

One Sacred Mantra:

Mantras are repeated sounds that sets up a positive vibration in the mind. Some faiths charge thousands for you to learn a secret mantra. Beryl Middleton offers this one for free. It's positively guaranteed to change your life.
   Breathe in, "sensa"
   Breathe out "humah."

Take your time and repeat again and again:
   Breathe in, "sensa"
   Breathe out "humah."

   ENJOY YOUR SENSA HUMAH, and TICKLE YOUR FANCY

Pray

"Beloved Pan, and all other gods who haunt this place! Give me beauty in the inward soul: and may the outward and inward be as one."   -Socrates
"The chosen people are the ones who listen with their hearts"
                              -Shelley Stockwell

The power of prayer is spectacular. God, or the higher power, as you understand him, her, it, taps superconscious awareness and allows spirit to co-manifest your dreams and goals. When you pray with all your heart, you easily receive guidance, truth and wisdom so that you learn to love yourself unconditionally. Sitting in a quiet place in nature also brings on altered awareness. Prayers and hymns help to bring about altered states of awareness by activating the sub and superconscious mind.

Amen is one of the oldest recorded affirmations. Originally from the ancient Egyptian language and then later from the Hebrew word meaning *truly*. Superstitions required a "God bless you" to keep your soul from slipping out, especially when you sneeze.

Friendly Persuasion
Use any hypnosis induction to put yourself in a relaxing state of mind and ask a friend to give you the positive suggestions you want.

Relaxation or Progressive Induction
The following inductions bore the conscious mind into a vacation somewhere out of town.

Fractional Relaxation
In this technique, you (just like a teacher you may have had) bore, fatigue, and tire your conscious mind as you move through your body or mind in details and simplicity.

One popular technique is to start at your toes, thinking about each toe in detail. Tense your toes, then relax them. Next move your concentration to the ball of the foot, to your arch, then to your heel. Tighten your foot and relax it. In the most minute detail, work your way up through your entire trunk, to your arms, hands, around your skill and across the eyelids.

Toning
Toning is great for those who are auditory and touch dominant. Hum with each breath the word "Relax." Let it vibrate your body starting from the bottom of the feet through the chakras all the way to the top of the head. Then combine all levels, each chakra, and go into trance.

Count Backwards
Count backwards from twenty to one, and sense yourself entering, step by step. A special place in your imagination with each count. Some picture a stairway some ride an elevator and visualize the numbers dropping deeper and deeper.

Count Breaths
Another technique is to count your breaths. With each inspiration, imagine white light. Hum softly the word "relax." If you are a visual person, see yourself relaxing. If auditory, use sounds. If you are kinesthetic, use sensations and feelings. Or, you can work with all of these senses together. I like to chart my breath as it journeys the body.

Count Blessings
Count each of my blessings, one by one, savoring each one, enjoying it completely with all your heart and each of your senses.

Eye Fixations

Staring
A popular technique is to stare at a pendulum. Try it, it works well. As you watch it swing from side to side, become the pendulum. Allow your body and breathing to feel the rhythm. Then, let your eyelids gently close down.

Or look upon and hour glass as the grains of sand fall. Falling, heavier and heavier, dropping one by one, as mist of drowsiness enfolds you and your eyes grow droopy, drowsy and sleepy. Eventually your eyes grow so relaxed that they just close down and you drift into a deep hypnotic slumber.

Or, look at a light or flashlight then close your eyes and let the light change colors and come and go behind your closed eyes and just let your self drift off.

❊ Gaze at the Moon
Imagine that there is a window that opens from your skull right in the middle of your forehead. When you close your eyes you can look up through that window and there you will discover a beautiful new moon, glorious in the night sky. As you gaze at the moon you begin to think about all the lovers throughout time who have gazed at this same moon...All the poets who have written about its beauty and all the babies snugly nestled in their small beds dreaming beneath this same radiant moon. As you continue to gaze you become sleepy drowsy and so comfortable and drop deeper and deeper into hypnotic slumber and the moon blesses you with its radiance...

💡**Hands Come Together**
Put your arms straight out in front of you, at eye level, palms facing each other. Look between your palms and imagine that there is a magnet pulling your hands together as you say to yourself or your subject 'Hands coming together.' When your hands finally touch you will drop into a deep trance and relax completely.

Misdirection Inductions
"What did Tarzan say when he saw the elephants with peanut butter on their feet running through the jungle?"
"Nothing, He didn't recognize them because they had on sunglasses."
-Jon Nicholas

Misdirection techniques are effective because the thoughts evoked are too much work for my conscious mind to track. As your conscious mind gives up control, you are entranced:

Out of Body
Lie on your back. Mentally float out of your body to a foot above yourself. Imagine you are suspended by strings and pulleys that pull you upward. As you float, become a detached observer and look carefully at your body. Describe it specifically and in great detail. Cover your entire body slowly, describing everything you see and hear, commenting on areas of tension and comfort.

Look With Wonder
Fix your gaze lightly on an object a few feet away. Silently talk to yourself about three things you see (pause), three things you hear (pause), and three things you feel (pause). Then you talk to yourself about two things you see (pause), two things you hear (pause), and two things you feel (pause). Good. Next, talk to yourself about one thing you see, (pause) one thing you hear (pause), and one thing you feel. (pause). If your eyes want to close, let them, and go on talking to yourself. Good.

As you go farther into a trance, you begin to wonder which of your arms or hands will become lighter. Lift it from the spot where it is resting with a true subconscious motion. Become aware of curious sensations of wondering about such a strange thing. You notice the lifting or other movements and their directions. And you wonder whether or how your hand will rise up and touch your face. When it does, you wonder if it return back to where it was resting. Or if the other hand will rise up first. Continue to enjoy this pleasant, curious experience of subconscious motion.

Track Your Thoughts
Become a witness, an objective observer to the thoughts you think. Observe your thoughts as they come and go. Notice how you, as the witness, can slow down or speed up any unpleasant thoughts. Simply open a door and let them leave and invite pleasant, serene thoughts from your imagination to instantly take their place.

Now, take a deep breath and become aware of the feeling of breathing. Hold the breath and when you let it go, take yourself even deeper into relaxation by saying "deeply relaxed." Let these words settle on the mind as a thought. Notice how you can observe your thoughts and your breath."

The Stockwell Thirty-Second Zap

When you do my thirty-second zap, you put yourself or your subject into a wonderfully refreshing hypnotic trance and in only thirty seconds! A visit to your inner world in this way is beautiful. This is where you live. This is who you are. Here's how to zap:

The First Blue
Say "blue" to yourself, then close your eyelids. Think and imagine the word blue. Blue as the sky, blue as a deep blue ocean, blue as a warm baby's blanket. Relax your eyelids so well that when you test them, they just don't want to open. When you've done a good job of playing this relaxation game you stop testing your eyes and say:

The Second Blue.
Say "blue" a second time. Then give yourself a positive suggestion, such as "I feel wonderfully refreshed." or "Calm, peaceful and easy." Then deepen your relaxation with deepening suggestions such as "with the next five breaths, I go deeper and deeper into the valley of relaxation. Deeper than I've ever gone before. (five, four, three, two, one)." Here in the valley, give yourself powerful suggestions and listen to your deepest wisdom.

The Third Blue
Return to room awareness (if you went into the valley count one two three four and five) "Wide awake, eyes wide open, feeling terrific."

Chason
Hold your non-dominant hand at eye level with your elbow slightly bent. Look at the back of your hand. Fix your eyes on a knuckle or index finger, keep your fingers close together and very tight. The hand is going to move towards your face. This is normal. Your fingers start to move apart as you move it towards your face. As this happens, close your eyes and enter a nice state of relaxation.

Ideomotor Responses
Ideo motor movements work as an induction, suggestibility test and a way to get feedback from your inner wisdom. French chemist Chevreul, gave this phenomenon it's name "ideomotor" meaning idea-movement because all thoughts "involuntarily and subconsciously" result in behavior. He used a pendulum, a string or chain with a ball or weighted object on the end.

Pendulum
Rest your elbow on the edge of a table, holding a string and weight between your finger tips in such a way that it dangles freely. You may stand or sit comfortably. Make no effort to move or not move the ball. Simply breathe and concentrate upon the movement the pendulum makes. Notice how it starts to move from left to right, right to left, backwards, forwards, clockwise, counter-clockwise. As you notice, each movement starts to happen in sometimes subtly ways or sometimes bold ways.

Now think the word "Yes, yes, yes!" As you repeat the word notice the movement of the pendulum. For this moment that movement represents "yes" for you.

Now the word "No, no, no." And again notice the movement. It will be different than the "yes" response.

And then "Don't know, don't want to say." and note that repose or movement. You're ready now to take another deep breath and ask

The Stockwell System

questions that you'd like your subconscious mind to answer.

Let Your Fingers Do The Talking

Relax by taking a cleansing breathe and say internally "Yes, yes, yes, yes!" Let the energy of the word move through the mind to the fingers. When you notice a twitch or movement, that is your designated 'yes' response for this process. Now establish a 'no' response by repeating "No, no, no." in the mind. And finally, the words "Don't know, don't want to say." and allow a finger to represent this response.

Review the three responses "Yes," "No," "Don't know don't want to say.' to make sure that they are clearly established.

To begin, take another cleansing breath and ask some simple questions that you know are true or false. For example:

- ✓ Am I breathing?
- ✓ Do I love God?
- ✓ Am I standing on my head wearing a pink tutu and combat boots?

You get the idea. Now ask questions you truly want answered and let your fingers do the talking. Since questions are limited to yes and no responses you can fact find like so:

- ✓ Is there a limiting pattern that's keeping me from making $100,000 this year?
- ✓ Am I consciously aware of that pattern?
- ✓ Will you let the pattern reveal itself to me as a thought right now?
- ✓ Am I aware of the steps I can make to change that pattern?
- ✓ Will you let me become aware of them now?

Non Verbal Inductions
Dance to Entrance

"Is there a man with soul so dead who has not been hypnotized while dancing with a beautiful woman."   -Ormond McGill

Dance and movement has been used to induce trance all over the world. Religious rites often involve ritualistic movement. The Whirling

Dervishes or Moslem Sufi dancers of the Middle East spin and alter state to drum and rhythm. The Hare Krishna use chanting and dance as a prayer or trance induction and the hypnotic trance dancers of Bali, Indonesia are world famous.

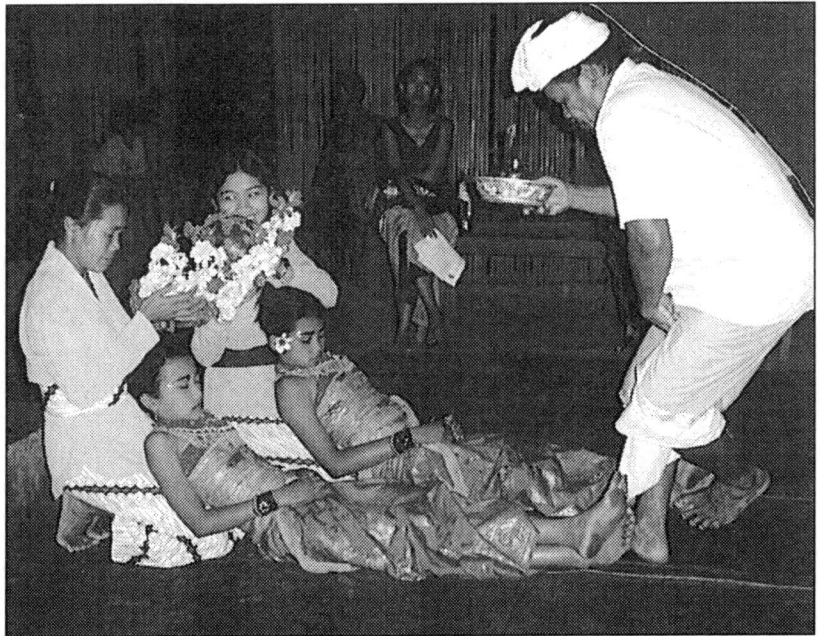

Photo by Shelley Stockwell

Dance creates mood as a suggestion: war dances, love dances, and gratitude dances. As both dancer and audience get caught up in the energy, the repetition of sight and sound combine with loss of equilibrium and away they go. The misdirection of the dance de-focuses attention from conscious awareness to altered states.

I have had a few clients who prefer movement to enter the trance state. When this is the case, I play repetitive, monotonous and riotous rhythm and instruct them to "spin. Just close your eyes and spin. Or just let the music move you with your eyes closed."

Cranial Sacral Induction

Photo by Shelley Stockwell

Thanks to Dr. Lilia Prada, O.D. and hypnotist for this one. The cranial sacral induction releases strain. Have the subject lie on their back as you gently place your hands on each side of their head. Close your eyes and gently feel the subtle motion of the head bones. Take your time.

"The bones of the skull are connected by sutures, there is movement between the occipital, parietal, sphenoid, frontal, and all the bones in the skull. Head trauma, birthing trauma or emotional trauma can form strain patterns between these bones and they become stuck."

♟ My version of Marx Howell's Induction

The patterns of moving and rotation induces trance. The configurations and pattern of hand placement can vary. Here is my version. Have the subject sit in a chair

"We're going to explore non-verbal communication. Are you familiar with non verbal communication? If I were to do this (finger in front of mouth like shush) what does that mean to you?"

If a minister was to do this (hands sweeping up like stand up) **or this** (hands sweeping down like sit down) **what do they mean?** (wait for answer) **So you see you know a lot more about non-verbal training than you realized.**

Now I don't know if your eyes will be open or closed but if I were to touch your neck like this (gently touch the side of their neck) you will open your eyes. So let's begin.

A powerful approach is to say; **"First I'll show you what will happen"** and then dialog with them as you go through the routine; the identical routine you'll perform silently the second time.

When complete, touch their neck so they open their eyes, and say **"Great, now lets do it non-verbally"** and do the whole routine again silently.

Here's a possible pattern to follow:

Rotate each arm.
Elbows loosely bent, one by one, slightly above eye level, rotate the arm so that their fingertips become the focal point of sight. If they try to help, gently shake their arm and hand and say "Relax, just relax, you don't need to help me. That's good." When motion is complete, place each hand gently on their leg or on the chair arm and then move to the other arm and rotate.

Eyes Closed
A sweep of your hand, or gently running your fingers down over their face, encourages them to close their eyes if they are not already shut.

Arm Positioning
Next, lift one hand and arm to be raised stiffly above the head and the other arm, elbow bent and hand touching behind the neck. Let the arm remain in this position for a minute. Then, gently bend the rigid elbow or gently shake the arm and return to lap or chair.

Repeat this movement with the other hand. Return the other hand to lap.

Gentle Press
Then press ever so gently on the lower arms thinking "deeper and deeper."

Breathe Together

Move around to the back of the chair. (It's a good idea not to break contact as you do) and place your hands on their shoulders. Synchronize your breath to theirs, using the same rhythm. Let them hear you breath in and out as they do. Each time they exhale, press gently down on the shoulders, and each time they inhale, lighten up.

Head Rotation

If they don't have a neck injury, place your hands on each side of the head fingers supporting the jawbone and thumbs behind the head and gently rotate the head randomly in one direction, then the other.

This Little Piggy

Thanks to Hypnotist Michael Ellner for this one.
Sit with the subjects' foot in your hand or lap or in front of you. Take your time and when you feel you have "permission" to enter their auric field, gently and firmly hold their foot in both hands, exploring it as if it is an angel wing.
Then, in slow motion, begin the wonderful childhood game of
This little piggy goes to market.
Gently pull each toe and think the words as you do:
This little piggy goes to market.
Gently pull the big toe
This little piggy stays home.
Gently pull the next toe
This little piggy had roast beef.
The next toe
And this little piggy had none.
Next toe
   And this little piggy cried wee, wee, wee, wee all the way home.
The baby toe is sweetly tugged. Then gently tickle up their lower leg to the knee and down again. Return to lovingly cradle their foot.

Mommy Mouse Cooks

Another version of this comes from hypnotist Franz from the Czech Republic and is called *Mommy Mouse Cooks*. Silently think this story as you begin gently moving your fingers in a circle on the bottom and arch of the foot:

"Mommy stirs the barley pudding in her big green pot. How many children does she have?"
One, two, three, four, five! First she feeds the big one
Gently pull the big toe
Then the next one,
Then pull the next toe
Then the next one
Pull the next toe
Then this one,
Pull the next toe
And the next.
Touch but don't move the baby toe
But this little one...Oh well, no more left!

◄How To Deepen The Trance

How Relaxed Can I Be?

To gauge how relaxed you are during self-hypnosis. Imagine if you are visual, pushing a measuring stick into the soft earth and reading the number on the stick.

Picture a mental yardstick and pick a number that represents your depth of trance at this moment. Move your attention down the yardstick and as the numbers grow bigger and bigger, go deeper and deeper into hypnosis.

If you are a touch person, measure your relaxation by the looseness of your hands or by the warmth of your body. If you are a sound person, notice the sound of your breath slowing down; and let it slow more.

If you choose to move to an even deeper level, say to yourself, "As I take five easy breaths, I am ten times more relaxed." Hold in each breath. When you let it out, say, "deeper, deeper, all the way down."

Photo by Jon Nicholas

Chapter 9

Affirm And Suggest

Reverse The Curse

The most powerful suggestions and affirmations reverse or positize negative ideas. Listen to limiting self-talk and simply change the word to reflect the result you want. For example:

Terrible with money	➡ **I'm terrific with money.**
I don't know how to do hypnosis	➡ **I'm great at doing hypnosis.**

No Sweat Exercise
Exercise the mind and the body will follow:

I hate to exercise	➡ **I love to exercise**
I don't have the time	➡ **There's plenty of time**
It's so boring	➡ **It's fun to exercise** **Each Step I take is a moving meditation**
I'm no jock or jockette	➡ **I am a jock or jockette**
I'm allergic to sweat	➡ **I love to sweat. Sweat cleanses, refreshes and revitalizes me**
I look terrible in spandex	➡ **I look great in everything I wear including spandex**
I've more important things to do	➡ **The most important thing in my life is to do good kind & loving things for myself**
It's too late to start	➡ **Now is the perfect time to start. Now is the first day of the rest of my life**
I feel guilty for not exercising	➡ **I forgive the past. I'm proud to take charge of my life**

When I'm My Own Hypnotist

Simple ways to use affirmations and suggestions when you're your own hypnotist, RRRRR you ready?

Repeat
Choose affirmations that focus upon your goals and repeat them after entering the trance state. You can use any induction found in this book.

Record
Make a recording of any induction, then recite these affirmations or some of your own, in your own voice and listen to the tape once a day.

Write
Write your affirmations down and post them in your field of vision at home or at work. Read them often.

Recite
Recite affirmations out loud or to yourself at least twice a day. Before getting out of bed, upon awakening, or prior to sleep are excellent since they utilize powerful natural trance states.

Rejoice
While getting exercise or while in the shower, chant or sing affirmations out loud or to yourself.

See Me At The Movies

Imagine a movie of the result you want. Create your fantasy exactly as you want it and as if it has already happened. So, if you want to lose fifty pounds, imagine yourself on a scale at his moment and read your ideal weight on the gauge.

If you are visual, visualize the results. If smell dominant, turn on your SV (smellivision). If sound rings true for you, hear the movie. The key is to enjoy a show your way and to project the end results you want in the present (un) tense.

Play it again Sam

If at any time the show is not moving the way you want it: change it. You are the director, the producer and the projector operator. You and all the other actors in the scene follow the instruction of the director. As the director, you make the movie exactly the way you want to create your reality.

Mental Rehearsal

Create a vivid fantasy of the results you want as if it has already The key is to make your movie as detailed as possible. Use your dominant senses and feel, see, smell, taste, hear and fully experience your goal as if you already have achieved it.

Suggestions For More Income
(For example, if you want to manifest more income):

I imagine myself receiving money from happy satisfied customers. I notice how good it feels as I tell my best friend I did it. I made two million dollars this year by working smarter, not harder. In my minds eye I see the money, smell the money, feel the money in my hands. I think back on how I did it, remembering all the steps I took that brought me wealth on all levels: Money, friendship, family, health. I am in my integrity.

Suggestions To Release Weight
If you want to release weight once and for good:

**I imagine myself stepping out of the shower weighing my ideal weight. I notice how I look in the mirror, the scale reads ___ . I feel so proud. I become aware of how it feels to be in that gorgeous body.
I imagine going clothes shopping and asking for a size 8 or medium or my ideak size. I employ all my senses: taste, smell, touch, sight, sound and beyond the senses as I focus on my success. I am healthy, slim and realistic. I am beautiful.**

Inner Wisdom
Suggestions To Release Weight

Enlist your inner wisdom to release weight:

I now make contact with the profound inner wisdom that is my true self. I am open to perceive the bigger pictures of my life. I trust my innate ability to take right action and I grow in wisdom and maturity with each and every breath I take. I am an open channel of love and light. I say yes to my deepest wisdom.

In trance is the best time to ask your deepest wisdom for answers to questions about yourself and how to proceed in your life. You may ask a generic question like: "What do I want? What do I need to do to have what I want? (How can I be happier healthier, more loved and loving, more successful)?

Your inner wisdom knows exactly what you need to do to make your life work on all levels. Ask your inner wisdom to brainstorm an issue. "I speak now to the part of me that is wise beyond wise. Since you know me better than anyone else, what steps might I take to become the biggest earner in my office?" Then allow your creative mind to answer. Do not sensor, edit, analyze or judge. Just let the answers fly into your mind. Allow the answers to pop like popcorn and listen well.

Monitor Self Talk
"When you say 'you drive me crazy' it isn't a drive it's a short putt."
-Jon Nicholas

Take advantage of your innate power of suggestion by being keenly aware of all things you say to yourself. The inner voice creates self fulfilling prophecies. When you say good, kind and nourishing things, you stimulate positive outcome.

I am keenly aware of all self-talk and I quickly and easily change any negative to positive. I say good kind and nourishing things to myself.

Hypnosis With Children

Photo by Jon Nicholas

Children love hypnosis. And since they're naturally in trance most of the time, induction and suggestion work rapidly and extremely well. Call your induction "imagination" and youngsters easily drift into the rhythm of a gentle swing or a rocking chair on a warm summer's night. The clip-clopping of a beautiful shiny horse as it prances through a dappled forest, the sound of gentle waves lapping on a quiet shore or the breezes that lift a glorious hang glider or balloon gently upward.

A magic carpet may lift them higher and higher too. Dolly dancing may open worlds of peace. If they have a favorite hobby, like skate boarding or surfing, just have them imagine themselves doing it. That easily puts young people into a glorious trance.

Take advantage of a child's sleep state. Talking to a sleeping child makes a deep impression on their subconscious mind. That's why no one, and particularly children, should sleep with the TV or radio on!

Make your phrases and suggestions vivid and active. Many children never close their eyes during trance. The job gets done just as well. Never be condescending toward children. They often know more than you do. Give them space to create their own solutions.

One of the biggest problems that face children is fear. Youngsters, until about age eight, are most often fearful of supernatural beings, strange animals, "bad people" and bodily injury. As they move from age eight to about twelve, fears can include changes in physical appearance, school performance and mortality.

After trance induction, have children take on an empowering role with which they can identify: a super hero, video game champ, space ship captain, king, queen, princess or a favorite TV character. Revivify the threatening pattern and have them "turn on their super powers" as you give them empowering suggestions.

The monster is getting smaller and you see that he unzips his funny suit and underneath is a funny, fuzzy bunny. Watch the bunny as it hops away, wiggling its cottontail. 'Good bye, Bunny' you say as you shine and sparkle your magic fairy dust.

You can have them call upon other protectors too. Let's say your young subject likes dogs:
Imagine yourself lying on your bed surrounded by 101 Dalmatians. Now let that funny looking green warted goblin come into your room and something very interesting happens! The dogs lick him and he changes. The funny fellow becomes silly and does a little dance a special dog dance that is hilarious.

Now, whenever you sleep, you know that your wonderful dogs are always there to lick any visitors and make them silly. Just the thought of it makes you want to laugh..."

≋ Imprints

When information is presented to you, it may come in the form of words, visual images, colors, sensations, taste, or smells. You needn't become analytical. Your subconscious mind gives correct information in the form best suited to your use at this time. Simply let it be and listen well.

Trance helps you discover imprints that don't serve you well so you can extract them and get what you truly want. Ask for limiting imprints to reveal themselves to you by saying: "If there is anything that has been getting in the way of my achieving success (happiness, etc.), I would appreciate this information."
With each thought that comes forward, say "thank you."

⚓ Anchoring

An an1chor is a physical gesture, word or phrase that trance-ports positive information from the trance state to the waking state. When you establish an anchor from a trance, when you are in regular awareness, it will trigger associated positive suggestions and reactions.

OK Sign

Touch your thumb to your forefinger (the OK sign) while in hypnosis and give yourself a post hypnotic suggestion like:

Whenever I touch my thumb and finger together like this I remember that I am in control of my behavior and I feel terrific.

Later, during waking consciousness, when I touch my fingers together in this same way, my post hypnotic suggestion is activated. All the positive conditioning from my trance returns.

☞ Hi Ho Trigger

Adopt a buzzword or phrase in you waking life that evokes a conditioned response. For example, a runner might say "passing gear," and they will automatically activate more energy. A weight releaser may say "Sophia Loren," and feel motivated to pass up on dessert to look just like her. A sexual enhancer might say, "blissful and vital," and feel sexier. And a test taker saying "I open my mind to all knowledge." activates the part of the brain that learns and remembers.

Judy Umansky's Unfolding Rose

Find a comfortable place to lie back and dream. You are about to go on a vivid journey to a place in your heart knows so well. Relax. Good.

Now as your right hand rests at your side, make a fist. Now counting backward, imagine that fist to be a rosebud unfolding with each number. Begin with your small finger and a deep breath in. Good. Again another deep breath. Good. Five, relax your pinkie as you see the soft white rose with red edges, begin to unfold.

Deep breath. Four, as you relax even more, you see the rose begin to take shape. Breathing deeper. Three, the rose is unfolding in its entire splendor. Soft white with red edges. Unfolding even more to tell its hidden secrets.

Two unfolding more and more. Beautiful petals each caressing each other, unfolding more and more. Relax. Deeper and deeper. Relax. Deep breath. One, the rose soft white and majestic with its red circumference is in full bloom with the sweet subtle sense of the rose itself.

The petals seem to form a spiral. You look closely at the rose, at the spiral closely, more closely as you find yourself spiraling down a beautiful, brilliant spiral pathway, deeper and deeper down deeper and deeper. The colors are so vivid you can touch them, each having their own wonderful sensation as you spiral deeper and deeper down.

Deeper with every beat of your heart. Deeper and deeper with each breath you take. Deeper and deeper, floating weightlessly down the spiral, so weightless, effortless, down deeper and deeper. Deeper than you've ever been before, spiraling weightlessly, effortlessly, down deeper and deeper, spiraling, deeper, weightless, deeper.

As you come to rest in this deep place within yourself, you see yourself in a mirror, you see yourself just the way you truly are, your true essence.

Self-Hypnosis Cassette Tapes

Self-hypnosis cassette tapes accelerate the learning curve because you can listen often and learn while you sleep or relax. Some enjoy subliminal (not audible) messages hidden behind soothing music. The value of subliminal messages is a subject of hot debate. Tapes can be ordered at the back of this book or you can make your own for yourself and others. Tapes give you opportunity through repetition, of making permanent and lasting impressions on the subconscious. Listen to a tape once a day for two weeks and you'll be amazed at the results!

The Brothers Pete And Repeat
As you hear each suggestion repeat it over in your mind or out loud. This vocal or sub vocal repetition reinforces the message.

A Sample - Self Hypnosis Script
With this sample hypnosis script you record your own self-hypnosis cassette tape or hypnotize another. It's lovely to play soft music (no vocals- they distract) behind your words. Take your time as you speak, and leave a few spaces so that the messages sink in. If you want to make this script for another person, simply change the "I's" to "You."

Induction
Hypnosis is a skill that gets better with practice. I love to practice hypnosis. I easily enter into the trance state whenever I choose. Each time I experience hypnosis, I enter trance more easily. Because I choose to relax deeply at this moment, I create a mental place where I can relax without being disturbed for fifteen to twenty minutes. Get comfortable. I stretch out comfortably on my back, with my feet eight to ten inches apart. I loosen any tight-fitting apparel that could restrict me. As I become aware of the feeling and sensations of my body. My body just relaxes and lets go as it rests upon the surface where I rest or sit. I become aware of my breathing.

Breath Awareness
I notice air going in and out of my lungs. It's as if I am fully in my body and yet, at the same time, I have flashes of knowing that I am

more than my body, more than my breath, more than my heart beating. I let my imagination drift off to pleasant scenes. Now, I think about a time when I was tired (perhaps sitting in front of a fire), when I just dozed off to sleep. In my mind, I picture that scene and remember when I began to breathe deeply and fully. I watch my breath, feel my breath, taste my breath, hear my breath, fully experience my breathing as it flows in and out, deep and full. I let myself go into deep relaxation the way I do it best. The way I do it when I am deep and sound in slumber.

Deepen the Trance

I give myself permission to take a deep breath. After I take the breath, I hold it in for as long as I am comfortable. When I let it out, I let myself go even deeper down; ten times more relaxed than before. As I let the air out, say to myself, "deeper and deeper." Now, take a second breath using the same technique. Now, take a third breath. If I like, imagine pushing a measuring stick into the earth to measure the depth of my trance. To go deeper I push it deeper.

Give Suggestions

Give yourself the affirmations, suggestions and programs you'd like. You may select the following affirmations or any others from this book . Or write your own. Make your goals as detailed as possible. Be repetitive. The more you repeat something, the more deeply you reinforce it. Remember that your subconscious mind is literal, so make your sentences simple and, at all times positive. End your suggestions with clear instructions:

Affirmations For A Perfect Life

Where I am today, is perfect. I have been on a journey arriving right here, right now, in this moment in time and space. I am welcome in the world. I'm part of the whole. I'm here to make a new beginning on my spiritual journey and to experience and accept joy in my life.

I'm in a perfect place for growth and change. Everything I have done in my life has brought me to this very moment. Today, I am open to be touched by love, joy, and nature. I am free to experience fully the joy of this very moment. As I breathe, my dreams are coming true.

It's up to me to bring out the best of myself. I have a boundless capacity for joy and pleasure. I am keenly aware of all self-talk and I quickly and easily turn any negatives into positives. I listen to the still, small, inner voice within, for I know that my senses tell me the truth. I trust my deepest inner wisdom. My inner self knows the truth about everything in my life, so I listen, hear and act from its wisdom.

social past

I remember every minute of my life. Any pain I may feel by remembering hurts less than the pain of knowing and not remembering. I accept the truth. The truth sets me free. I don't need to cover up past hurt with self-destructive thinking, behavior, food, drink, drugs, or sex.

My parents and their relationship are separate from me. I am not a reflection of my parents or children and they are not a reflection of me. I am whole and perfect in my singularity. I forgive my parents and others for any mistakes they made. They did the best they could, given the way they were.

I forgive myself fully for mistakes I made; I did the best I could and I do better and better every day. I understand that my behaviors in the past were learning experiences. Everything in my life teaches me valuable lessons. When I know what doesn't work I can choose what does work.

My life is now, at this moment in time. The past is over and is but a memory. The future is only the confirmation of what I dream or create in this moment in time. Right now is my life and I enjoy the experience of being 100% alive in this moment in time.

love

I am lovable and capable. It is easy to love me. A unique and priceless person, I love myself fully, just the way I am. I'm enough, and perfect just the way I am. I'm kind, gentle, and compassionate with myself. I grow and learn every day. Everyday I learn new ways to celebrate myself.

My honest, loving spirit draws other honest, loving spirits into my world. I am enriched every day through my loving. The more I love, the more I receive love. I deserve to be loved for myself, just as I am. I easily receive and give my loving.

I give myself permission to be myself and express myself. I express my ideas easily. I'm worthy of the respect of others. Others respect my point of view, just as I respect theirs. I am a good listener. I listen well to myself and others. People respond when I reach out. It's safe and rewarding to love others. I am my true self with others and I am loved just for being me.

I accept compliments easily. I am proud to be me. No matter what others say to me, I know, in the deepest level, that I am a worthwhile and special person. I enjoy complimenting others.

positive emotions

I breathe light into any real or imagined fears or limits I may have had in the past and they leave easily. I am filled with true serenity. I feel worthy, safe and secure.

My emotions flow freely. I learn from my emotions. My emotions are messages from within. I stand tall in my emotional magnificence, crying or laughing freely. My emotions easily flow through me and I always return to joy. My inner brightness shines through and others are attracted to my light.

I hold myself in high esteem, I am self-confident and can easily express and assert my own ideas.

physical well being

I breathe fully and freely. I am a sensuous being, able to allow myself pleasure, fun, and spontaneity. I approve of my sensuality and sexuality and the gifts they bring me. My body pleases me. I enjoy my sensuous self.

I am healthy. My positive thoughts create my healthy body. My body is my perfect friend. I feel my body. I love my body. I am my body. I do good, kind and nourishing things for my body. I am fully in tune with my body. If my body is uncomfortable, it's communicating with me that something needs my attention. I listen to my body and I take whatever actions are necessary to bring myself back radiant wellness, natural balance and homeostasis.

I love moving my body; stretching, flowing, dynamic movement makes me look and feel terrific. I feel so glad to be alive and moving.

success

I am a growing and maturing personality, and the changes I make nurture me. I accept change easily. I easily transform any limiting behaviors, those that no longer serve me well, into ones that bring me joy and inner harmony. I approve of my actions and myself. It is OK that I am sometimes unpredictable, after all, I'm human.

I am powerful. I enjoy taking and accepting responsibility for myself. I am responsible for own happiness and fulfillment. Life's most challenging and important task is to grow up and take responsibility for my own joy. I love being responsible for my joy. I love the joy I bring to myself. I choose to be happy.
I deserve to have whatever I want. I follow through easily and harmoniously in things I start. I live my dreams. Life is good to me. I am abundant.

Come On Back

Take time now to receive and review your journey. Let information and relaxation sink in and make a deep permanent and lasting impression. When this is so, it's time to come back. A simple closing brings you back to regular awareness. All you have to say is:

I remember everything that has transpired during this session. Each of these suggestions has made a deep, permanent, and lasting impression on my mind.

I choose to return to my regular awareness. When I open my eyes, I'll feel refreshed and invigorated, and I'll remember clearly this journey, complete with all the information that I have received. Or

Count from one to five and at the count of five, my eyes spring open. One two, three, four, five, take a deep breath and stretch. Or

As I count from one to five, I return to room awareness. Becoming more and more alert, refreshed and invigorated with each number. If I chose to sleep now or for the duration of the night, at the count of three I will turn off my cassette player and return easily to deep slumber. Slowly and calmly returning. All my muscles, nerves and ligaments relaxed, two coming back more and more, three perfect in every way.

If I choose now to return to sleep I may do so however, if I want to come back; four, feeling terrific and five alert and feeling great and the word is 'yes.'

Illustration by Shelley Stockwell

Chapter 10

FEEL TERRIFIC
🌴 Less Stress For Success

🌴 Wellness: *Fare Thee Well*

> *I am my body.*
> *My body is me.*
> *We live together*
> *Harmoniously.*
>
> *I love my body.*
> *My body is me.*
> *We live together*
> *In harmony.*

🌴 Less Stress For Success
Hang Loose And Don't Sweat The Small Stuff

Everything about and within you is energy. Energy is used to keep you functioning and alive. Some is expressed in movement, words and actions. Some is stored up inside of you. Some is shored up and trapped inside you. Trapped energy in the body is called pain, tension, tightness, fat or illness. If you discover one of these areas, replace saying, "My back is killing me," to "I have energy here. I release it." Releasing trapped or stored energy gives you the gift and a lift.

      Releasing energy is so much better than behaving like an energy pack rat. Holding back emotional energy is like trying to hold a beach ball under water, that requires a concerted amount of extra energy.

Think of something that stresses you or makes you emotionally uncomfortable. An unpleasant thought or memory you that sticks with you.

Be outrageously brave and feel it strongly. As you do, notice what's going on in your body. Take an inventory of your responses; are you going tight in the stomach, heart, head, legs and hands? Just notice. Be aware also of your breathing. Is it more rapid or do you hold your breath? Is your heart rate faster? Notice.

These body changes signal where you store your stress and, if repeated, take their toll on your body. They become the precursor for migraines, colitis, ulcers, arthritis, vascular constriction, heart attack and cancer. Thank your body for giving you this awareness.

The second important awareness is how you, in the past, have coped with these bodily messages. Some use sugar, prescription pills, pot and street drugs, excessive eating, smoking, alcohol or coffee to numb the stress. But these substances cause even more stress.

Some throw themselves into work, or spiral into obsessive repetitive thoughts or behaviors to ignore trapped energy. That's a little like constantly touching a sore tooth with your tongue or picking an old sore again and again. If we allow ourselves to repeat such strategies, we repeatedly add more stress, more trapped energy.

To change these patterns you must give up the idea that this is how life is supposed to be and choose to find a new and better way to use this energy in the pursuit of joy, peace and movement. Take a deep breath. Release the stored energy you felt a moment ago. Let it free. Any time you notice it breath there and let it loose. With such practice you learn new skills for balance and peace.

What Happens When We Free Trapped Energy?
Freeing energy can bring up feelings; all kinds of feelings; boredom, depression, sadness, body shaking and relief. When that happens, you realize that these were the emotions that you used to push down your

enthusiasm and joy. Freeing energy can also manifest in physical ways; a heavy period, more perspiration, and other body cleansing. All this activity brings you closer and closer to your purest self. That's the you who relaxes and is in radiant motion. Your heart opens to the expanded universe that is you.

How Do You Release It?

Patterns you use to store energy can control you. If you eat when you are uptight, the part of you that digests your food stops dealing with the actual situation that upsets you. The solution: make the part of you that wants at eat look at what it is doing. Then allow any energy that is with you to flow through you. It's just old patterns coming to the surface to be cleaned out and replaced with your love and willingness to feel your freedom and joy. Then, let your heart flood your mind and you will release this energy pattern.

SUGGESTIONS FOR RELEASE AND RELAXATION

Photo by Shelley Stockwell

The next few moments will return me to balance, peace and relaxation. I take a deep breath. All that my lungs can hold and as I let it out I begin to get into center. Now a second deep breath. This time, I breathe to the mind and let go of any tight thoughts.

A third deep slow breath as I breathe to the body and then the mind. I begin now to relax all the muscles in my body, for this is a time of renewal and regeneration.

The release of tension isn't something I make happen, it is something I allow to happen. In this moment, I allow myself on the cellular level, to release any trapped energy and relaxation begins. My muscle are now automatically releasing, relaxing, letting go. My body knows where to go next, which muscles need to release and relax. I breath to each muscle group as they smooth and let go. I am so glad to be alive.

And now a deep cleansing breath; inspiration (in) and letting go (out). My muscles relax as they release any tension from my nerves. Any suppressed feelings, any tight thoughts fade away.

I now focus my attention on a particular muscle. One, that in the past, may have carried tension. (pause) I notice how my breath and awareness relaxes them. As the muscles relax, my nerves relax too. Any emotional build up, any stored energy around my nerves is washed away by my breath. What a great feeling.

If I choose, I can track the delicate circuitry of every nerve in my body. I explore them as a great adventurer would explore a new-found paradise. As I journey this grand and glorious network of energy, I am aware that my nerves relax. Any stored emotions are cleansed from my nerve sheaths and carried away as uremic acid by my body's natural cleansing system. (pause) Any limits leave as breath, perspiration or elimination. I am entirely cleansed from head to toe. My nerves are cleansed and renewed.

I breathe through my spine to my brain. As I breathe to my deepest mind I hear the word relax. Relax. Relax. Relax. Every molecule, cell, nerve, muscle, ligament, and organ in my body is now cleansed and renewed. I am at peace. When I sleep I relax.

When I work I relax. When I play I relax. If I encounter a bump on my road of life, I relax. I go with the flow. I live my life with ease.

I am at peace in my body and in my mind. My feeling and thoughts are appropriate for my best health and happiness. I feel confident, balanced, alive and vital from head to toe.

Health Benefits of Hypnosis

Hypnosis, also called Therapeutic Visualization, Placebo Effect, Hypnocounseling, Motivation, Biological Reprogramming, Neuro Linguistic Programming (NLP), Engram Therapy and Faith Healing taps your innate ability to return to balance and wellness. Here are some ways hypnosis is used:

- Address each individuals special needs
- Restore homeostasis and build energy and vitality
- Strengthen the immune system
- Evoke and accelerate healing and recovery
- Pain Management
- Mental Anesthesia
- Overcome resistance and accept necessary treatment
- Accelerate recovery time
- Eliminate addictions and destructive habits
- Eliminate compulsions like eating disorders
- Eliminate stress and phobias
- Build trust
- Build self-esteem
- Uncover the sacred gifts hidden within wounds

WELLNESS

Fare-Thee-Well

"Hypnosis doesn't cure us, it stimulates our body's natural healing power. Your wonderful body and mind heal you daily without conscious effort. You are constantly in the process of maintaining, repairing and renewing our physical body." -Shelley Stockwell

"Every cell in your stomach lining is replaced within five days, so if you still have an ulcer in five days, how can this be?" -Deepak Chopra

Suggestions For Wellness

I am healthy. My positive thoughts create my healthy body. My body is my perfect friend. I feel my body. I love my body. I take care of my body. I am fully in tune with my body. If my body is uncomfortable or saying "ouch." it is telling me something that I now listen to and hear. I take whatever steps are necessary to bring myself back to a natural state of comfort and homeostasis.

I am my body.
My body is me.
We live together
In harmony.

In this moment, I focus my attention on my toes. I breathe to them and they relax. I move now to my feet and then the ankles and they too relax. In this moment I release any tightness with my breath. I focus now on my calves, my shins, my entire lower legs and feet and they completely relax. Now my knees, my thighs, and up to my buttocks. Relax I say, and all the muscles, nerves and ligaments relax.

My hips, my solar plexus, and my belly relax too, as I focus now upon my spine, my chest and my shoulders. Relaxed and easy. Good. Now my attention moves to my neck and down my arms to my hands as I relax. As my face relaxes, I might notice a smile across my lips. I feel glad to be alive and comfortable and I drift off. Deeper and deeper into relaxation.

From this moment I am a person who is well, physically and mentally fit to enjoy my many interests, desires and talents. I begin by holding healthy attitudes and positive awareness. Healthy bodies emerge from healthy thoughts. Healthy minds live in healthy bodies. My mind is healthy and positive. My body is healthy and balanced.

I begin a new life as the person I really am. Any suffering I may have experienced in the past belongs to the person I called myself a moment ago. My true self is the person I am right now. My true self is free, confident and does exactly what is best for me. I become more whole, complete, balanced, cleansed and joyful with each breath.

I have within me a creative intelligence that knows how to make, restore, and renew me. It is operating right now. I am now aware of it and I am grateful. The same intelligence that keeps my heart beating and lungs inflating heals me. I give myself to my highest power; I give myself to the part of me that knows exactly what I need to do to be happy, comfortable and radiant. I think now about my miraculous heart. It pumps blood to every cell in my body. It is efficient and works perfectly. Thank you heart for doing such an excellent job.

Nothing, even an old limiting me, can keep me from feeling terrific. I forgive myself for any mistake I have made. Any toxins out, out and away. I learn from the past and in this moment I am cleansed. I am joy. The past is just a memory. Tomorrow is a fantasy. In this moment I am radiant.

Your state of mind is the single most important factor in physical wellness. Your body, which houses your essential self, is made up of billions of atoms and 98% of them are replaced each year. It's a dynamic structure that constantly renews and reinvents itself. Your cells, mind and spirit have an intimate interrelationship. And the subconscious and superconscious mind knows exactly what you need to do to revitalize the body.

The behavior modification of hypnosis has been effectively used to speed up the healing process, overcome physical and mental *dis-ease*, extinguish phobias, and alleviate chronic discomfort. For a person suffering from degenerative illness, hypnosis helps them detoxify, cleanse, and fortify their immune system. Think back to a time when you had a sore or wound that took forever to heal. Was it a particularly stressful time in your life? Most Likely. That's because stress hampers healing. Since the by-product of all hypnosis is relaxation, hypnotic "slumber," gives the body time to regenerate and renew.

Researchers at the Ohio State University College of Medicine removed a pea-sized circle of skin from the inner arm, below the elbow, from a group of healthy women with the average age of 62. Thirteen of these women had spent about seven hours a day for seven years or more caring for a husband or mother with Alzheimer's disease. Stress with a capitol S!

There was no differences between these care givers and the control group in the use of alcohol, physical exercise or body weight. The control group however, had more that smoked and were unmarried.

The stressed care givers wounds took an average of nine days longer to heal, and blood samples taken before the biopsies showed lower levels of interleukin-IB, an immune system chemical that stimulates the healing process, showing a strong link between stress and healing. That's why hypnosis and its by-product relaxation, enhances healing.

Photo by Renee Parenteau

We're born with an innate immune system. This amazing defense mechanism fights imbalances (illness) and regularly returns us to homeostasis or wellness. When we cut our skin, our blood quickly clots so we don't bleed to death and the wound reseals itself. When toxins enter the body, our blood calls out special cells and organisms to destroy the hostile invaders. If we are exposed to a virus or bacteria, our immune system develops antibodies that protect us if they show up again. That's why most of us only have the mumps once.

Hypnosis taps the body's natural desire for wellness. It goes to the source of a problem and offers the steps needed to solve that problem. Often a simple attitude, life style or dietary change restores radiant health. Prescription drugs generally do not.

When we stress ourselves, feed ourselves junk food, smoke cigarettes, don't sleep or take drugs, our body works overtime to do its perfect work. When adrenal stress and an overloaded liver say "enough already," and we experience pain, more stress, depression or illness. We are then forced to stop and learn to consciously tap innate body wisdom and the subconscious.

That's where hypnosis takes over. The deeper mind knows exactly what you need to do to revitalize your body. You can use hypnosis and, while in trance, dialog with your symptoms or illness. Ask that part of yourself "What do you need?" and notice what you get.

All you need to learn is how to trust your body and its natural ability to heal. Your body and higher self want to return you to homeostasis and will tell the truth if you will only listen! When you use hypnosis, you discover the source of any problem and what steps you need to take to solve it. Often a simple attitude, life style or dietary change restores radiant health. Prescription drugs, like darts from a blindfolded dart player, usually do not.

Seeing a medical doctor can be important because doctors are trained in the diagnosis of a problem. When we know what the problem is, we can actively enlist the body-mind in the "treatment." Too often we get drug relief that masks symptoms and doesn't cure the problem. And, even more often, the cure itself becomes a worse problem. Modern medical treatments too often sow the seeds of illness in the future. Eighty percent of the pharmaceuticals prescribed today are either optional or of marginal benefit because they don't affect the outcome of the disease, says Dr. Deepak Chopra.

Additionally, what a doctor or article says to you can become a powerful suggestion that makes things worse. Let's say that you have been "diagnosed" with Multiple Sclerosis and you read in the pamphlet from the M.S. Society: "As yet there are no known drugs to influence healing or to affect a cure for Multiple Sclerosis." This can be discouraging.

You go then to your doctor who says "M.S. is a progressive illness and you can be sure that over time you'll lose your mobility." This "life sentence" suggestion may then be magnified by well meaning friends. If you accept these suggestions, they become self-fulfilling prophesies that you reinforce by limiting thinking. But what about those who have gone into remission? How did that happen?

Those who go into remission do not reinforce the advancement of illness; they reinforce the advancement of wellness. They stubbornly attach themselves to a positive attitude and choose *to change their condition for the better* on both the conscious and subconscious level.

Perhaps Doctors of Oriental Medicine have the right idea. They assist the body in balanced flowing energy and wellness. They won't receive payment if you are ill. You pay them for preventative medicine.

What a health practitioner says to a client has an enormous impact. They offer the power of suggestion with every word that they speak. Under general anesthesia every word spoken makes deeper imprints on the subconscious mind. If a doctor gives positive suggestions in these vulnerable times, the patient is much more likely to recuperate faster and need little or no painkillers.

CASE STUDY
Carolyn

Only 27 years old, Carolyn had a "female problem" that left her with less than perfect bladder control. Her doctor recommended surgery that not only didn't help but made things worse. This is what we discovered during a hypnogression. The results were full bladder control.

Shelley: "I'm talking directly to your bladder; was the surgery a success?"
Carolyn: "Yes"
Shelley: "Then what seems to be the problem?"
Carolyn: "The Doctor has just completed the operation. He says to the nurse 'Give me that. If you don't give me things when I ask, this bladder will never be right. What's wrong with you."
Shelley: "So you believed what he says?"
Carolyn: "Yes, I think something is wrong with my bladder. It will never be right."

Shelley: "Well, examine your bladder carefully. Is it right?"
Carolyn: "Yes."
Shelley: "Then you have complete control of your urine flow?"
Carolyn: "Yes"
Shelley: "Very good. All of this information is now making a deep lasting and permanent impression on all levels of you your body, mind and energy. You now know and understand that you body and your bladder work perfectly."

The Placebo Effect

"The doctor told me to take one pill three times a day."
"How can you take a pill more than once?"

Illustration by Shelley Stockwell

Ask any mother and they will tell you that "Let mommy kiss your booboo and make it better," makes it all better.

For a placebo to be positively effective the receiver must believe that they are going to get better. When that happens, their body responds by producing the right chemistry to return them to homeostasis. Placebos were used in World War I when the morphine ran out. Told that the water injections were powerful anesthesia, many experienced little or no pain.

The British Medical Research Council offered a lady with high blood pressure a placebo, telling her it would bring her pressure to normal. For the 5 years she took the placebo her blood pressure remained at a safe level. When she stopped taking her "medicine" her blood pressure skyrocketed, so they gave her real drugs for her pressure!

Hypnotherapist Steve LaVelle tells of the case of a Medical Doctor Bruno Klopfer. One of Dr Klopfer's patients was dying from numerous cancerous tumors. The patient enlisted the good doctor to get him an experimental drug named "Krebiozen" that he had heard would cure cancer. The drug, which was later proven to be "useless," melted the tumors away. Dr. Klopfer then gave the man sterile water telling him that it was a fresh, more potent Krebiozen. His report read: "The tumors melted like snow balls."

A positive attitude by a caregiver can also evoke healing and become a sort of placebo effect as well. Conversely, negative suggestions from a caregiver can push us to quit and get worse. Hypnosis is a fantastic way to put the placebo effect into action. Here's how:

Put yourself in a trance and imagine that you are taking the miracle cure for what ails you: the perfect herb, potion or medication. Imagine it moving through your blood, to every cell in your body. Let it cleanse away any impurities and heal you. Feel the miracle, smell it, taste it, hear it, see it and know that it is done. You are in radiant wellness.

Miracles do happen The True Story Of Ken

"I had a series of tests; CAD, x-rays, an ECG -Electrocardiogram, and a stress treadmill. Three Doctors said that I needed surgery for my heart was in serious jeopardy.

Instead of closing down as I might have done; I reached out to many for their support and prayers. I sought and received Reiki energy from friends and myself. I asked for help from my guides, teachers, ascended masters, my line of gurus, my higher self, angels, and a team of medical Doctors from the 4th dimension, to assist me. In a two-week period I had three experiences from my sleep but not dream state.

I saw myself in a room of light with no walls. I could see only myself yet, I knew others were with me. The atmosphere was milky, misty, as though a fog machine was being used. I was completely undressed and lying on a silver metal like table.

I was observing myself from a vantagepoint outside my body. I was at my head looking down, when "they" began to operate on me. My chest cavity was opened up, to lay bear and expose my heart. The operators were deft and efficient. Busy hands moved with extreme swiftness to complete the operation and to close. The procedure was almost over as quickly as it began. I was passive, detached and felt no pain and I awakened.

Again I was in the same setting, on the same table although, this time, I was not aware of my surroundings. I viewed myself from the same vantagepoint. An unseen friend and guide, named Master Alondro, and a team of medical practitioners and ascended masters were present.

As before, I couldn't see them. I simply felt their presence. They wrapped a one-forth inch thick and four inch wide copper-metal band starting at the center of my chest, under my armpit on the left side and around to the center of my back. Then a second band (but only three inches wide) was placed in exactly the same way and under the first band. Then, they placed a third band this time two inches wide under them both. They did the same procedure on the right side of my chest. When all the bands were in place, they administered charges of electrical impulses into the plates that entered my chest cavity.

"Wait a minute, I can feel this!" I cried out in fear. They calmed me down and completed the procedure.

Again I am in the room with the no perceivable walls. This time, I am standing and facing a man. I see this as if I am standing behind myself. The man has no discernible features. His attitude and stance show that he is the Questioner.
"Who do you think you are? What do you think you are?" he says. I am calm and reassure him: "Why, I am a being of light; let me show you." and I focus my attention and thoughts directly to my heart.

Instantly a spark of white light radiates outward and a feeling of joy and beauty flood me. The light encompasses my total being and I am elevated upward into the air. My arms are outstretched and my head faces upward. I float in front of the Questioner and show him my truth. This glorious white light now replaces my body and my voice says simply: "Now, do you see?"

Two weeks later, I was admitted to the hospital for another angiogram. If the die running through my heart showed that the arteries were blocked the Doctor would operate. Well guess what? All my arteries were open and clear.

The Doctor couldn't explain it but no surgery was required. I had experienced a healing.

-Ken White,
Graphic Artist, now Healer

Optimism For Optimum Wellness

Positive thought stimulates hormones that in turn boost the immune system. Ever since Norman Cousins (Anatomy Of An Illness) "welled" himself with laughter and positive thinking, researchers have explored the body/mind connection. In one study, scientists measured the substance in saliva that protects from catching a cold. Subjects with positive attitudes showed higher immunity in the saliva. Their blood too yielded higher levels of disease fighting cells.

Your self-talk determines how you perceive the outer world. That information then colors what your senses perceive, how you feel and what action you take. Optimists tend to use affirmative action and are more likely to make positive changes in behaviors that aren't working.

We come to believe that the stories we tell ourselves are true. If you're going to distort reality anyhow why not do it in a positively self-serving way? Positive self-talk and positive mental rehearsals crate positive results.

I'm healthy.	I'm sickly; always have been, always will be.
When uncertain I expect the best.	If something can go wrong it will.
The glass is half full.	The glass is half empty.
The future excites me.	The future looks bleak.
I'm lucky.	I'm unlucky.
Things have a way of working out.	Things never work out for me.
My abilities make me a winner.	I faked 'em out; my success is a fluke.
I can be difficult sometimes.	I'm a horrible person.
It's easy to love me.	Nobody will ever love me.
We've had a bad day; we'll get over it.	We can never get along.
Money comes easily to me.	I'm terrible with money.
I like people.	I can't trust people.

Be well and prosper

Hypnosis is a perfect tool to shift self-talk, replace negative patterns and entrench healthy attitudes. Are you negative? Are you positive?

Which of the following phrases do you usually say or think?

Affirmation For Affirmation
I think and act in positive ways: ways that nourish me. I am in control of my thoughts. I choose positive thoughts and actions. Negative thoughts have no power over me. I am keenly aware of all self talk and I quickly and easily change any negatives to positives. Every day in every way I am getting better and better and better; feeling so glad to be alive.

Pain Management

Pain is a natural response that lets us know when we are injured or ill. It reminds us to immobilize a part of the body or tend to it in some way. Hypnosis lets us discover what contributes to the "ouch" and lets us tap the mind's pharmacy to promote natural anesthesia.

Here's how it works: If you stub your toe, chemicals near the affected nerve endings, are released. They send a message via your spine to the brain saying "I've been hurt." You respond with an "ow!" These chemicals also increase the circulation in the injured area. This is what causes the swelling and redness. Extra blood heals and fights off bacteria. Your brain and spine then send chemicals that relieve some of the pain. That's why as moments go by pain usually decreases.

How you feel about the pain, your past associations and your state of mind at the moment, have a profound effect on how much something hurts.

The causes for temporary or chronic pain may vary depending on injury, surgery, or illness. Pain management for them all is successful with hypnosis and there are no unpleasant side effects. With hypnosis there are no addictions and no cases of the solution being worse than the cure.

Of course, medical problems are best evaluated by a physian and then hypnosis is a phenomenal adjunct to well you.

Use Your Brain To Control Pain

This simple biofeedback exercise gets better with practice, and the results—physical and emotional relief—are astounding. In this process, you trigger your body's natural painkillers (endorphins and enkephalins).

Take a deep breath, relax your jaw, and close your eyes and imagine a place about one-and-one-half inches above your eyebrows in the center of your skull. This spot is called the septum pellucidim.

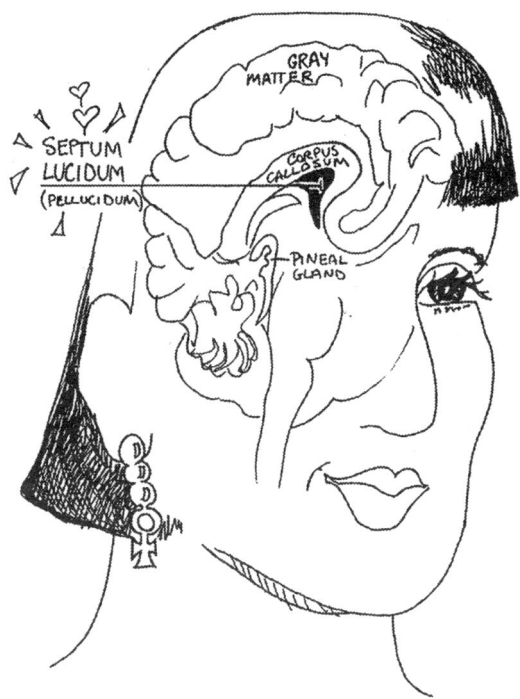

Hold your attention there by picturing or imagining a beam of energy caressing and stroking your septum as if it were a furry pet. Keep attention light and relaxed. You'll feel a gentle "AHHH" when you reach this magic spot.

Continue to stimulate your sweet septum, and notice any discomfort melt away.

Adopted from Pete A. Sanders, Jr.'s "Joy Touch" technique

Dialogue With Symptoms

Get into center with your favorite induction.

I'm talking to the part of your body that's trying to get your attention. Will you communicate with me?
Very Good.

Why are you getting our attention?
What is it you'd like to say?
What purpose does your illness or statement serve?
What can he/she do to make you well?
You've been heard, thank you. He/she now agrees to do what you request so you can relax, you needn't get attention any more, we're on your team.

Suggestions for Nerve Regeneration

Get into center with your favorite induction.

I realize that I am a miracle of messages and impulses that travel through my central nervous system. As I breathe, my breath travels to the parts of my body that needs healing and regeneration. With the next breath, I breathe between the nerve and the protective sheaths around it. My breath cleanses away any congestion or blocks.

Any interruption is now bathed away and replaced with fresh and revitalizing energy. Every nerve is now coming back into balance. Every nerve sheath is comfortably lubricated and rests easily to protect and comfort me. As I breathe, every nerve, ligament, bone, fiber and organ in my body comes to balance. I feel terrific.

Suggestions for Surgery

Get into center with your favorite induction.

I am choosing to have surgery so that I can fix what is broken, repair what is damaged and cleanse away any blocks or limits. I am being repaired, overhauled, so that I may return to radiant health. My doctor, my nurses and the hospital staff are all here to help me return to vibrant well being. We're a team. We cooperate. We work together.

What I picture or imagine in the theater of my mind becomes reality. I now do a mental rehearsal for my surgery as I imagine myself before, during and after surgery. I notice that I am confident and positive. It feels so good knowing that I am in charge of my thoughts and feelings. Each time I do this mental rehearsal I grow more calm and confident. I smile with confidence and pride. I congratulate myself. I am positive and doing great.

My body relaxes easily, whenever I ask it too. I ask it to relax now, before, during and after my surgery. I am in control of what happens to my body. My body cooperates with my surgical procedure. I experience everything as sensations without the least bit of discomfort. I am comfortable. I yield easily to my surgery. Any anesthesia I need is taken in easily and I require very little. "I am doing fine," I say to myself and I know it is true.

Before surgery I sleep and relax well. I am keenly aware of self-talk and keep it positive and uplifting. I know that I have hired a team to repair and revitalize me. When it is time for the anesthesia I relax even more and need only a very small amount to get my body ready for the procedure. "Thank you body for cooperating," I say as I relax even deeper.

Sounds go on around me and I pay no attention to them. I enfold myself in a bubble of healing light and my mind drifts off to beautiful scenes in my imagination. Perhaps a gentle swinging hammock, a crystal lake or a glorious green pasture. A favorite place I have visited or one I make up in this moment. Calm and relaxed I enjoy each scene, noticing all the wonderful details; the sights, sounds, smells, tastes, and energy of my beautiful sanctuary.

Surgery Can Be Grimm

In 1794, before the advent of anesthesia, pain management was often handled by hypnotic distraction, the same way it is today. Legend has it that a nine-year-old lad while having a tumor removed, was told a gloriously engrossing story.

"If you pay full attention to the tale being told, you will feel no discomfort at all." he was instructed. It worked! The procedure was painless and the story made a deep impression on the child. Eighteen years later, at the age of twenty seven, he submitted the story Snow White to a publisher.

Jacob Grimm was as proud of that story as he was of all his Grimm's fairy tales.

from Hilgard, J.R. and S. LeBaron,
Hypnotherapy of Pain In Children With Cancer

My body cooperates with the skillful hand of the surgeon. It opens easily, and has the exact amount of blood flow necessary to maintain perfect balance. My body knows exactly what to do and is in concert with my surgeon. All my vital signs are in perfect order; blood pressure perfect, heart rate perfect, breathing relaxed and easy. I am doing fine.

My body knows exactly what it needs to do to heal. It's interesting, how from the very moment I decided to have this surgery done, my body began its healing process. That's because I knew exactly what to do to bring me to wellness. All systems are go. The healing system and immune system are doing their work perfectly. All of my blood cells do their job perfectly. In fact, this is the easiest surgical procedure my medical team has ever done. The reason is that I am giving the orders to my healing system to cooperate fully with my medical team.

All of these thoughts, concepts and ideas make a deep permanent and lasting impression on all levels of my body and mind. I know that they are true because the profound wisdom of my body agrees. (one minute pause). Good, I'm doing great.

When my medical procedure is complete, I come easily to full consciousness. I notice how relaxed and comfortable I feel. All of my organs function normally and naturally. I have an appetite and can eat easily. I have a thirst and can drink easily. I can void easily. I feel wonderful and grow stronger and stronger with each breathe. My blood pressure is normal. My blood count is perfect. My lungs breath easily and effortlessly. My body forgives my team and me for any disruption in its normal patterns and now returns to balance and homeostasis.
I notice how good I feel and continue to feel as I heal.

Of course, I am aware that my surgery has been completed because I may notice sensations there. These are the feeling of healing. I notice any sensations and pressure as energy, healing energy. I am in control of the healing I began during the surgery and it now continues. I am well. The creative force within heals me.

adopted from Ann Spencer Ph.D.,
founder of IMDHAInternational
Medical and Dental Hypnotherapy Association

Suggestions For Comfort and Ease

Get into center with your favorite induction.

Focus your attention on the part of your body that is getting your attention. Give it your undivided focus. Put your awareness there. Notice everything about the way it feels. How large of an area is stimulated as you put your attention in that place?

Imagine what this place of your body looks like, as if you have you have x-ray vision. Imagine that you can see every microscopic cell. Notice the sounds that come from this place.

Imagine that this part of your body has gotten your attention for a very good reason. It is literally trying to speak to you, to make itself known. Listen with your heart. What is it that this place, in your being, is trying to communicate to you? (pause) Very good.

Let your body speak to you in symbols or words and listen with your kindness. Now decide if you are willing to take these steps. If so tell your body "I agree to take the steps you recommend right now today."

Ask this part of yourself what it needs from you. What can you do to ease its sensations? Is there something you can eat? Something you need to avoid eating or drinking? Is there any attitude or notion or motion that aggravates it? If you rested a little more would it be more comfortable or more radiant? What would happen if you moved more gracefully, like a cat? Would it like that? Maybe you could drink more water? Laugh more? Or released your worry?

Now, respond to your body's requests. You might say. Since, dear body, you have communicated with me and you have told me what you need, you can relax, heal and feel great. You no longer need to get my attention. I promise to honor your requests so now you can be calm, comfortably and easy.

Thank you for letting me know that there was a problem so that I could solve it.

The Stockwell System

☺☺☺ Three Headache Remedies

ONE
Tell the Truce

Imagine a war going on in your head; guns cannons, warriors and bombs. Focus your attention to your feet and see the soldiers marching and running. Count from one to three and the war is over.

TWO
Magnetic Magic

My hands are giant magnets and as I pull them from your head all pain and tension will move from your head to my hands.

One two three the war is over.

(Draw hands away and say:)

"How good it feels!"

THREE
Hawaiian Sacred Pool Meditation

As you follow these ancient directions you will experience the sacred healing ritual of the Hawaiian Huna. When you activate and drink the healing waters you are renewed.

Fill up an 8-10 oz glass with water and put it in front of you on the table. Breath four full breathes in through the nose and out from the mouth. Now take two regular breathes. Place your hands around the glass, but don't actually touch it.

Repeat the breathing cycle 3 more times and as you do, visualize or imagine energy going into the water. Sometimes the water is said to boil). Those who drink this charged water will be healed.

Hypnodontics
Bits for Dental Hypnosis

"When I work with someone who has really difficult handicapping facial and dental abnormalities, I help them clearly visualize and use self-hypnosis. I find that they are able to achieve results they would not be able to obtain any other way."

Dr John Goode, Orthodontist,
Trance-formations (video)
Creativity Unlimited Press

What a relief for dentists and hygienists when their patients release the "death grip" on the arm of the dental chair. When they relax their face, jaw and mouth, follow requests, mentally manage bleeding or pain, and leave happy. Steve Martins song "You want to be a dentist" represents powerful painful (though in this case funny) imprints many have regarding the dental experience. Hypnosis is the perfect tool to help us mellow out and actually enjoy the process of good health.

Hypnodontics is a term coined by Dr. Aaron Moss, DDS and describes a wide range of hypnosis applications for dentistry. Hypnosis helps patients override dental anxiety, anesthetize the mouth to eliminate pain, evoke healing and enjoy putting their mouth in order. Bruxalism (teeth grinding) is easily eliminated when the subconscious is programmed to relax during sleep.

Some hypnotists offer relaxation suggestions half an hour before the patient moves into the dental chair. This soothing preconditioning is reinforced during the actual dental procedure. Hypnosis helps the patient feel in control in a situation where they previously felt powerless. Because of the time distortion quality of trance, the visit goes "quickly" and as a result of hypnotic distraction and anesthesia, nothing "hurts."

When managing pain always avoid the word "pain or hurt." Use suggestions like: "You will enjoy the cleansing and renewal of your visit with Dr. Smith today. Any procedure he uses you will understand and interpret as sensation without the slightest bit of discomfort. Your mouth is cool and numb. All sensations are experienced as just sensations; cool touch, pressure and healing." You get the idea.

The Stockwell System

Glove Anesthesia Technique

For Dental And Medical Procedures

Get into center with your favorite induction.

Put your attention on your hand. Focus one finger at time and imagine that each is cool and growing numb. It is as if a cool white snowy glove is being placed on your hand and fingers. Your hand feels a lot like it does when it falls asleep; a sort of tingling sensation. Perhaps you notice it now in your fingertips. Notice too a warmth gently spreading from the palm of your hands. How interesting that is.

Your palm becomes cooler and cooler. Numb and peaceful. Want it to happen, let it happen, feel it happen. Your hand grows numb cooler and cooler. So heavy, so numb. It's as if you don't even feel the air around your hands anymore, as if you are so cool and numb anything that touches you hand doesn't feel at all.

That feeling that started in your fingertips, that numb feeling like a glove, grows even stronger now as you breathe.

>   Deep comfortable breaths.
>   Numb and cold.
>   Cold and numb.

Place your hand now to your (jaw if dental work) and notice how the cold numb feeling spreads into your body. Wherever you touch your body you notice this delightful cool numbness. Any procedure that is done to this, or any part of your body, will feel cool. And you will notice absolutely no discomfort what so ever. The numbness leaves your hand and numbs the place you touch completely.

Later, when your procedure is complete, both your hand and the part you have numbed will be renewed restored and revitalized. Pleasant feelings return and your healing is quick and easy.

Asthma

Asthma usually has its origins in childhood. If you go back to the 1lem through forgiveness and inner dialog. A simpler more direct approach is the one I call "Up Your Symptom and Breath Again."

Up Your Symptom and Breath Again

Get into center with your favorite induction.

Recall a recent time when you had an asthma attack. Actually be they're remembering what that was like for you.

Imagine that you can gauge the strength of that experience. You might imagine a gauge like a thermometer or a dial with the numbers one through ten on it. Or you might feel the numbers with your fingers. Or simply sense the intensity of your gauge. Ten on your gauge would be the biggest asthma experience in the history of the world. One would be a very small, almost nonexistent one, not there at all. You get the idea. Good.

As you stay deeply in hypnosis remembering that time when you experienced asthma. Notice what the number reads on your gauge. When you know say it out loud or simply nod your head.

(If they are at a one, two, three or four) **Very good. Lets bring it up to a higher number lets say a five, six or seven. And let me know when that has happened with a nod of your head. Excellent.**

(If they are already at a high number) **Bring it up slightly higher. Great.**

Now back to where it was when we began.

Now, in your minds eye, picture or imagine a beautiful tranquil valley. A perfect place where you feel secure. A beautiful place that brings you great joy. When you put yourself there, let me know with a nod of your head. Good.

Notice the gauge of your breathing, as you bring it down, down, down to a much lower number. When it is down lower, lower to an easy comfortable level. Let me know with a nod of your head. Great. You now understand that you can turn your asthma up or down anytime you choose. You are in control.

Go now deeply into that beautiful sacred place your own natural sanctuary and touch your thumb and forefinger on one hand. That will serve as a kind of anchor that reminds you that you are in

control. If ever you feel the sensations of tension in your breath you gently bring the gauge down and you feel terrific. I breathe with ease.

Multiple Sclerosis

The symptoms and progression of M.S., like other illness we know little about, can be bypassed with the right mind set. The first ingredient for success is your sincere desire to be well and mobile. You might think that anyone with M.S. would certainly choose remission, but that's not the case. Some like being waited on or catered to or enjoy playing poor me. To release M.S. you must release any "payoffs" you receive by being ill.

It's important that you take an active role in your positive advancement. You make the appointment with the hypnotist. You actively affirm wellness.

Childbirth

The same mind that can produce a false pregnancy, complete with real hormonal changes that cause the pigmentation of the face to change and the breasts to give milk, can produce a pain free and easy childbirth. Hypnosis is a phenomenal tool for pain free birthing. With it, labor is shortened by an average of 2 hours and mothers have some 56% fewer cesarean sections. This encourages drugless birthing with little or no medical intervention.

Hypnotists are often in as midwives or to assist a midwife. As a hypnotist I have had the honor of assisting both home and hospital births. Hypnosis is great to encourage support from fathers, and can be taught to both expectant moms and dads in unique birthing classes or as a lovely adjunct to the Bradley Method classes. Hypnosis births are beautiful and non-invasive. Hypnosis slows the overly exuberant panting breaths recommended by the Lamaz system. Such over breathing limits oxygen to mother and child.

Resources
Leboyer's, Frederick, Birth Without Violence, 1975 Knopf. Focuses on a nurturing birth for both mother and baby. Reminds us how conscious babies are at birth.
Natural Childbirth The Bradley Method

Illustration by Shelley Stockwell

CHAPTER 11

Sweet Dreams

ZZZZZZ

My dreams are the daddies of real.
How much I love equals how much I feel.

Easy, slow, watch me grow
time moves us gentle in his palm
as our faces wrinkle some
and you and I our dreams become.

My dreams are the Daddies of real.
How to forgive. How to heal.
How to love. How to feel.
And celebrate life is what they reveal

-Shelley Stockwell

☾ SUGGESTIONS FOR RESTFUL SLUMBER

I remember my dreams. I wake sufficiently to write my dreams on paper and, when complete, I easily return to restful slumber. I sleep soundly. The sounds of the night go on and I enjoy a deeply relaxing time in my bed. If there is a reason for me to awaken, I easily attend to what needs to be done and then I easily doze off again. I awaken refreshed and revitalized when I need to start my day.

I think therefor I am, I think
"Any thinking physicist must come to the conclusion that time and space are illusions." -Albert Einstein

Dreams are powerful tools that expand consciousness. They help resolve conflicts, inspire solutions, refresh thoughts and offer new approaches to life.

Bushmen of the Kalahari and Australian Aborigines believe that their human experience is only God dreaming them. Other indigenous ones receive prophesy in dreams that shape the future. For the industrialized, the idea that we are dreamed up by a higher power is challenging. The idea that we, in turn, dream our own reality may be tough to grasp [or not grasp].

Ancient Greeks and Romans visited dream temples where they searched their dreams for massages from the gods. Artemidourus, a Greek philosopher, said that dreams "hold the future, analyze them and they prophesize."

Many inventors have had their inspirations while snoozing. Chemist August Kekule's discovery of the structure of the benzene molecule in a dream. "One night I turned my chair to the fire" he wrote "and sank into a doze." He then dreamed of atoms swirling and settling into six circling "snakelike" patterns "One of the serpents caught his own tail and the ring thus formed whirled exasperatedly before my eyes. I awoke as if by lightening and spent the rest of the night working out logical consequences of the hypothesis."

Before going to sleep ask your subconscious to offer a solution to something your wanting to explore or resolve. If you've lost or forgotten something that you want to retrieve say, "When I awaken I will remember. It will come back to me."

The Mexican Indians train children to relieve worry by telling their trouble to little yarn wrapped dolls. Then they put the dolls under the pillow and sleep. When they awaken the dolls have solved the problems.

When a dream reveals itself to you, listen to your inner symbolism and "interview" your inner voices and guides. With dreams you can explore altered states like out of body experiences, past lives and spiritual encounters. These insights enhance your present day experiences and lets us re-member that we are body, mind and spirit or conscious, subconscious and superconscious.

Dreaming Becomes Me

KNOW WELL
Jingle bells, jingle bells
the Christmas season's here
It's time to manifest your dreams
and watch them all appear. -Mary Silva

You've got to have a dream, if you don't have a dream
How you gonna have a dream come true? -Richard Rogers and
Oscar Hammerstein
South Pacific

More than half of your life is spent lying supine; apparently out for the count. Yet, in actuality, you are in for the count. As your brain waves shift throughout wake and sleep, you access and process memories in the form of mental "images," emotions, and physical changes.

These mental images have amazing power. They inform you of feelings and thoughts and offer keys to resolve unresolved issues. They give symbolic clues to your history and imprints. Dream images give you an opportunity to explore feelings and work out conflicts. Stress and drugs often interrupt dream and sleep patterns. That's why sleeping pills are so harmful.

If dreams frighten you, the trick is to not wake up, but to take the dream to its completion. Then, ask for a gift. Before you go to sleep, request a beautiful, restful slumber, flying, sex to orgasm, and to remember your dream. Ahhh. Zzzzzz. These are the goals of healthy sleep time.

"Our unconscious existence is the real one and the conscious world is a kind of illusion, like a dream for a purpose, which seems real as long as we are in it." -Carl Jung

HOW DO YOU GRAB DREAM?
Take a space between a gap in the tide of word.
Hold my heart at even beating then my dreams are heard.
Let my mind dance helter skelter, let my day begin.

Sandman:
Levels Of Waking And Sleeping

Wanta Beta?	20-13 Cycles Per Second (CPS) I'm awake, you're awake.
What's it all about, Alpha?	13-7 Cycles Per Second (CPS) Laid back, easy, and creative.
State A Theta	7-4 Cycles Per Second (CPS) Laid back and easily impressed by suggestion. This is my meditation/hypnoic state where I go just before sleep and when I first wake up.
Delta Dawn	4-0 Cycles Per Second (CPS) Sleep, dreams, and visions.

My dream returns on kitten fingers, I'm my dream again.
-Shelley Stockwell

SUGGESTIONS FOR A DREAM CATCHER
When asleep or when awake, I enjoy noticing if I am dreaming or not. I ask myself; Are you dreaming or not? Is this my body or is it a dream fragment? Are these my emotions or are they also fragments of a dream? I am conscious of all dreams. When I awaken, I make mental notes of where I went and what I did. If unclear, I return to sleep and make a vivid notation of my dream. When I awaken I write down my observations.

For fun, I give myself assignments before sleep. That way I know that I am in a lucid dream. I can look at the palm of my hand. If I want, I can write the letter 'c' there. That means I am *conscious* of what is real and what is a dream. I can tie my shoe or pet a dog. Any assignment I carry out gives me a great sense of satisfaction.

You easily reconnect with your dream world and reframe any old pain. This conscious interaction with dreams is often called lucid dreaming. It's amazingly simple to "enter" a dream, change a script, bring in new characters and expand creativity and possibility. It's as if you create an interactive movie, as you simultaneously create fantasy and observe the fantasy unfold. Lucid dreams are intense, and sometimes short yet they always make an indelible impression.

Some philosophies believe that your waking state is the dream and that your sleeping state is your only true reality. Aborigines travel the dreamtime and heal. Patricia Garfield studied the Senois society in her book Creative Dreaming and discovered that Senois are believed by their aggressive neighbors to be too magic to fight. The key to Senois "magic," peace, happiness, and personal power, is their deep respect for the dream state. A Senois is taught from birth to actively manipulate their dreams. This interference creates a positive outcome. The positive goal of Senois dreaming is to fly, receive gifts, or have sex to orgasm. In pursuit of these goals, there are no taboos.

Dreaming in western civilization is often a nightmare, repeated. Let's say I am being pursued by a big, nasty, ugly brown bear to the edge of a cliff. As I fall off the precipice, I wake up in a cold sweat. My fear never gets any resolve.

Highly Senoi-ing

"To those who are awake, there is one ordered universe, whereas in sleep each man turns away from this world to one of his own."
-Heraclitus,
Greek Philosopher

The Senois do it this way: A Senois child has the same big nasty brown bear chasing him to the edge of a cliff. At breakfast he tells his family. His Aunt Tilly says, "That was a wonderful dream, but you should not have awakened. The next time you have such a dream, make sure you hit the ground. And if you die, be sure to ask the bear for a present. Or you could turn around and fight the bear. And if you kill the bear, be sure to ask for a present. The next time you have the dream, everyone wants to hear about it."

That day is spent celebrating your "gift." Songs are sung, dances are danced, and paintings are painted—all to celebrate my "completion of dream." We may not have such a group of partyers, so why not be a party of one? Write down your dreams. Talk about them with a friend or read your dream journal. Let your wonderful stories weave you to release conflict and confusion and meet your unlimited creativity.

Embrace the Senoi goals. Each night, fly anywhere you want and any way you want. You can have sex with any recipient you want, any place, any time. There are no taboos. What fun.

Hypnogogic Gadgets

Steven La Berge of Stamford University modified swimming goggles with red lights that flash when the wearer enters REM (rapid eye movement) sleep. The eye-dia is to become aware of your dreams so that you can influence them.

Catch A Dream Exercise

We all dream. The trick is to train ourselves to remember. Analyzing dreams lets us discover our beliefs and solutions.

As I drift to sleep tonight, in that hypnogogic state between wakefulness and sleepfulness, I will remember my dreams and I write them down.

Start tonight. Keep a note pad or tape recorder by your bed. Dreams quickly slide away from conscious memory unless you record them immediately upon waking.

Shape Shift a Nightmare

The next time you have a dream where you are in danger, immediately say, "Enough of this dream." And reframe it, which means, choose to replay the dream or re-script it so it has the ending you prefer. When you interfere with defensive patterns and behaviors, and replace them with positive action and behaviors, you return to joy.

Explore Dreams

God speaks in dreams and visions. -The Holy Bible

There are many ways of interpreting dreams. Fritz Pearl's popularized "gestalting a dream," where you become each part of the dream. So, for example: "Two people on horses. My horse, Frosty, looks good from the outside, but is in bad shape. My horse is sick and tired, and can't go any further. My horse is dying. I realize I am dying." I become all parts—each of the two people, each of the two horses—and I explain the dream from their point of view. This gives me the sense of responsibility for everything in my life.

Another way to explore dreams is to reframe any uncomfortable images.

Write down your dream
For example, two people are on horses. My horse, Frosty, looks good from the outside, but is in bad shape. My horse is sick and tired, and can't go any further. My horse is dying. I realize I am dying.

Magnify your dream
Look more closely at the dream and see what it is trying to tell you. In this example, I think this dream is talking to me about relationships, since there were two horses.

Dreams are surprisingly literal. They are naked symbols of what goes on inside of us. They're really not farfetched and they really do not require psychoanalysis.

Ask myself what the images tell me
What do the images want you to know about your feelings? In this case, I feel sick and tired on the inside, as if I want to quit.

Play it again, Sam
Make up a story creating a new image that reconstructs your feelings and the way you really want them to be. In this case, I bring my horse to a gorgeous brook, I brush his coat, feed him a fresh carrot, and we rest. In the morning, I find my horse and myself revitalized.

Interview The Dream

*"Come walk into the golden room unbridled and arrayed
Here you shine in full delight. Do not be afraid."*
-Shelley Stockwell

Dialoguing with parts of the dream are popular techniques used by many. This interview brings forth a meaningful guide from a young man's deepest self.

Case Study:
The True Story of Val

Val had two "lucid" (vivid) dreams about a "purest gold" Egyptian ring. The first one involved a sacred ceremony where a male showed him the ring. The second dream (three days later), a woman with long black hair whom presented the ring to him. The powerful impact from these dreams prompted Val to explore them using hypnosis techniques.

After inducing trance, I asked to talk to the part of Val that is keenly aware of his dream world. Here are the transcripts. Notice the success of answers when I "active listen" by repeating his exact phrases in my questions:

Are you familiar with the Egyptian Ring made of the purest of gold?
   Yes, it is the ring of wisdom created in the beautiful land of Alexandria by our seven fathers, the builders of cities.
Do you know in what year or time frame the ring was created?
   Yes, thank you.
   (note: A case against asking yes and no questions)
What cities did the seven fathers build
   They built a beautiful city with big, perfect beautiful stones. People building stones. Beautiful, beautiful stones. Beautiful buildings. Temples.
What is the function or purpose of these perfect, beautiful buildings?
   Eternal Life.
May I talk to one of the seven men please? (nods) *Who am I speaking to please?*
   Pharaohs Cousin or Jeremiah. I am one of the seven men and the builder of the perfect buildings for eternal life? I walked the earth plane

in linear time, seven thousand years ago. The six others are very wise brothers.

Are you walking the earth plane now, or are you spirit?

I am a guide. I come from center earth and I remain with the earth.

Have you been contacting Val in dreams? (nods) *Why have you chosen to communicate with Val?*

He is a clean soul.

What is your message?

Live life. Wisdom will come. Focus on the power within to receive. Val has been given a gold ring. It must be on the right hand. The fourth finger. This ring will give him much power.

Is he wearing the ring at this moment?

No

Will you place it upon him now, please?

(pause) It is done. A spirit ring is as present as a real ring.

Will you tell us who the woman with the long dark hair in his dream was?

You speak with her directly.

Am I the woman or am I speaking to the woman? What are saying to me?

You are the wise woman. You are Isis.

(note: A chill ran through me. Unbeknown to Val, I am a trance channel who channels the spirit guide Isis)

Val is very wise. He is learning now to accept this gold ring. Have you any advice to give him about the ring?

He is eager and ready to receive. He is not to remove the ring until the time comes when he will pass it on. He is to cleanse your spirit and soul. He must learn to concentrate a little more. So it is written.

Where is it written?

By the temples in Egypt; Alexandria.

I have recently visited many of the temples there. Were Val to visit them, would he find these writings?

Yes, they are in the temples that no man has seen yet.

In reality, in terms of physical being, can he stay in Los Angeles and see these temples which no man has seen yet? Or must he travel to see them?

He will go.

Val has been dreaming about you and you have been entering his dreams for some time now. Is there anything he can do to assist his understanding in connection to you?

He will know. And he is to breathe.

I made a tape called the Mer-Ka-Ba. It is an ancient Egyptian Breath of the Sun. It is a channeled process of breath that takes one from the 3rd to the 4th dimension. Is this the type of breathing that you were recommending or a different kind?

That will do nicely. He is learning to concentrate. He is doing well.

Shift The Dream
If the illusions of the past aren't working, reframe them to happier ones. Dreams are flexible when we give our imagination free reign and our superconsciousness permission.

Analyze The Dream

To Sleep Per Chance To Dream
What do you do if you have difficulty sleeping? We all have a bout now and then with too much anxiety, too much food on the stomach, or good old-fashioned jet lag. Problems arise when sleep patterns are chronically upset. The most important thing is that you don't get in a fight with yourself over it. Good sleeping is easy with a little wisdom.

What Causes Sleeplessness?
What you put in your body mainly. A cup of coffee or a piece of chocolate cake may make it impossible to fall asleep or may come back to haunt you in the middle of the night with nightmares or sleeplessness.

Over the counter drugs, irregular heartbeat and lots of sugar can also be the night stalker. Side affects of prescription drugs like beta-blockers, steroids, antidepressants, diuretics, inhalers, nicotine patches, nicotine gum, tobacco and even cholesterol lowering drugs give sleep disturbances.

There is no right amount of sleep for any one person. Some need 6 hours, some eight and at different periods of your life you may require different amounts.

Sleep Like A Baby?

Up every 3 hours and crying. Don't despair, prepare. Here's how to change your patter:

Avoid napping in the daytime. Keep yourself awake by being exposed to sunlight during your waking hours. Maintain a fairly regular schedule and create a late evening ritual like closing the shades, playing soft music and sipping an herb tea like chamomile, valerian root, passion flower or hops, forty five minutes before bedtime. A warm evening bath and gentle breath can really put you away

Most important avoid all drugs, stimulants like caffeine (coffee, tea, sodas and chocolate), sugar and nicotine after three in the afternoon.

Resources:

Garfield, Patricia, Creative Dreaming
An excellent book that studies the shamanistic
Senoi culture and how to conquer dreams. A must read.

Tholey, Paul Lucid Dreams

Stockwell, Shelley, Hypnosis cassette: Sleep Beautiful Sleep
Creativity Unlimited Press- order form at back of this book

Ronda and Friend

Illustrated by Shelley Stockwell

Chapter 12
MAKING MONEY

$ Laws of Abundance
$ Get Rich Quick
$ How To Negotiate

How To Manifest Goals

To manifest dreams and goals it is essential that you harness your thoughts for positive results. Positive thoughts coupled with positive actions create predictable and positive results.

You can have it all when you learn hypnosis. Hypnosis sets the mind for positive thought. Additionally, choosing to practice hypnosis as a career brings untold wealth and the self-satisfaction of helping others.

The Laws Of Abundance
Expect Success And Celebrate The Journey

Affirm Success
I am a winner. Everyday, in every way, I am more and more abundant. I am grateful for all I have at this moment.

Rich rewards come with the decision for rich rewards. Affirm your desire every day in every thought and action.

Train your thinking to make yourself a winner. Recycle negative thoughts into positive ones. Turn obstacles into challenges and opportunity, stress into excitement, and defense into proactive offence. Monitor your self-talk carefully and positively create positive results.

A BUN DANCE

Illustration by Jeff Bucchino

✚ Positive Changes
"Why are you begging? Why don't you go to work?
"Go to work! Why, to support a bum like me?"
New attitudes require flexibility and a willingness to have new experiences. If you find resistance's to letting it go of any limiting attitude or behavior, ask yourself: "If I don't change this how will it effect me in the long run?"

Stagnation is really the painful road. Life is an exciting dynamic experience of newness. Associate pleasure with change and you enjoy the journey. Constantly challenge yourself to grow.

♪ Celebrate The Now
Always make affirmations in the present tense. Celebrate your blessings in the here and now. The future is always going to be in your future. Right now, at this moment, you are abundant.

🦅 Birds Of A Feather Flock Together
To be successful, observe or hang out with others who are successful. Read their books, listen to their tapes, attend their classes, make them your friends and model yourself after their victories. Success is contagious. When you are around it you begin to act successful too.

Negativity is contagious also. Avoid negative or frustrating folks. Many limited people try to project their fears and limits on others. Stay away from those who are not supportive of your gifts and your successes.

✉ Affirm Success
Ask yourself: "Is it my intention to have more money? Is it really?" If your answer is "yes," take a moment now and affirm that for yourself. Many of these affirmations come from The Money Tape I made with Joan Lessin:

I am wealthy in body, soul, mind, spirit, and material possessions. I am abundant in all ways. There is always enough and more. My time is my most precious commodity. I use it for my highest good.

I'm always enough. There is always enough. I easily achieve my goals and my dreams. I visualize, smell, taste, hear, feel and imagine my success as if it's already happened.

When I do my part, the universe does its part. I ask the universe, and the universe comes through for me. I have more money now and every day. I deserve to be successful and paid well for my efforts. I am honest and honorable.
I surround myself with successful, positive, nourishing people and avoid toxic ones. I allow others to assist me and I remember them and their thoughtfulness. I enjoy mutually supportive relationships. I enjoy giving and receiving. I enjoy my successes just as I enjoy helping others be successful. I easily revel in my success and the success of others.

I say "No" when I want to and I take good care of myself. I say "Yes" when I want to, and I take good care of myself.

I deserve money. I appreciate money. I enjoy money. I take good care of money. I love money. Money appreciates me. Money loves coming to me. Money comes to me in many safe and appropriate ways. There are many good and honest ways that money comes to me. I am open to the easy flow of money. More safe and appropriate channels are continually opening. Through them, money flows to me. As I breathe right now, money is finding more safe and appropriate ways to come to me.

One way that money may flow to me is through clients, employees, or others. I attract many high-level people who enjoy giving me money. The work I do with and for others is good work. The people for whom and with whom I work notice me. They love me and encourage me.

My work becomes more and more fulfilling, satisfying, and lucrative. My work satisfies me at all levels, mentally, emotionally, and physically. My work brings me more and more money. I love my work, and my work loves me. My work is play, and play is my work. My playful work brings me money.
The peace I receive from my work brings me money. I am peaceful with money. I know I will always have money.

$ Laws

Affirm Success
I deliver what I promise. I have an honorable code of ethics. I honor my commitments. I am timely. I do what I say I will do. I do unto others, as I would like them to do unto me.

To manifest abundance, I put my plan into action. I promise myself that I will be diligent: doing a little everyday. I deliver to myself what I promise.

When I work for others I establish rapport with them, and close the deal. I am diligent. I deliver to them what I promise.

The Laws Of Asking

$ Ask! Ask! Ask!
I ask for what I want. I ask myself, my friends, my family and past clients for help in achieving my goals.

To be successful *ask, ask, ask*. Never stop asking for what you want. Ask your subconscious mind to assist. Ask others for their support. Pray and ask the higher power for your dream to come real, now. Imagine that you have already manifested your goal.

$ Affirm Now and Every Day,
I ask myself "What do I want?" and I listen well to my answer. I act as if I already have it.

$ Dial "Yes" For Success.
I call or write my friends and acquaintances and ask them for referrals. I share with them my vision of success. Saying, "This year I want to be (the top salesperson in my office). Please help by giving me referrals? Is there someone that I can call today?"

$ Group Dynamics
I join clubs; service organizations and network groups and ask.

$ Makin' A List, Checkin' It Twice

I list ten people or ways that I will ask for the results I want. Next to each one, I write down the date that I will ask: Do it now!

$ I'll Buy That

I enjoy finding warm bodies who enjoy paying for my product and services.

You need buyers to sell a product or service. Here are some simple ideas: Call everyone who you have ever done business with. Follow through on every lead you have received from work or from friends. Make no less than five cold calls a day.

List ten ways to make more contacts with your buying public:

_____

_____

_____

_____

_____

_____

_____

_____

_____

_____

$ Smile

Smile, smile, smile! I put a smile in my voice. I put a smile on my face and I put money in my pocket.

Apes bear their teeth to diffuse aggression. We operate much the same way.

To put yourself and others at ease and sooth defenses, smile.

Your energy, even on the phone, speaks much louder than words. That's why you instinctively know when someone on the other end of the phone has stopped listening to you. If you are scowling and saying "how nice" it still comes across as scowling.

Since your facial expression is transmitted over the wires, a great sales trick is to put a mirror in front of the phone. When you answer the phone, watch yourself in the mirror and make sure that you have an enthusiastic and genuine smile on your face.

$ Play The Match Game

The match game helps you strikes accord and warms rapport with other warm bodies.

I enjoy marching along with other people's drummer. When I active listen, breathe, and emulate others, they become part of my team. Others enjoy supporting me in my pursuits. I understand others and they understand me.

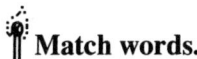 Match words.

Repeat back the words and phrases others use to express themselves. This lets them know that they are heard and this allows you to get out of yourself and stand in their moccasins. Active listening is possibly the single most important technique in successful communication and rapport.

Ask someone something, listen to their answer and then restate his or her reply back to them. This proves to them that they've been heard, a critical factor in establishing rapport.

Here's how it would sound:
Me: *"Why did you buy the house you are living in now?"*
They: *"I love the view and it had a feeling of spaciousness."*
Me: *"You really enjoy a nice view and the feeling of space."*
They: *"Yes!"* (And *I love you too*, they think.)

🕯 Match breathe.
Notice the other person's breathing patterns and stay with their rhythm.

🕯 Match pace.
Speak with a matched volume to the other person and a matched separation of time between words. If the person speaks rapidly, pick up the pace. If the person speaks slowly, slow down.

🕯 Match dress.
Dress in a similar style or color range to others you want to emulate or attract. It is okay to dress slightly more professionally than they are dressed. But if the person is wearing shorts, wearing a tuxedo makes rapport more difficult. In business, wear the style of someone two rungs above you on the ladder. It makes a difference.

🕯 Match gesture.
If the person folds their arms, fold yours. If the person sits down, sit down. This monkey imitation is an amazing subconscious cue that puts the others at ease.

$ Give and Receive Compliments
I easily acknowledge others success, wisdom, beauty and kindness.

Take a moment and think about compliments. Do you give compliments easily? How do you receive compliments? The art of selling (yourself, ideas, and products) is immeasurably enhanced when you practice the art of giving and receiving. If you are uncomfortable receiving a compliment, or discount them with an offhanded remark, such as "this old thing, I've had it for years," change your response immediately to a simple "thank you" or a warm "coming from you that is a really a special compliment."

$ Remember People
History is loaded with people who were successful because they trained

themselves to remember; names, faces and important information about others. George Washington was said to know the name of every soldier in his army.

To remember names, make sure that you hear the name in the first place. Pay attention and then quietly repeat the name to yourself several times to help it stick. Spell the name that helps you recall it later. The main reason we forget names is that we weren't paying attention or were distracted. Invite the person to tell you a little bit about their name.

Make an association with the name. Visual mental pictures work well as memory pegs for some. If the name is Farmer, imagine them in overalls. Then go on and use their name in conversation and call them by name when you say, "So long."

Next time you see them you'll remember their name and more about them and guaranteed they'll be impressed with you.

$ Say Thank You

Don't forget your friends. If someone gives you a referral, drop him or her a quick thank you note. If someone hands or sends you money always remember to say, "thank you."

$ Get Personal

I share myself as fully as I am able, because, in expressing my truth, I stay healthy and clear-minded.

It is okay with me if you do not open or share yourself with me at this time. People have different styles of opening. Some are slower than others. I encourage myself to be open as quickly as I am able.

The less you share of yourself, the more difficult it is for others to feel close to you. Open your honesty and enjoy the respect of others.

$ Diffuse Complaints

Diffuse complaints by the "ATSAC" Solution:
Active listen
Tell the truth
Seek a satisfactory solution
Ask for acceptance of your solution
Commit

Active listen
> To diffusing an irate customer or upset friend acknowledge their complaints through active listening. Let them know that you empathize with them. For example:
> ✓They: "I'm furious! You told me that you would have the papers to me yesterday, and they still have not arrived."
> ✓Me: "I understand that you're upset. You were expecting those documents to arrive yesterday."
> ✓Listen well to their response. Let them know that they have been heard.

Tell the truth
> Give the facts. Take responsibility. Avoid the urge to blame someone else for the problem.
>
> ✓Me:"It was my responsibility to get the papers there on time. I didn't get them in the mail until today. I am sorry."

Seek a satisfactory solution
> See if you can come up with a solution.
> ✓Me: *"So that this never happens again, I'm thinking of some steps I can take. One thought I have is that my time line was unrealistic. In the future, I think it would be more realistic to have the papers mailed out on Wednesday instead of Thursday."*

Ask for acceptance of your solution or co-create another
> ✓Me: *"Would that work for you? Or do you have another possible suggestion we could use?"*
> They: *"It's okay. Don't worry about it. But next time if you're going to mail it late, please call me and let me know."*

Make a binding commitment that responds to their request
> When you agree to do something, mean it. Make your commitment your bond.
> ✓Me: *"Yes, that's fair. If it ever happens again, I'll be sure to call you right away."*

If their solution is not satisfactory, offer another solution *without* discounting their ideas. A good way to do that is to repeat what they say and use "and another idea" with your solution.

✓ Me: "Calling you to let you know is a good idea and another idea that might work better for me would be to e-mail you as to my timeline."

Get Rich Quick
Muster A Cluster

Dreams become reality. How much money would you like to receive this year? Be expansive. Go on, exaggerate: five million dollars? Six? To manifest money, or any other goal, the process of clustering works superbly. Graphically setting goals puts your thoughts into a concrete form and clarifies the steps necessary to make fantasy real. The "cluster" technique helps you to identify, clarify and realize dreams. Here's how you do it:

Brainstorm Your Dreams

Begin with a dream shower. Write down an unedited list of things you want. Perhaps these are things you liked as a child, or things you like now. Write down everything, even if it sounds absurd. See how many things you can come up with. One hundred is a nice round number. Twenty is OK, too. Keep writing things as they come up, but make sure you have at least twenty. When complete, put a star by your favorite ones; those that give you the most energy.

1	31	61
2	32	62
3	33	63
4	34	64
5	35	65
6	36	66
7	37	67
8	38	68
9	39	69
10	40	70
11	41	71
12	42	72
13	43	73
14	44	74
15	45	75
16	46	76
17	47	77
18	48	78
19	49	79
20	50	80
21	51	81
22	52	82
23	53	83
24	54	84
25	55	85
26	56	86
27	57	87
28	58	88
29	59	89
30	60	90

Clarify

Now pick a dream. Any of your starred dreams will do. Don't worry if that dream seems impossible. Anything you want can come true when you create it as a concrete goal. Write your dream here:

My dream _____

Cluster

Let's say, for example, that the dream you chose is to have more money in your life. Write that goal in the middle of a sheet of paper and draw a circle around it, like this:

This is your target. When you write down your target, it makes a deeper impression on your central nervous system. Writing things down makes ideas more concrete.

If you think of obstacles that are in your way put those thought aside for now. You can deal with obstacles at another time. For now, just focus on your target.

If your goal is more money, it helps to be specific about how much money you want. The bigger the better. Write that down.

It's now your job to brainstorm. Think of all the possible things that you can do to make this dream become real. Write down a list. If your goal is to have $4,000,000, your list might look like this:

✓Do something I like to do
✓Work smarter not harder
✓Save more money
✓Become a hypnotist
✓Develop a new skill
✓Borrow money

Cluster these random thoughts around your goal and make them spokes connected to your goal.

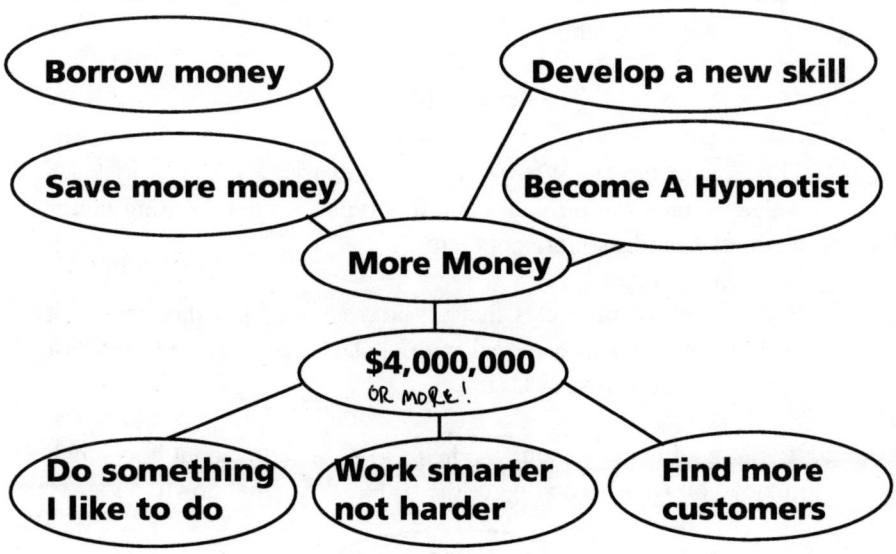

Let each of your idea "spokes" spring forth more ideas. For example, "Find more customers" may spark an ideas like:
  ✓Ask friends for leads
  ✓Be friendlier
  ✓Join a club
  ✓Go to church
  ✓Be more receptive
  ✓Advertise
  ✓Hand out business

Now, focus on each of these subgoals. Let's take
  ✓Ask friends for introductions

Write a list of people you might ask. Write down everyone you can think of: friends, family and previous business contacts. This might be a stretch, but don't worry. The results are the happiest stretch of all.

You might write under
  ✓ Be friendlier
  ✓ Ask someone to have lunch with me.
  ✓ Smile more

So this is how your chart might look at this point:

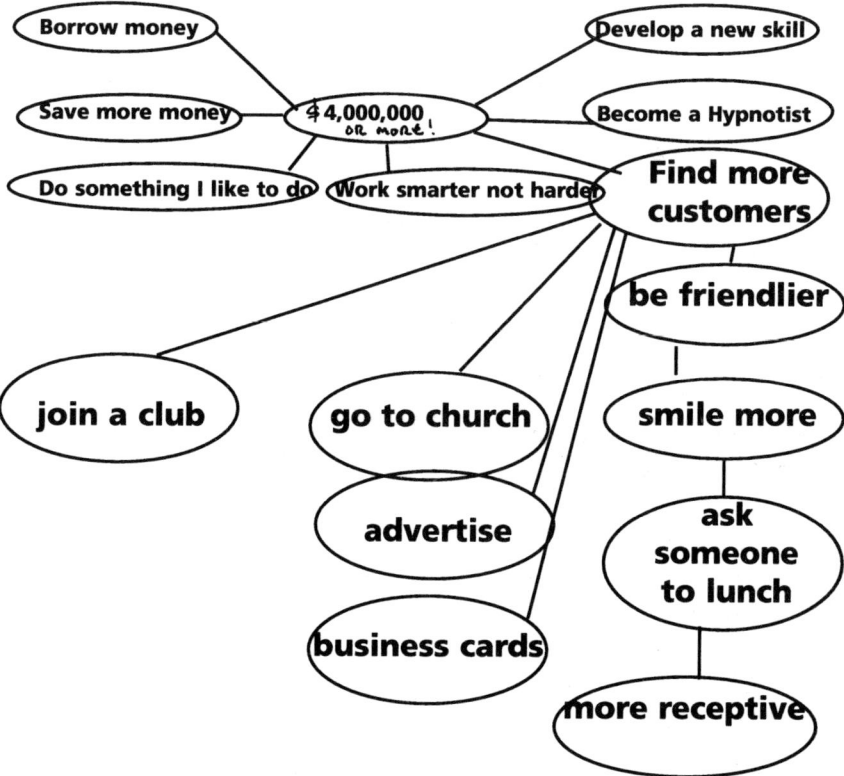

Prioritize the cluster groupings by numbering them; "find more customers" may be number one for you, and "joining clubs" number two, and so on.

The Stockwell System

Action

Give yourself a time line as to when you will take the action step that makes your idea a reality. Perhaps you will "call Betty" and tell her you are ready to meet new friends. Make a date with yourself to take action. Put it on your calendar.

One Week At A Time

The process of reaching goals happens one day at a time, one week at a time. Know that you can only eat an elephant one bite at a time. Goals are like that. They can seem monumental and unattainable unless you break them down into workable steps.

To reach a goal, break it down into simple cluster components. Start with the farthest reaching ones, one at a time, and work inward toward the core of your cluster: your dream, your goal.

One Day At A Time

Each morning, write down the list of steps you will take today toward achieving your goal. You may use the outreaching spokes from any or all of your clusters. You may choose to work on one cluster a day.

Illustration by Shelley Stockwell

A Star Is Born

If you like, cluster each of your starred dreams on separate pieces of paper and then put them in a row in front of you. That way you can prioritize which cluster you choose focus your energy upon first.

Certifiably Committed

Take all bulls' eyes (the centers of your clusters or the starred items on your list) and write them down on the affidavit on the following affidavit. You can have a friend read your affidavit and sign it to make it official.

Obstacle Obliteration

Obstacles are simply sub-goals that need to be clustered. For example, if you have an obstacle that says, "I can't meet new people because I'm too shy," put a square around your limit and then cluster solutions to the limit; "more self confidence and creativity" would be a fine spoke. Around that thought, brainstorm simple steps to build confidence. "Get books from the library on how to overcome shyness," "take a drama class," "talk to a friend about your feelings of being shy," "become outrageously brave and talk to a total stranger in the supermarket, a waitress in a restaurant, or the mailman."

AFFIDAVIT

I CHOOSE TO FOCUS ON THE FOLLOWING GOALS:

_____
_____
_____
_____
_____
_____
_____
_____
_____

I LOOK FORWARD TO TAKING THE STEPS NECESSARY TO REACH EACH GOALS. I DESERVE TO HAVE IT ALL!

_____
Signed

_____
Date

_____
Witness

How To Be A Great Negotiator

Any time you exchange information with the idea of making a change, you negotiate.

Negotiating skills develop with awareness and then help you develop your awareness even more. In business and in life, you don't get what you deserve; you get what you negotiate. Think about the last time you negotiated with someone: yourself, a friend, a loved one, an employee, a sales person, a customer, a vendor.

I was stunned one day in the market as my then five year old negotiated with me to buy him a ball. (He had dozens at home)."If you get me this ball it will make a complete set; one in each color. Won't they look great in my room? (selling the benefits).

"Mommy doesn't have the money for that ball."

"Well let's put some paper towels back and then we'll have the money." What could I do?

One of the best low key negotiators I ever saw was my agent at the Frankfort Book Fair in Germany. A buyer picked up a book and said, "Why would I want such an awful book!"

My agent smiled, remained neutral and said "Would you like a cup of tea?" As the client continued to thumb the pages of the book, the agent actively listened, nodded, smiled gently and never addressed the barrage of forthcoming criticism. I watched in awe as the buyer talked himself into buying the book!

Prepare to Negotiate

Watch what goes on within you and around you. Observe the everyday conversatilons of yourself and others and you'll see folks negotiating all the time. Listen to your own self-talk and hear how you talk yourself in and out of things.

Attend workshops, read books, and think about negotiations that you've made in the past. Maybe you didn't think of your interactions as negotiations before. Observe them from this viewpoint now.

How did you get what you wanted as a child? What negotiation and agreements (both spoken and unspoken) went into your marriage agreement? How did you purchase your last car? And what are you like in a flea market?

Be A Good Planner

Do your homework. Plan out what points you want to make and your bottom line. When it comes time to negotiate, listen well to what the other says so you can repeat back their ideas and then add your main points, again and again.

Think then speak. Plan your communication; don't run off at the mouth.

Hold High Expectations

No one will give you more than you charge. Open positively: Where you start effects where you finish. Be confident. Expect to do well. Studies prove that people who expect more get more. Expect happiness, peace and joy from yourself and see how they manifest too.

Be In Good Shape

Negotiation takes energy and can create tension. Good negotiators are in good mental shape and good health. Get enough rest and eat well. Most importantly, don't drink, take drugs, or load up on sugar or caffeine. Any substance that throws you off balance will hurt your bargaining power. Negotiators are in a good mental place. Feel good and others will feel good about you.

Look Good

If at all possible, dress like the person you're negotiating with. Be clean and smell good. And, of course, smile. A little self-hypnosis before meeting each other face to face will make you look relaxed and comfortable.

Visual impact can make or break a negotiation. Studies show that people make judgements within seconds that can decide the outcome of a negotiation. Books are truly judged by their cover. To prove this point, when I lecture, I often get three people dressed in exaggerated attire and one dressed in a blue, color coordinated suit to stand in front of my listeners. I then have my listeners answer these questions:

✓What kind of personality does this person have?
✓What Kind of family?
✓How much money do they make a year?

- ✓ What are their strong and weak points?
- ✓ How educated are they?
- ✓ Would you trust them in a business situation?

The well-dressed one is always judged as smarter and a more likely candidate for a successful negotiator.

Be A Good Listener

"It is better to keep silent and let people think that you are a fool than to open your mouth and remove all doubt." - Abraham Lincoln

Listen to the other's desires and repeat them back to them so they know that they have been heard. When negotiations get going a good technique is to repeat their request and tag on "and also." For example, they say "I think twelve thousand dollars should get the job done." But you think it will take more, you respond with, "Twelve thousand dollars would get the job done and fourteen thousand dollars will be a little more realistic given the expenses we'll accrue."

When actively listening and repeating back their desires, remember the points you want to make and your bottom line. The trick is not to get sucked into commenting or responding to their points. One trick is to say "I understand." and then, like a broken record, bring up your points again and again until they come around to your way of thinking. This determination is the same skill a hypnotist uses to bring you into trance. They don't take no for an answer, they just keep plugging away until you let go and enjoy deep relaxation.

The one who speaks first usually sets the tone. Greet the person with a smile and a firm (not killing) handshake. Make eye contact. Begin by saying something positive that gets the other person's attention. Be sincere. No one likes to feel manipulated.

Be a good listener to yourself. What is your bottom line?
What do you want for yourself?

Ask Questions

The person who asks the most questions usually controls the conversation. They receive the most information and information is power. One well placed question shows that you're listening to their viewpoint and needs. The one who asks the questions controls the conversation. I once got a job by asking my interviewer: "You have a very interesting job, talking to people all day long. How did you get into this?"

An hour later after telling me their life's story said:

"You are perfect for this job you're such an interesting person."

If you're asked a question restate or rephrase it before answering. Don't make up answers that can be proven as wrong. If you don't know the answer say so. Thank the person for raising a good issue. And promise to look into it. To be credible, follow up. If the question is irrelevant, gracefully move on to another topic. Remember that the only dumb question is the one not asked.

Stay Positively Neutral

If you're greeted with hostility don't engage in it. Go into neutral or tell a lighthearted story. Or divert their attention to aspects that they already have agreed upon.

Persistence Pays

Don't quit when rejected. "No" often means, "Give me more information."

Analyze Your Negotiations And Learn From Them

Win/win negotiations are the most successful.

Resources

The Money Tape
Affirm abundance and your subconscious mind creates abundance. The audio Money Tape motivates through a conscious pep talk, a hypnotic closed eye guided journey and the delightful Money Song. By Joan Lessin, Ph.D. and Shelley Stockwell, Ph.D., with music by Ed Sakota and Billy Krodel.To order send $12 to: Creativity Unlimited Press Casilina Drive, Rancho Palos Verdes, CA 90275

STEP THREE:

HYPNOSIS IN ACTION

Give one your wisdom and they might succeed. Give one tools to tap their own wisdom and they most definitely will succeed.

How can you use hypnosis for yourself to create joy and abundance? How do you let your conscious, subconscious and higher self manifest money, love, wellness, creativity, peace and harmony? How do you get out of your own way, bust limiting thinking and go for it?

Read on.
Love,

Shelley

Photo by Gerry Lumian

Chapter 13
Life Attitudes: Weed It And Reap

LOVE
"Momma I love," he said with purist heart.
And he did.

*I left him long ago in a childhood filled
with my mother driven to succeed.
I left him alone to struggle with the demons.
Independent and self sufficient,
lost in a computer screen, lost in cyberspace,
while I traveled my own world
built on dreams.*

*Somewhere in the crack of my defiance,
I left him sitting on my dead mother's knee.
Smothered in my mother's demanding tone
that I dance her dance.*

*I don't know how to love.
I know how to smother.
I know how to run away.
How do I learn to love?
Show me the way.*

-Shelley Stockwell

To create joy and abundance, it's important to clear up any limiting attitudes or imprints. Limits are weeds in the garden of your mind.

Positive attitudes and imprints are flowers. Plant new positive seeds and their blossoms overtake your thoughts with beauty and joy. Any weeds don't stand a chance! They lose their power and fade away.

Fertilize and till the soil by identifying and clarifying limiting life scripts, beliefs or patterns. Move past any defenses and honestly evaluate if and how you create limits or pain. If you notice a limiting pattern, take responsibility and change it into an expanding pattern that works better for you. Happy gardening!

Affirm:
It is now okay for me to have a healthy relationship with myself. It is now okay with me to have a healthy relationship with others.

I am a growing and maturing personality and I find new ways to love others and myself. The past is just a memory, the future a fantasy. My life is now in this moment and I find new ways to feel terrific. From this point forward, I only do kind, considerate, nurturing things for myself.

My higher self uplifts me. My higher self makes me naturally high. I no longer do anything that harms me in any way. I only do things that bring my precious body to radiant health and my mind to clear and positive thinking. I am now a full-fledged pleasure seeker. I create a positive and happy life for myself.

I put my hand on my heart and affirm that it is so: I choose joy. I choose wellness. I choose peace. I choose success.

The world has now entered into a conspiracy to do me good. And, even if I try to sabotage it, the world will prevail in bringing me pleasure, joy and abundance. I choose to flow with this glorious world that brings only good into my life. And so it is.

What Causes Limiting Imprints?

Imprints come from society, familiar traditions, emotions and awareness'. Most start in childhood and reverberate through adult life. Every time we repeat a limiting thought or action, we reinforce it to stick.

Limiting and out-of-control behaviors are simply an attempt to cope with wounds to our psyche. These strategies help us by attempting to increase thrills and avoid chills. Unfortunately, if our coping mechanisms are self destructive, they eventually cause more chills and fewer thrills.

Many limiting imprints are a result of accidental hypnosis, when you're in a spontaneous trance (brought on by trauma, shock, illness or infancy). Powerful thoughts, with strong emotion, bypass an undeveloped, preoccupied or confused conscious mind and you do not consciously consider or reconsider them. These suggestions make a big impression on the subconscious and may show up at various times thereafter.

We all have impactful suggestions from our early years. Prenatal thoughts were passed from your mother to you during your pregnancy; birth itself made a big impression on your sweet self; and strong emotions, like fear, allow messages to bypass the critical mind (of you the small child). These can create thoughts so powerful that may rule your entire life.

Belief As Cause

Most hurtful imprints, addictions, compulsions and phobias reflect the underlying beliefs that make us **SUFFA**:

Stuck

We believe we're stuck with no way out.

Unaware

We're unaware of how our behavior affects others or ourself.

Familiar

Painful patterns appear normal.

Family

Family traditions make toxic behavior seem like old home week.

Afraid

We sometimes fear change or think 'I cannot.'

Trauma As Cause

Anything real or imagined that hurts or traumatizes can create powerful imprints that linger long after the original imprint was implanted. Fear induced and implanted suggestions are often referred to as "accidental hypnosis" or "waking hypnosis." The conscious mind paralyzed by emotion imprints or implants a thought or an emotional response.

Hurt, trauma and disappointment make big impressions on our attitudes and behaviors. Most traumas result from feeling unloved, unprotected or abused. Such trauma turned inward can create self-destructive behaviors and attitudes.

Acts of violence, natural disasters (earthquake shipwreck, war) shock, and hurt, bring up coping strategies. War veterans suffer "flashbacks" or "shell shock." So do victims of tornadoes, childhood abuse, invasive surgery, drugs, toxic chemicals and stress.

If we turn to drugs to cope with hurts and traumas, they cause more hurts and traumas. Phobias, compulsions, insomnia, panic or guilt, set off by anything that shocks the central nervous system, causes more stress and trauma.

Pain As Cause

The more distorted a response becomes, the more distorted a response becomes. Pain we avoid is overshadowed by pain we create with destructive coping patterns. Initially, we repeat behaviors for good reasons. We want to feel good and/or numb underlying pain.

Destructive behaviors we choose may hurt immediately or catch up with us later. If the beer we slug down when we are upset becomes a compulsive beer, followed by another, we might not notice the damage until it's too late.

Sick people too are highly suggestible and open to accidental hypnosis. That's why it is important what a doctor or caretaker says to the very ill. There is a distinct difference between "With such a serious illness fifty percent of the people die." or "Certainly you are ill now but at least fifty percent of people recover. And from what I see about you, you are in the fifty percent that will snap right back to wellness."

Effect As Cause.

Question: *What's the world's most prolific manufacturer and user of drugs?*
Answer: *The brain.*
The body cannot determine whether chemicals enter the brain through the mouth, nostrils, skin, internal gland or from itself. Negative imprints

are reinforced or caused by the body's tendency to be hooked on chemicals we find agreeable.

We get 'hooked' on destructive behaviors because of the exaggerated pleasure or relief we experience during them and our payoff can be intoxicating. Stress, for example, changes brain functioning by causing the brain to release too many or too few neurochemicals, which in turn, stimulate or deprive other parts of the brain.

Emotions and thoughts also evoke profound neurochemical responses. Physically hooked on cigarettes, may also mean hooked on the pleasure response one gets from the ritual associated with smoking.

Positive, nourishing behaviors also stimulate the brains natural neurochemical responses. Positive thinking and healthy choices return us to chemical balance and please us. We may not get the same "rush" we got from over taxing the brain chemistry: true pleasure is more subtle.

> "I didn't just quit smoking cigarettes. I had to give up my ritual of lighting up and holding those white devils. The way I did it was to interweave breathing fresh air, while holding an imaginary cigarette and enjoying a quiet break to reconnect with myself."

Imprints From Society
If someone wants you to follow their train of thought, make sure they don't have a loco motive.

Denial, compulsion, addiction, fear, and depression are often socially transmitted mental blocks. We adopt cultural ways to see and be in the world. We're taught how to act in that world by our society.

Limiting behaviors and attitudes of unhappiness, frustration, and loneliness are often taught to us by others with their own agenda. We automatically adopt rules of the day, and of caretakers and teachers.

What we see on TV, read, and hear on the radio also hypnotizes us. These imprints influence thinking and behavior. Even when rules shift and change with time, old ones return like crop circles in the meadow of the mind.

If a tribe says that we must lather ourselves with cow dung to ward off evil spirits, we modern folks may laugh. Yet, if we take a tranquilizer or down drinks at a cocktail party to ward off our insecurity that may seem O.K.

Sneer at the Massai, if you will, who smear ochre on their head or paint their face blue to attract a mate; we dye our hair and put on our cosmetics to be appealing.

Society and its values imprint us with "distorted trance strategies" to help us cope with issues. Coping strategies might be as mild as a party to lighten up a funeral. Or as far flung as mass suicide to take us from here to "the Promised Land."

Denial

Jon: "There are three things I can't remember.
Shelley: "What are they?"

Denial means lying to yourself. Lying is often socially acceptable. Do you write your true weight on your driver's license? Or tell the whole truth on your income taxes? Or pay your taxes at all? Did you cheat on an exam? Or tell the cashier if they gave you too much change?

Little white lies don't hurt Aunt Tillie's feelings. Bigger lies allow us to deceive ourselves. We may ignore our inner voice of truth and pretend that we don't hurt our body with abusive habits like tobacco, caffeine, sugar, drugs or other self-destructive behaviors.

Family secrets keep up images so we may walk out of the room while children are beaten. Or pretend that we are loved when we ourselves are being abused.

An "honest politician" is an oxy•moron. And a criminal is usually the one who gets caught. Business associates may feign teamwork while stabbing each other in the back. We may ignore air, water, land, and food pollution and choose to ignore human starvation or injustice when it doesn't concern us directly. Instinct tells us that if it's unpleasant and we are helpless, maybe it's better to ignore the whole thing.

Denial is an elephant under our living room or global rug that we pretend isn't there.

Compulsion, Obsession, Addiction

"I finally got my son to stop biting his nails.
"How did you do that?"
"I bought him some shoes"

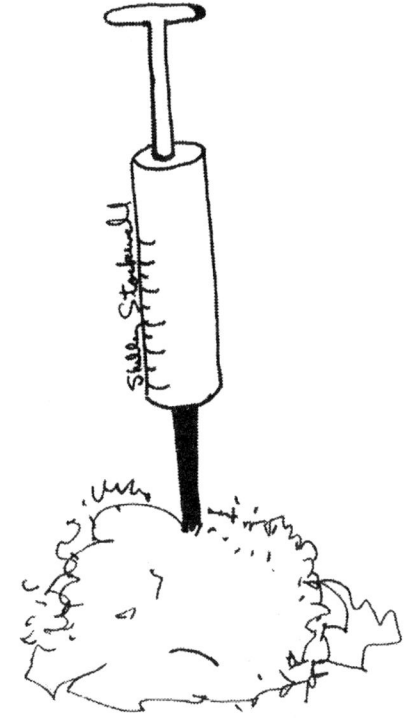

Illustration by Shelley Stockwell

FURRY WITH A SYRINGE ON TOP

Out-of-control thoughts (obsessions) or behaviors (compulsions) happen to all of us on occasion. They smoke screen underlying hurt and depression and make everything worse. If you are obsessive, you've "got to think 'it' again and again." If you're compulsive, you've "got to do 'it' again and again." Obsessions and compulsions capture so much attention that you have little time for anything else.

Compulsive behavior may run the spectrum from slight peculiarities ("I must eat dinner from the left to the right side of the plate.") to massive obsessions ("I must eat my plate.").

Over eighty-percent of the people, who have obsessive or compulsive behaviors, experience both intrusive thoughts and ritualistic behaviors.

Oy phase mere

Out-of-control behaviors numb underlying pain, temporarily. Yet, over time, make pain and depression worse and often lead to more out of control behaviors as one "hypnotizes" themselves through repetition.

Compulsive/obsessive patterns are a downhill spiral. All tend to follow the same three-phase progression.

- **Behavior becomes a crutch** (Phase 1). "I drink just to get by." "I shop to feel OK."
- **Increase in tolerance** (Phase 2). "I need more drink to get by." "I shop more to feel OK."

- **Behavior creates a bigger problem** (Phase 3). Stress from out-of-control behavior, coupled with underlying pain and stress, intensifies out-of-control behavior. "I hurt more; I drink more." "I am more anxious; I shop more."

Isn't this hysterical?

This Swell Ganglia of Mine

Doctors speculate that self-destructive behaviors are a result of stress and swollen basal ganglia in the brain. Swelling affects the thinking processes. Drugs are often offered to reduce the swelling. Unfortunately, the drugs themselves can cause additional stress, and furthermore, may not address the underlying cause of the pain in the swell brain.

Compulsions

"There was an old man from Peru
who dreamed he was eating his shoe.
He woke in a fright,
in the middle of the night
and found it was perfectly true."

Compulsive behaviors are often honored in society. If you are a workaholic, you may be killing yourself, yet be respected in the working world as a high achiever. Everyone will praise you for that—at your funeral.

A compulsion is an irresistible impulse to perform an irrational act. When the irresistible meets the irrational, compulsion runs behaviors and attitudes.

You have a compulsion if you find yourself doing any senseless repetitive action or a behavior that harms you. Usually these ritualistic behaviors are accompanied by a feeling that something bad will happen if you stop. Compulsive behavior is repetitive, restrictive, rigid, and not any fun.

Obsessions

An obsession is an "overboard" preoccupation of thought. You are obsessing if your thoughts run you, and you don't run them.

Each of us occasionally gets a thought stuck in our head or checks a few times to make sure they turned the heat off on the stove. But when these thoughts are so intrusive, or they check the stove so many times they can't go about their day, then this unwanted preoccupation causes stress and anxiety.

Ironically, compulsively driven people, often think they are decreasing stress while, in fact, their imposing thoughts create more stress. The pain of hiding senseless obsessive and compulsive behaviors is enormous.

Some define obsession as being besieged, taken over, or possessed. "The devil made me do it." But obsession is not possession, demon or otherwise. It takes place inside the brain, not outside. Patterns of thought, imprints and repetition reinforce crazy thinking on the cellular level. Brain cells seek stimulation and opening. Think of obsessions as mental masturbation. Better you should get excited by creativity and learning.

Compulsions and Obsessions:

Take a deep breath and read this list of compulsions and obsessions. Being outrageously brave, check any that run you.

___Addictions
___Adrenaline junkie
___Aggressive
___Anger
___Arguing
___Boating
___Busy body
___Chaos junkie
___Co-dependent
___Collection freak
___Competition
___Computers
___Control freak
___Counting
___Dare devil
___Do gooder
___Eating disorders
___Emotional freaks
___Exercise mania
___Eyebrow plucking
___Exhibitionist
___Fanatic
___Fishing
___Foot tapping
___Football
___Gambling- lottery
___Garage sale hound
___Gossiping
___Hair combing
___Hermit
___Hit me, hurt me
___Hockey
___Hypochondria
___Hysteria
___Inhibitions
___Jogaholic
___Leg bouncing
___Lip biting
___Love obsession
___Lying

___Masochism
___Masturbation
___Miser
___Money
___Movies
___Nail biting
___Neatnik/perfectionist
___Nose picking/eating
___Packrat
___Passive aggressive
___Picking
___Politics
___Pornography
___Promiscuity
___Rageaholic
___Reading
___Religion
___Resentment
___Sadism
___Scamming
___Seminar junkie
___Sex
___Songs-in-my-head
___Shopaholic
___Shoplifting
___Sports addict
___Super jock/jockette
___Superachiever
___Temper tantrums
___Thrill seeker
___Ticks
___TV
___Video games
___Videot
___Washing
___Worry wart
___Workaholic
___900 numbers
___Name your own

Lose Of Impulse Control

Everyone has numerous impulses and feelings—some good and appropriate, some inappropriate and perverse. In a healthy mind state, you censor and do not act upon crazy impulses. In chemically imbalanced mind states, you may not censor and instead act out wacky impulses.

Drinking alcohol and taking drugs lowers impulse control even more. Self-destructive and numb, we may yield to crazy impulses, and say and do inappropriate things. This hurts others and us. Later, we regret our behavior.

The truth is that all feelings and impulses are human. You only get in trouble when you act out the inappropriate ones.

In a stunning study on brain cell activity, Dr. Belluzzi determined that single brain cells exhibit addictive behavior. When you have a low metabolic rate, or lots of idle neurons that are not being opened, your cells choose excitement anywhere they can get it.

Addiction

The word addiction comes from the ancient Latin addicene: *someone who is captured and enslaved*. Addictions are out-of-control craving and dependency for a substance. This dependency runs you; you don't run it.

Over time you may substitute one substance for another (sequential addiction) or indulge in more than one hurtful substance at a time (cross addiction). You may exchange substances for compulsive behaviors or phobias.

Addictions stimulate the brain's emotional and motivational centers by creating dopamine. Dopamine, in turn, causes psycho-active effects and drug-dependency qualities, which motivate more of the same addictive behavior. Nicotine is a perfect example. A smoker, while smoking, wants to smoke more.

INNER·VIEW QUIZZES

Substances That Hurt Your Body
Take a deep breath, get centered, and let your true self answer.

I use the following substances to "cope:"

___Aerosol spray
___Alcohol
___Antidepressants
___Aspirin/pain killers
___Barbiturates
___Chocolate
___Cocaine
___Coffee
___Cola
___Cold remedies
___Cough medicine
___Overeating

___Decongestants
___Downers
___Drugs
___Ecstasy (the drug)
___Hallucinogens
___Heroin
___Inhalants
___LSD
___Marijuana
___Tranquilizers
___Methadone
___Glue sniffing

___Morphine
___Nose spray
___Peyote
___Salt
___Sleep aids
___Solvents
___Steroids
___Sugar
___Tobacco
___Mescaline
___Uppers
___Name your own

No Excusals
It's Me I Bamboozles

I bamboozle myself with _____ (drug of preference).

I use it because:
___ It's glamorous.
___ I feel grown up.
___ It's what partying is all about.
___ It makes me a big shot.
___ I handle it better than anyone else.
___ I need it to relax .
___ I need it to get going.
___ Things go better with it.
___ My friends do it.
___ My family does it.
___ Movie and rock stars do it.
___ I won't get hooked.

Taking Back Control
"If you don't stand for something, you'll fall for anything."
— Bonnie Dean
"What? Me worry?" —Alfred E. New Man

The proof that irrational behavior can happen even to the most rational person is obvious if you notice yourself in any of the preceding lists of addictions, compulsions or obsessions.

✓ Why do we go off center?
✓ Why would we choose to hurt ourselves?
✓ **What crazy payoffs keep** us out of control?

The answers live in the subconscious, or deepest parts of the mind. If the logical, conscious mind were able to stop self-destructive behaviors, everyone would have quit hurting him or herself long ago.
When you ask your *conscious* mind to change a behavior that lives in your *subconscious*, it's like asking a plumber to fix the electricity. It doesn't work. Subconscious patterns are changed in the subconscious mind.

That's where self-hypnosis or hypnotherapy comes in. Hypnosis is the fastest way to change the deepest mind. And when you learn to tap your inner mind, you find inner strength, discover the source of limiting behaviors, and release old pain. As you extinguish old hurts, you take back your power and replace limiting attitudes and behaviors with healthy ones.

You Can Change Any Habit
"Unless you change your direction, you might wind up where you're going." —Chinese Proverb

AFFIRM SUCCESS
If I change a negative behavior or attitude for a positive one, for just two weeks, I will shift into a fresh new start and get positive results.

It takes only two weeks to permanently change a behavior. If you chose to brush your teeth using the opposite hand, it would feel a little bit strange at first. Yet, in two weeks time, it would feel normal. Behaviors change by repetition and reconditioning.

Change works like this.

I choose it.
I consciously perform my choice.
I reinforce it repetitively with thought, word, and behavior.
I accept my new patterns comfortably.

Change Can Be Uncomfortable

A man lived next to the train tracks and slept through the midnight train whistle for 50 years. One midnight, the train whistle did not sound. The man woke up with a start, "What was that?"

Change, an inevitable part of life, unsettles all of us. Even the release of painful old patterns to yield rewarding new ones can throw us off for a while.

Withdrawal from the drugs or the internal adrenaline rush of compulsions can be off centering or disturbing. But it is well worth it if the final result is joy and peace.

I Honor the Change Process

"How do you eat an elephant?"
"One bite at a time."

There is nothing to change but the fear of change itself. Change is inevitable, essential, and can be uncomfortable. Nothing stands still. Change is a large part of life. The only thing certain is change. Fear is much more uncomfortable than change. With the right attitude adjustment, change can be exciting and fun.

Your body changes as you go through the seasons of your life. Families dissolve and reform. Jobs come and go. At work, people are asked to adjust to a new boss, a new job, a new work process, a new computer system. Even the way you act at home may change. You now may have to lock your doors and your car, and strap your purse around your waist.

Everything In Moderation

One way to successfully deal with change and handle things rationally is to stay below your "change threshold." If you feel irrational or confused, it may mean that you are making too many changes at once. Handling each one separately, one at time, and make change easier.

Stay below your personal threshold point by limiting the number of changes you make at one time. Don't pile change upon change. Take them one at a time and notice when you make too many changes at once. Being aware of the amount of change helps assimilate each one more easily.

Dump Obsessing About Being Dumped
"You done stomped on my heart and mashed it flat.."
-Country Western Song

"...how the heck can I get over that?"   -Shelley Stockwell

Have you been jilted, dumped and devastated? Or, even worse, been the one who dumped another? Love is supposed to be a bed of roses, so what happens when it turns to thorns?

To stop your achy breaky heart, obsession of the mind and that holler feelin' in the gut, here are some pointers. Each soothes, comforts and puts you back in the saddle again.

Love is forever. The relationship may be over, but the loving goes on forever. One of the glorious things about love is that it can last forever. Each relationship allows us to reflect on our loving emotional self. Let your love for that significant other stay in a special heart compartment forever.

Love is a mirror. All love starts with self-love. If you were not beautiful you would never have noticed the beauty in another.

Forgive and live. Stored resentment hurts you more than it could possible hurt anyone else. If someone has harmed you with insensitivity, they will pay a dear price of having to live with that. What goes around comes around. Let it go.

Love is Therapy. Relationships are always an opportunity to look at your "stuff." Your childhood patterns, what Mommy and Daddy showed you about love, is not always what you want for your relationships when you grow up. Some relationships are training wheels to show what works and doesn't work in love. You can let go of the wheels (the past) with a new and more compatible bicycle built for two.

Now is a golden chance to observe what worked, so you can do it again in the future, and to observe what didn't work, so you can give that pattern up. If you're not sure what healthy love is, now is the perfect time to become a love scholar. We go to school to learn all sorts of things.

Lopsided love loses. Love is both giving and receiving. If you've just been doing one and not the other, it's like breathing out and never breathing in. No wonder this relationship keeled over.

Finally, heed the most profound words ever written on the subject again from a country and western song:

"You got to know when to hold 'em."
Know when to fold 'em.
Know when to walk away.
Know when to run.
You never count your money
while your sittin' at the table.
There'll be time enough for counting
when the dealin's done.'

NLP For CPR

Hypnotist Kate Ellis has a gorgeous NLP (neuro linguistic programming) technique for mending a broken heart. Here is my version of Kate's approach. It works well with folks who have keen imaginations and are visually dominant. Try it, you'll like it:

Imagine yourself sitting in a posh chair in a movie theater. On the screen is a super big color photo of yourself. If you are not a particularly visual person, you might notice how you feel being that photo. What is around you? What are you wearing?

Next imagine yourself in the projection room and about to show you a movie about your "relationship." When both the you in the theater and you in the booth are ready, run a movie about the great things that happened in your romance; the fun, the passion, the gentle moments, all the sweet memories. If you get misty watching the movie, that's fine.

Now rewind that movie all the way back to before you ever met. Take it off the projector and put on the next feature: A movie about all the bad parts of your relationship. Your pet peeves, the injustices, the hurts, and the disappointments. It's OK to growl watching this movie.

When it's done, rewind that one too and just relax in your comfy seat. How happy you are as you look up at the screen and see a happy picture of yourself smiling at you saying: "I'm glad that's over."

Finally, project a movie of yourself five years from today; happy in a new life surrounded by love. That old relationship is the past. You are now in a new moment of joy. And you say "thank you" to that person and that relationship that didn't work out five years ago. "You taught me so much about loving myself and making healthy choices in love. All the past is forgiven and I have matured and grown into a happy, successful and loving one."

You leave the theater and enjoy a beautiful night sky and, if you happen to see that old flame again, you feel comfortable and complete.

Addiction

"Why did you take up the piano?"
"My beer kept sliding off my violin."

Getting high on drugs and alcohol is often acceptable behavior. I toast the bride and groom with a bit of the bubbly, and although I am toasted and feel terrible the next day, I say to myself, "Boy, that was a heck of a party."

Culturally, bingeing on soft drinks, chocolate, and sugar are considered cute. Within my body, they're considered poison. Coffee is marketed as "the best part of waking up," but they forget to mention what I'm waking up: irritable bowel syndrome, ulcers, arthritis, stress, and depression.

Is the "real thing in the back of your mind" the pounds of caffeine we ingest each year? Soft drinks and coffee get us started in the morning, move bowels, and get us over the 2:00 p.m. slump. It also overtaxes the nervous system, pulls fluid and vitamins from your cells, stresses the adrenal gland, weakens the immune system, and makes us jittery.

Ice-cream-slurping anorexic models claim that sugar brings beauty, joy, love, and popularity. But the 135 pounds of sugar we eat each year may not to be serving us so well.

Happy slim families are shown bonding during fast-food orgies on television, while we cruise the drive-through window and eat the hamburger, french fries, coke, and fried apple turnover in the car alone.

Is the break you deserve today the 63.6 pounds of fat and oils you'll eat in fast food restaurants this year? Seventh and eighth graders surveyed said their favorite food was pizza, with hamburgers and ice cream second and third. Give us a break! Clogged arteries and cellulite scream, "No!"

Speaking of no, we're told to say "no" to drugs, in multi-million dollar advertising campaigns. While we pop over-the-counter remedies, the medicines hyped by drug companies and prescribed by doctors, and hidden ones (preservatives, and steroids fed cows and chickens) in food.

> **This HRTs**
>
> Hormone Replacement Therapy (HRT) is being sold to millions of menopausal women to strengthen bones, moisten the vagina, and lower heart disease risk. It also, unfortunately, increases the risk of endometrial cancer and has been linked with breast cancer (now an epidemic affecting one in three women). Herbs, such as licorice, a healthy diet, lots of water, exercise, and avoiding alcohol, caffeine, and hormone-laced food might be a better solution.

Fear

"When did you get paranoid?"
"When they were all out to get me."

If you're not living in Sarajevo, you can watch it on television, read the newspaper, or listen to the radio in your car. Bloody gloves can be your life. Merchandisers present vivid scenarios of why you have to have a home security system, a car phone, and estrogen. CEOs of insurance and pharmaceutical companies make the highest salaries, on average. And life insurance is sold on the unlikely "probability" that you will keel over at any moment. Scared? Who me?

Depression

No wonder many get depressed.

There Are Solutions

Read on.

Photo by Bryce Stockwell

Chapter 14
Limits & Unlimited Solutions

Childhood Games That Limit

"Every few years 'repot' yourself so you can grow new roots and go in new directions."   -Helen Lessin Shaw

An exciting and rewarding life begins as you release limiting patterns of thought and behavior. Bring forth calcified notions and get moving. Here's how:

AFFIRM SUCCESS:
I am a maturing and well-functioning personality.
No other person or event is responsible for what I experience in this moment. I am the one who creates what I experience. If I react in a certain way, it is I who pushes my own button.

If I don't like the way I am thinking and reacting, I change it for behaviors and thoughts I like better. I release any limiting patterns. I am unlimited. I notice how change takes place automatically. It's easy to change.

Change any negative responses to positive affirmations. (fill in the blanks:)

If I were 10% more responsible for creating more happiness for myself: I would_____.

If I were 10% more responsible for creating peace for myself: I would_____.

If I were 10% more responsible with my beloved: I would_____.

If I thought for myself: I would_____.

I now make an agreement with myself to take these steps toward responsibility and I bring joy to myself. I'm in charge of my life.

History Revisited

"Long after we leave the home we grew up in, we continue to create situations in which we are mistreated, ignored, put down or controlled. These life traps determine how we think, feel, act and relate to others, even when we appear to have everything."
-Jeffrey Young and Janet Klosko
Reinventing Your Life

Most behaviors that don't serve us well are a result of patterns set in childhood. Painful past patterns pollutes pleasure. You must be bold, brave and honest to investigate and reframe limiting patterns. If you do, the results will be awesome. There are few things written in stone that can't be corrected. No more blaming, alibis or self-pity.

We can easily become attached to coping mechanisms we learn from the past. And model ourselves to be just like mommy, daddy, and our caretakers or the opposite of them. Either causes distorted ways of seeing and acting. Most of life's problems are the consequence of such distorted viewpoints.

Each of the following sections about childhood imprints begins with a quiz. Take each and then decide if it fits. If it does, repeat the affirmations three times, click your heals and seize the day.

Mummy-Fied?

"When you arrive at your future, will you blame your past?""
-Robert Half

AFFIRM SUCCESS:
I accept the fact that Mom, Dad, and my family were just actors in the movie of my childhood. Their behaviors don't have to be my behaviors anymore. I am perfectly myself and my behavior is of my own choosing; not the same or opposite Mom's or Dad's.

I become my own perfect Mommy and Daddy. I treat myself with respect, encouragement, and support. I forgive. I am willing to grow and learn new ways to love myself.

Reverse the Curse

"Self reliance is something you develop on your own."
                                    -Jim Riley

"Reverse the Curse." is the flip side of "Like Mummy" and equally limiting.

Do I Reverse The Curse

From childhood: I often think, say, and or do: (fill in the blanks)

___ "My worst and best traits are suspiciously like Mom/Dad/ my caretaker."
___ "They drank and smoked; so do I."
___ "They screamed at me, now I scream at my kids."
___ "They made me eat everything on my plate. Now, I eat the plate, too."
___ "They called me stupid. Now I call myself stupid."
___ "They compared me to my brother or sister and I felt inferior. Now I compete with others."
___ "Mom was afraid of snakes, so am I."

If any of the above statements sound familiar, it means that I choose Mom and Dad's behaviors in an attempt to feel close to them. To take back my individuality, I choose to be like ME!

Am I The Opposite Of Mummy?

"If you don't stand for something, you'll fall for anything."
— Bonnie Dean

Do I often say, think, and/or do: (fill in the blanks)
___ "I'll do anything not to be like Mom/Dad/ my caretaker."
___ "They were never there for me. Now I control others with an iron fist and smother with love."
___ "They screamed at me. Now, I ignore my kids."
___ "They insisted that I eat everything on my plate. I'll show them, I won't eat at all."
___ "They called me stupid. Now I'm a super-achiever."
___ "They made me insignificant. So I make myself Mr. VIP."
___ "They compared me to my sister. Now I don't compete with anyone."
___ "Mom was terrified of snakes, so I'm becoming a rattlesnake trainer."

Yes to any of the above statements, means that I've programmed myself to be the opposite of Mom and Dad. This is my subconscious attempt to be close to them. To take back my individuality, I choose to be like ME!

AFFIRM SUCCESS:
I accept the fact that Mom, Dad, and my family were just actors in the movie of my childhood. Their behaviors don't have to be my behaviors anymore. I am perfectly myself and my behavior is of my own choosing; not the same or opposite Mom's or Dad's.

I become my own perfect Mommy and Daddy. I treat myself with respect, encouragement, and support. I forgive. I am willing to grow and learn new ways to love myself."

In•turned
Rather than cope with impossible situations outside of ourselves we save our own life by withdrawing. This works well, until our whole life seems to stagnate. Do you shut up and shut down? If so, you've chosen

negative patterns to make yourself disappear. If this is the case, you withhold yourself from others. Anger, TMJ, and people who have sore joints at their jaw often have trapped anger needing to be expressed.

Do I Shut Up?

"Who is it that is dragging this corpse around?" — Zen Koan

Do you often think, say, and/or do: (fill in the blanks)
___"If I get fat, he won't molest me again."
___"If I go inside (lay low/ shut up/ be perfect/ work hard) I won't get hurt again."
___"If I stay helpless, maybe I'll be rescued."
___"If I disassociate from my body and my life, maybe I won't feel the pain again."
___"If I have panic attacks, I won't have to go to work and fail."

Yes to any of these means that I have been giving up my personal power in an attempt to be close to the past. I now take my personal power. I am open to communicate.

AFFIRM SUCCESS:
I choose positive behaviors and claim joy and vitality in my life. I am keenly aware of all limiting self-talk and behaviors. I easily change any negative to positive.

I express my truth and myself easily. I do good, positive things for myself. I am awake. I enjoy and seek out the company of others. I choose healthy people who are safe to talk with.

Ashes to Asses

In an attempt to right old wrongs, and release trapped pain we sometimes turn our anger inward or strike out. Do you "show them or hurt and insult yourself?" If so, you most likely insult, smack, rage, and abuse others and yourself. This attempt to get even or to vent buried frustrations always hurts you the most.

> ### *Do I Show Them?*
>
> I often think, say, and/or do: (fill in the blanks)
>
> _____"If I get sick, he'll (she'll) be sorry."
> _____"If I hurt myself, I'll show him (her)."
> _____"If I insult all women (men), I get even with Mom (Dad)."
> _____"If I'm a nervous wreck, she'll (he'll) know it's her (his) fault."
> _____"If I kill myself, she'll (he'll) blame herself (himself)."
>
> Yes to any of these is my attempt to fill my needs that were not met long ago or to avenge a deep hurt. I now release this pattern, once and for my highest good.

AFFIRM SUCCESS
I find positive ways to release any buried frustrations. I bash the heck out of a tennis ball, punch a pillow, or sing at the top of my lungs. I know that all my disgruntled behavior is simply energy wishing to be released. I now release it in non-destructive ways.

Echoes from the Past
Oh, the frustration of repeating the same behaviors and hoping for a different outcome.

We re-create an original trauma that caused pain and despair in a futile attempt to re-solve it. Do you obsess about what happened before? Do you relive old hurts, again and again?

If so, you are hoping that in some crazy way they'll get resolved. Past trauma becomes repeated as present drama. "Maybe this time they'll change and love me." Sound familiar?

Is It Old Home Week Again?

"If you always do what you've always done, you'll always get what you've always gotten."   -Dr Bernie Seigel

I often think, say, and do:
_____ "They didn't love me; nobody ever will."
_____ "Dad (Mom) beat me, now my husband (wife/mate) does."
_____ "Mom (Dad) abandoned me, now everyone else does."
_____ "Mom (Dad) made me eat everything on my plate, now my boss forces me to keep my desk clean."

I now create a new, happy home within myself.

AFFIRM SUCCESS:
I give up the myth that others will change. Others do themselves

perfectly. They are never going to change. They are responsible for their behaviors. They have chosen their behaviors.

No matter how many times I replay the old scene; if I play my part, 'they' will always play the flip side of my part. I put on a new movie.

Instead, I create a new glorious home within myself. I become my own perfect mom and dad. I live my life joyously in the now.

Controlling Others
"Eyes the boss."   —Dick Tator

Controlling others is an attempt to cope with uncertainty and out-of-control caretakers from the past. We keep a tight grip trying to get a grip. Controlling yourself, all others and the world is an impossible and exhausting game.

In truth, you are responsible for your own peace of mind and it is essential that you learn to be response-able to the needs of others by letting them run their own lives. Assist others when needed, but don't try taking their power from them. That makes them resentful and you lonely.

To Cope with Fear, Do I Puppeteer?

"The only things worth learning are the things you learn after you know it all."   -Harry S. Truman

I often think, say, and/or do: (fill in the blanks)

_____ "I control my environment and the people in it with my systems, rules, and beliefs."

_____ "I starve (or binge) because, finally, I can do whatever I choose with my own body."

_____ "I go overboard."

Yes to any of these means I need to relax my death grip on the world.

AFFIRM SUCCESS:
I hold everyone else fully capable to run his or her own life (except little children). I empower myself and take response•ability for running my own life. I allow spontaneous fate to co-create exciting change and adventure in my life.

Games That Limit

With the best intentions, we sometimes indulge in limiting patterns, habits or manipulations that undermine peace of mind. Do you play any of the following games?

Game of Blame

"Nobody can write your autobiography but you."   -Helen Shaw

SOME PEOPLE TAKE THEIR ROLLS SERIOUSLY

Illustrated by Shelley Stockwell

Most people live life by default: "de fault ain't mine." To be healthy, happy and centered we need to take responsibility for what we do in our lives. True, some things are beyond our control. But how we react to everything that happens to us is within our power.

Do I Play The Game of Blame?

I often hear myself saying or thinking: (fill in the blanks)

____ "It's not my fault."
____ "The computer (my car, the bus, Internet...) was down."
____ "My secretary (boss, husband, wife, kids...) screwed up."
____ "I drink (eat, smoke, cry) because of my wife (boss, mother, father, my illness...)."
____ "If it wasn't for ____ I could have what I want.

If I marked any of these statements, I've let the fickle finger of fate focus fallaciously. This kept the heat off of me.

The Stockwell System

AFFIRM SUCCESS:

I replay the scenario when I blamed another as if I was the only one in power. That way, I see how I created the situation and what the payoff was.

In the same circumstances, how would I play this scene?

I take full responsibility for my behaviors and actions. If I make a mistake, I honestly admit it. I notice what I have learned from any mistake. This situation from the past gave me a gift. What is it? An insight? A strength? An awareness? I now play 'The Game Of Gift.'

If necessary, I apologize to any person I have insulted or blamed. I right any wrongs by honestly owning up to the situation as my responsibility. I forgive myself for harming anyone with insensitivity.

I don't allow that mistake to happen again.

I congratulate myself for growing in wisdom and responsibility.

Game of Complain

"Oh, Am I hungry. I'm so hungry."
She eats.
"Oh, was I hungry, I was so hungry."
☆
"How is Mable anyway?"
"She is as we say, enjoying ill health."

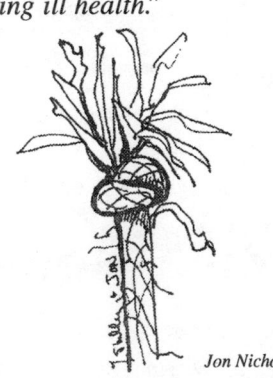

Illustration by
Jon Nicholas & Shelley Stockwell

FRAYED KNOT

Do I Play The Complain Game?

I often hear myself saying or thinking:

"Ain't it awful."
"I'm so tired."
"I'm so sleepy."
"My hair is coming out by the handfuls what should I do?"
"He never comes home on time."
"School sucks"
"Work sucks"
"Life sucks"
"I've got troubles, I've got worries, I've got my gal who could ask for anything more."
"Oh, my aching bones."
"Poor me"

Sufferin' succotash! If you've heard these kinds of messages from yourself you've tuned into a painful victim game. Here's the way to change this negative pattern:

If Another Plays the Game Of Complain

Don't get engaged in the game. Give them a hug. Say only once; "It sounds like you're having a rough time." or offer one helping hand solution. Then notice their response. If they discount your ideas and continue playing ain't it awful say; "You're wise. I'm sure you'll figure out what to do to make you happy." If they appear eager to negotiate a solution, jump right in, the game is over.

AFFIRM SUCCESS:

In the past, complaining was a way to get attention and engage another in conversation. It's a lot more fun now to have positive exchanges. I now enjoy getting attention in more positive ways.

If something bothers me, I enjoy discovering and creating positive solutions. I find creative solutions to problems. I enjoy telling

The Stockwell System

others what's on my mind so we can brainstorm solutions together. If so, I listen to their ideas. I don't wear others out with problems that I can easily solve myself. I now get attention from myself and others in positive ways.

I am thankful that I have been able to complain. It proves that I am alive. In fact everything in my life is miraculous. The fact, that I can think, see, hear, speak are all part of the miracle of me. As I reflect on these and other precious gifts of being alive. I am filled with pleasure. I submerge every muscle nerve and ligament in this pleasure. How fortunate I am to be alive. As I return to the here and now I experience this same pleasure. I now embark on the pleasurable task of celebrating my life.

I've Got A Hippo In My Backyard Game

"I've got a hippo in my backyard."
"I've got a hippo in my backyard and it weighs two tons."
"Mine weighs four tons and is green."
"Well mine won an Olympic gold medal..."
This never-ending game of one-upsmanship is an unsuccessful attempt to feel "better than."

Do I Have A Hippo Hang Up?

I often think or say:

"I'm big, you're little"
"I know you don't know"
"I'm right, you're wrong"
I'm smart, you are stupid"
"Mine's bigger than yours"
"Mine's better than yours"
"I am, you are not"
If so Hippo's got to go.

If Another Plays Hippo: Let them have the last word. Your response can simply be: "How nice, you have a hippo in your backyard!"

AFFIRM SUCCESS:
I value myself. I am perfect just the way I am. I have nothing to prove. I am a growing and maturing person. Everyday in every way I find new ways to respect and honor my gifts, my growth and my potentials. I like it when I shine. I like it when other people shine.

Garbage Bag Game
This is a silent victim game until the end. In the mind of the garbage bag player, it goes like this:

"You did this bad thing to me, but I won't say anything. I'll just take it and throw it here in my garbage bag. Oh, oh, you just did another bad thing, but I won't say anything again. I'll just throw it in my garbage bag...(on and on)."

Somewhere down the line, when the bag is nice and full, the garbage collector takes their overstuffed bag of resentments and dumps it on their offender's head saying, "You SOB!" or words to that effect.

AFFIRM SUCCESS:
I am direct about how I feel or what I think as soon as I notice that I am angry. I communicate things that bother me as they happen, before they build and bulge. Simply and directly, I tell the people who hurt me that they did so. When I say I am angry, I feel better. In the business world, expressing anger is sometimes difficult, yet, it is safe if I honestly express my hurt in this style, "When you did _____, I felt _____."

If it's not appropriate to express my truth out loud, I pretend I'm looking through the back end of a pair of binoculars. I see the obnoxious person several thousand miles away. I detach, take a deep breath, and do something else.

Put Down Game

JUDGE-MENTAL

Illustration by Shelley Stockwell

Do the faults of others seem like bright headlights on a passing car and more glaring than your own? Some hide this game behind humor. Humor is no excuse.

The two versions of this game both can be played silently or out loud depending on your style: Version one "I put myself down." Version two "I put another person down by fingering their faults or inadequacies."

The faults we see in others are usually a reflection of our own. It's an unconscious attempt to distract ourselves from handling our own limits. My faults are a part of myself.

AFFIRM SUCCESS:
I take a deep breath and ask myself, "What is it that I want or need right now ? What is it that I am not getting? Then I find another way to get it. Asking for what I really want is good.

I forgive others for any mistakes they've made and I say good, kind and loving things to and about them. I look upon them with "soft eyes." I forgive them for me. It makes me feel so relieved not to hold such painful resentment.

I forgive myself for any mistakes I've made and I say good, kind, loving things to and about myself. I look upon myself with soft eyes.

Better Than Me Game

Competition is another name for this game.

AFFIRM SUCCESS:
I am my best; no contest.

Alone Again Game

"Suppose I threw a war and nobody came?" -Unknown Soldier

This game is played to re-experience disappointment and abandonment. Set 'em up, so they can let you down. When playing the alone again game we choose unavailable people and then are shattered because they let us down.

AFFIRM SUCCESS :
I actively pursue loving relationships with others. If I don't know what a healthy loving relationship is I find out. Everyday in every way I learn new and better ways to love myself and others.

Paralysis Game

"I can't move. I can't breath."
"What if..."
"What if I make a mistake?"
"If I start writing now I'll be too tired. If I wait 'til tomorrow I can use the computer. If I have a good dinner I might be too sleepy..."
"I'm so overwhelmed I don't know where to start, so I don't."

AFFIRM SUCCESS:
I move my body, my thoughts to positive ones and my face to a smile. When I'm in action I feel terrific. I break tasks into small action steps. I enjoy beginnings, middles and endings. My life is an adventure. I love to move my body and my mind.

Coulda, Woulda, Shoulda Game

Words like "kind of," "sort of," "I'm not sure," "I'll try," and "would of," "could of," should of," are nonproductive and make you feel terrible. Take back your power and affirm success.

AFFIRM SUCCESS:
I don't should on myself. As I change my words, I change my mind for my highest good.

I change 'I'll try' to 'I will or I won't.' or 'I choose to or I choose not to.'

I change 'woulda, coulda, shoulda' to 'I did, it was, and oh well.' The change is a relief.

Yada, Yada, Yada Game

Photo by Chris Gordon

Do you talk just to talk? Do you talk to yourself while someone else is supposedly talking with you? This non-communication game is a one way street with several versions:

Yada, yada, yada version #1:
"What do you think I should do?"
"Whatever."
"Oh thank you, thank you, thank you."

Yada, yada, yada version #2:
"What do you think I should do?"
"Whatever."
"That's not true, it's this way. What do you think I should do?"

Yada, yada, yada version #3:
"What do you think I should do?"
"Whatever."
'(I ignore whatever you say and keep talking.) Yada, Yada, Yada."

AFFIRM SUCCESS:
I listen well to myself and others. I give myself time to think, to listen and to learn. I am a keen observer of myself and others. If I need to express myself I get involved in Toastmasters or discussion groups.

Never-Always Game

"How Come You Never?" "How Come You Always?" Players of this game use sweeping generalities. Does someone you know always do that?

Distorted Mirror Game

Self fulfilling prophesies are what we create when we project our beliefs upon the world. If you tell someone,
"You don't love me (anymore)," eventually, you'll be correct.

If you tell another, "You can't be trusted," eventually, you'll be correct. If you tell them, "You're going to leave me. You're glad we're apart." Eventually, you'll be right. If you tell yourself, "People hurt me," you're correct. If you tell yourself, "Men/women are impossible to get along with," you'll be right.

AFFIRM SUCCESS:
I allow the world to mirror my beauty, love, and kindness. I look and see the beauty in others.

I ask for positive results in all situations. I trust the goodness in others and in myself."

Excitement Junkie Game

If you love the thrill of the chase, if pursuing the unavailable turns you on, if unstable, rejecting, on-again-off-again people are intensely interesting to you, beware. You may be an excitement junkie. Intensity and stress are often cross-wired with pain and distress.

AFFIRM SUCCESS:
Though life may seem quiet at first, I adjust and find large thrills in subtle things. I remember that I'm coming off a nerve-wracking drug. And just like any junkie I need time for my body to withdraw from my adrenaline addiction of the past.

My true self takes pleasure in the subtleties of life. I am calm, peaceful and clear minded.

Seduction Game

"Everyone comes on to me."

Do you wear fetching clothes, stick out your chest, swing your rump, use sexual innuendoes, dirty jokes, pat or rub or touch others excessively, and when they come on to you say to your friends or yourself; "I'm amazed. Men (women) always come on to me. Men (women) are like fleas. I just have to slap them off. Or yell 'off with their head,' I just can't understand it."

The seduction game is a power trip that often hides anger, and insecurity and a desire to control others. The temporary ego rush is always burdened by an awful feeling that you are lying to yourself and others.

AFFIRM SUCCESS:
I stop playing the seduction game at once. It isn't any fun.

I'm attractive and desirable. I don't need to keep proving it at the expense of others. I don't need to keep hurting myself. I now carefully select who and what I draw to my life. I put out my sexual beam when I'm interested and available for real relationships. Otherwise, I take my energy and put it into more rewarding and productive efforts.

Upside Down Seduction Game
"Nobody comes on to me."
The upside down seduction game is a control trip that says, "Off with my head!"

If you don't bother to groom yourself, make no eye contact, your posture is pathetic, and you hold yourself away from others, you may be playing this game.

If someone shows an interest in you, and you immediately turn him or her off, that is the seduction game in reverse.

AFFIRM SUCCESS:
I stop playing "them and us," and view every human being as a precious individual with feelings and needs just like my own.

I am proud to be me. I like looking and feeling my best. I stand tall. I am open to receive a lot. I like others and they like me. I enjoy looking at myself in the mirror. I love being clean and well groomed. It shows me how proud I am to be alive.

Collecting Votes Game
"Don't you think she is boring?"
"Do you think I should call my sister today after she did that to me?"
"Should I stay with my husband or leave my husband."

Rather than take responsibility for your behavior, attitude, decision or feelings, do you take votes?

AFFIRM SUCCESS:
I take responsibility for my feelings, responses, decisions and behaviors, and accept the consequences. I can ask for other people's opinions if I need to make a decision. I no longer use indirect means to gossip or berate another. I take responsibility for my behavior, attitudes and feelings.

Vampire Games

> Psychic vampires talk to themselves
> and hook you in their game
> of "poor me," "gotcha," "gimme some"
> and "it's really quite a shame."
>
> For underneath their record stuck
> dwells a sacred soul
> but for now I won't be suckered in
> to a game that takes it's toll.
>   — Shelley Stockwell

Are you being eaten by a psychic vampire? Some relationships can suck us dry. You may not notice it at the time, but afterwards, you feel drained, headachy, with a vague feeling like you've been had. Suck relationships are based on your giving and their taking.

If you work hard emotionally, but nothing comes back, you're not acknowledged for your efforts, and the kinder you are, the greedier the suck becomes, watch out! There lurks a psychic vampire.

Psychic Vampires play three variations on the theme: crisis junkie, broken record and gotcha.

Crisis junkie

Ask a crisis junkie, "How are you?" and they'll drone on in hour-long dissertations about their latest drama, wrapping it up with, "To make a long story short" or "Enough about me, how are you?" and "What do you think about me?" often followed by; "What you just said reminds me of this terrible thing that happened to me..."

Broken record
No matter what the situation or conversation, it will come back to the same old story, played in three-part disharmony.

How many times have you heard this story of that "son-of-a-bitch?" or what "so-in-so did!"

Gotcha
These folks criticize, so you agonize. Gotcha vampires know exactly which buttons to push to create resentment. They love pointing out how you don't give them what they need. If you give them a lovely plate for their birthday, they might say, "You were three days late for my birthday and I don't like blue," leaving you to apologize for your insensitivity. Try this approach "I'll show you how insensitive I can be, take a hike."

AFFIRM SUCCESS:
I commit myself to hang around only with nourishing people. People, who play these suck games, probably won't hear what I say, because all they are really doing is talking to themselves. If I expect them to change, good luck. If I expect them to be helpful and nice, good luck. The best advice I can give myself is that if this relationship is not fun, I'll cut bait and find a better one. I'm no longer the sucker at the end of the line.

I tell them the truth, the whole truth, and nothing but the truth. I say something like, "When you obsesses about your past, I get bored, and my mind drifts off. So if you want to have a relationship with me, you need to be sensitive to my needs, just as you are demanding that I am sensitive to yours. Otherwise, I don't want to hang out with you any more."

I verbally set limits, by saying, "I don't want to hear about your _____ today. If you'd like to talk about something pleasant, I'll meet you for lunch."

I make sure I always have a fast escape route. The last thing I'd ever want to do, is take a three-day car trip with one of these sucks. If I'm trapped by a vampire, I remove myself mentally from their auric field. I think about a beautiful place or beautiful moment in time.

It Reminds Me Of... Game.

When you play this game, you are never in the moment; you're living in the past. Another version of this game is, "tomorrow, I'll..."

AFFIRM SUCCESS :
I am present. I talk in present "un-tense," so that I am not tense. I stay conscious, awake and alert. I easily listen to others without adding my story. It is safe in my world.

Poor Me and The Fan Game:

"No one appreciates me?"
"Poor me and after all I do."
"I'm shattered, I'm devastated."
"I have the worst luck."

Poor me like all victim games keep us feeling helpless and hopeless. Stanislofski, the inventor of "method acting," said that to suffer is to live, he must have loved these games.

In the Fan Game, the victim stands below a spinning fan. When the sh__ hits the fan and they are well splattered, they point to a clean place on themselves and say, "You missed a spot."

The Rescuer Game

A rescuer becomes responsible for every one but themself.

AFFIRM SUCCESS:
I support others to solve their own problems.

Perfectionist Game.

The perfectionist always focuses on what has not been done. Instead of praise, a perfectionist gives criticism. If a perfectionist happens to be a parent, they usually get the opposite result. Instead of the child trying harder, he or she often quits.

Worry Wart Game

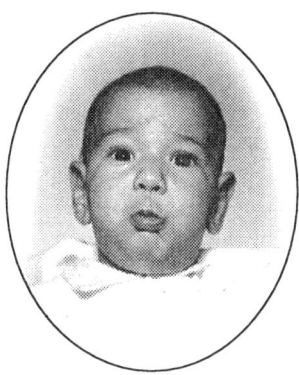

Worrying is usually an attempt to make things come out our way. Usually we are schooled in the art of fretting from someone in our family. Worry takes up the mental energy that we could use creating positive action. Energy drains away when we fret.

For many, worry is their favorite recreational activity. When they worry about others they take the heat off themselves. When they worry about themselves they get to feel weak and powerless.

Far from a release, worry causes and builds tension in the body and robs us of living our life in the present. Worry certainly doesn't solve problems, it creates more problems.

In truth, worry warts are highly creative people or they wouldn't find such a myriad of things to worry about; being too fat, too slim, too poor, what others are doing or not doing, the list goes on and on.

AFFIRM SUCCESS
I turn my creativity toward interesting pursuits like drawing, painting, building, designing, writing, sculpting, or making positive plans that put me in the driver's seat.

If I learned to worry from someone else, I give this pattern back to his or her. It's theirs I don't want it and I don't need it. I choose to enjoy my life.

If my mind goes back to an old pattern of obsessing of worrying I say to myself "enough!' and I think of new ways to move forward in my life. I move my body, I make new plans and I get a life.

Illustration by Shelley Stockwell

CHAPTER 15
Recycle Old Patterns

"As a man thinkith so he is."   -Jesus
"We become what we contemplate."   -Plato
"You take a hundred pounds of clay..."   -Playdough

"Sunshine wonderful, absolutely yes!
When you're happy feeling fine,
you can't be depressed"

CHOOSE YOUR LIFE QUIZ

Choose Poem one or two, whichever best represents your life.

Poem One

Mother loves me forever.
Father is there 'til the end.
Brothers and sisters, best buddies,
I'm never in need of a friend.

Truth is the mode of communing.
Laughter: the tone of the day.
My talents & dreams;encouraged.
"You're terrific" is what they all say.

My energy bubbles elation,
I relax right up to the soul.
Love and peace are so easy
I am healthy, happy, and whole.

Poem Two

Mother abandoned me early.
Daddy beat me instead.
My sister & brother betray me.
I was sexually molested in bed.

Family secrets are sacred.
Survival: the tone of the day.
My talents and dreams are insulted.
"You're a loser" is what they all say.

My energy's always hysteric,
To stop the pain is my goal.
Shame, guilt, rage, and heartache
Keep me sad and out of control.

Poem Three

I become my own good mommy
And a daddy I love and adore.
I really am my best buddy
For that's what friends are for.

The truth is what has freed me
I laugh and smile and grin.
My talents and dreams are respected
I hear the voice within.

I do kind things for my body
I take back control at last.
I honestly express each emotion
I release and forgive the past.

If you chose poem one, congratulate yourself. You're blessed.
If you chose poem two and prefer poem one,
choose poem three and you will be blessed.

Suggestions For A TERRIFIC Life

I have to accept the fact that my past probably won't get any better.
— Shelley Stockwell

Take a deep breath and put yourself in center, into relaxation, the way you do so well. Good. Now read these ideas slowly so that their meaning sinks in.

I am 100% response•able for everything in my life—my health, my behaviors, my relationships, my success, and my peace of mind.

I allow others to run their own life. I regard others with positive neutrality. I honor others right to make their own choices and learn their own lessons. I lovingly guide children, teaching them to love themselves.

I am keenly aware of any games I play. From this moment forward, I choose to play victor, empowerer and supporter. I choose to play happy and peaceful.

I maintain clear and well-defined boundaries between myself and others. I am in charge of my life.

In all situations, I ask myself: "Whose problem is this, anyway?" If, in the past, I played victim, I now lovingly reclaim my power, and the game stops. If I played rescuer, I now give others their space to grow. If I played persecutor, I now find healthy ways to release rage as energy without hurting others or myself. I control my emotions and express them in appropriate ways, times, and places.

When I choose to assist others, I do it with love, and I'm not attached to the outcome. I choose joy. Joy is my compass.

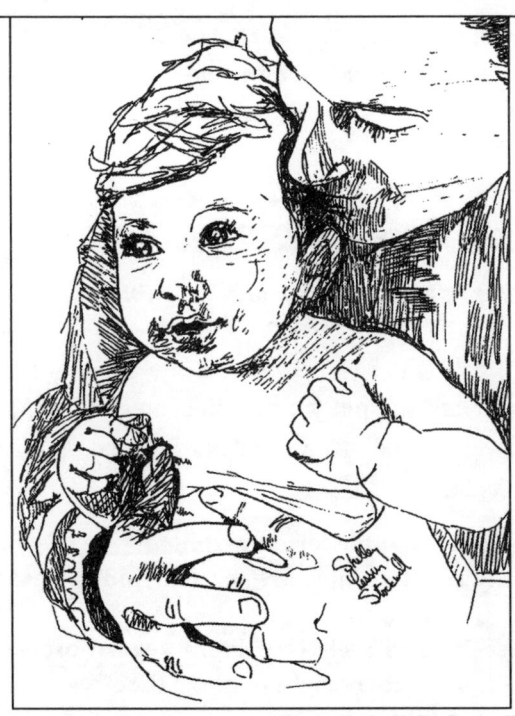

Illustration by Shelley Stockwell

Limiting Imprints:	Empowering Imprints:
"I can't live without you." **Co·dependency**	*"I support my dreams and I support your dreams."* **Inter·dependency**
"I know nothing." **Denial**	*"I tell myself the truth. I listen and act from my truth."* **Truth**

Bust Limiting Imprints
Imprints from Home

Come on Mom, don't be mean,
Think about my self-esteem.
You dropped downers, you popped speed
and took a toke, when you felt the need.
You sipped white wine so you'd relax
(No need for you your brain to tax).
So why complain because I party,
am sometimes stoned and often tardy?
Let's face the facts we know are true
I'm growing up a lot like you.   —Shelley Stockwell

"*Long after we leave the home we grew up in, we continue to create situations in which we are mistreated, ignored, put down, or controlled. These life traps determine how we think, feel, act, and relate to others, even when we appear to have everything.*"
—Jeffrey Young
and Janet Klosko
Reinventing Your Life

We are like balloons; when we expand, we are light and fly. If not, we lie on the table thick-skinned. To change your life, all you need to do is change and expand your mind. To change your mind, you must mind your mind. When we pay attention and understand how the brain and mind work, we're able to influence thoughts in a positive way.

Imprints (pieces of information in the subconscious mind) influence the way we think and act. Limiting imprints, ones that don't serve us well, are easily replaced with suggestion. We recognize these "limiting" thought patterns when we stay conscious, tell our truth and explore the subconscious through hypnosis.

The most powerful imprints come from the people who raise us. The conscious mind doesn't develop until around five years of age. From conception to age five, fueled by our genetic coding, we absorb as gospel, information from the "big people" (the worlds best hypnotists!). We model their behaviors, and enforce their actions with our life experiences.

Mommy and Daddy are our natural role models. If Daddy raged, we might become a rageaholic too with outbursts and tizzies. Or, we may adopt our own style of rage. Instead of blatantly tantruming, we may don a 'nice' mask and express rage in sneaky 'gotchas,' or choose life partners who vent rage for us.

If Mommy numbed with food, we may do that too. Family traditions sometimes die-hard.

Co-dependency

"I'd join Co-dependency Anonymous if I could find someone to go with me."

Deep•end Quiz

I often think, say, and/or do:
_____ "My problems are caused by others."
_____ "It's hard to tell where others end and I begin."
_____ "I know what's best for the others in my life."
_____ "I control others by manipulating, pouting, yelling, ignoring, threatening, or intimidating."

If I answered true to any of these four statements, I use co-dependent relationships to smoke screen my frustrations.

What is co-dependency?

Co-dependency is a pattern of thinking and acting that makes other people responsible for your feelings or makes you responsible for their feelings. It is founded on a belief that you and I are not separate individuals with our own path and purpose, but rather, that we merge in a designated "pecking order." If you believe someone or something outside of yourself controls you or that you must control others, you're working a lot harder than you need to.

Co-dependency keeps you from taking responsibility for yourself and your life. If you blame someone else for what happens to you, that blame is the outward sign of your internal feelings of being helpless and powerless.

You make others responsible for your situation because you have not learned how to take responsibility yet. You learned about relationships at home; if this is how they did it, perhaps you do it this way too.

How did you catch co-dependency?

Photo by Carole Powell

Without support as an infant, you would have died. As a baby, you were still partially fetal and, therefore, dependent on your caretakers. How well you got along with them, or if they took care of you was a matter of life or death.

If your family was co-dependent, they found your independence threatening. Were you trained to believe that you were incapable of being on your own? Were you taught dependency: to always be taken care of or to take care of others—i.e., "Father knows best." "Mommy can't cope, you have to be Mommy's mommy." If so, you were taught to be responsible for what other people think or feel. When this happens, we subconsciously are attracted to others with the same mindset. And thus, co•dependency blossoms.

Are you dying to be taken care of?

Limiting Imprints: fear driven	**Empowering Imprints:** love driven
"I depend on you to take care of me, because I don't trust myself." **Dependence**	"I take care of me; I expect you to take care of you." **Independence:** "I trust myself to take care of me." **Inner·dependence:**
"I expect you to take care of me; you expect me to take care of you." **Co·dependence:**	"We are each self reliant, and when we combine our individual creativity's, we enhance each other's lives." **Inter·dependence:**

Self-sufficient caretakers teach children to be self-sufficient. If your family was not co-dependent, you can comfortably stand on your own two feet. You would have learned that being in·dependent is safe. A healthy family would have shown you, through example and reflection, to trust your own inner wisdom and become inner·dependent. You would learn honor your feelings and thoughts, be self confident, and hold yourself in high esteem.

Inner confidence attracts others who are self-assured and inner dependant. Together you form beautiful inter·dependent relationships. Healthy love allows us each to support ourselves in having what we want and need and lovingly supports each other to fill those needs.

Trauma vs. Drama

Co-dependency is often an attempt to resolve past trauma by recreating it in a present-day drama. For example, if you were a victim in your childhood (and most children are), you may "hire" someone to play the role of persecutor in your current drama. You'd do this hoping, in some bizarre way, that you could work it out, this time.

That's why you may marry the "same" person again and again. Dramas that attempt to resolve trauma always come out the same. You can even play a different role and the scene will end the same. If you recreate your life as it was in your childhood, you never meet a new person or have a truly new experience. Same old, same old.

Dominance and Submission

Another reason for co-dependency is an exaggerated pattern of natural dominance and submission. In all the animal kingdom, a pecking order develops. Maturity over youth, male over female, blondes over brunettes, muscle over flab, brains over brawn. Children fight for their parents' attention. Men and women worry about how they "measure up" in acquaintances, accomplishments, admiration appendages. Competitive sports are a global addiction where we cheer the top dog and jeer the bottom dog.

If your family was out-of-control, and you felt weak and powerless, you might decide to be exuberantly dominant or powerful. Or you may take on a passive role and submit to another. Parental patterns of dominance and submission may become yours as well. Such competitive tomfoolery is possibly the main source of violence acts in society.

> To ward off an aggressive dog, lower your head, lower your hand, make a limp wrist, and whimper. To ward off an aggressive ape, bear your teeth in a smile.

Magnetic Attraction

As a victim, we find "professional" rescuers or persecutors. Later, we secretly resent them for power-tripping us. "You never let me think for myself. You never trust my judgment."

If the victim complains, rescuers may put on their persecutor hat: "You ingrate. How dare you talk to me like that, after all I did for you." The victim, now more victimized, might cry or withdraw. On with the rescuer hat: "Don't cry," they say, "I'm sorry. I'll make it up to you."

Victim, Rescuer and Persecutor

"A person can move throughout the victim triangle without needing other players. For example, let's say you feel out-of-control with food (victim). You decide to rescue yourself by going on a diet (rescuer). When it does not work, you become angry with yourself by feeling guilty and putting yourself down (persecutor), making yourself more of a victim, feeling more helpless and out-of-control."

— Diane Zimberoff
Breaking Free From the Victim Trap

The Problem: Co-dependent Triangle

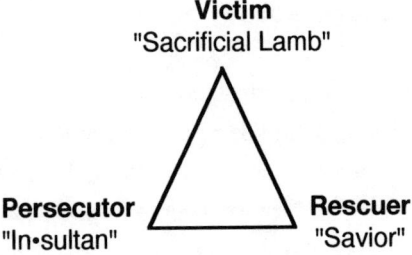

Some people spend their whole life in this boring, repetitive pattern. Not you, anymore. You now create new, fun, and dynamic relationships.

The Solution: Interdependent Triangle:

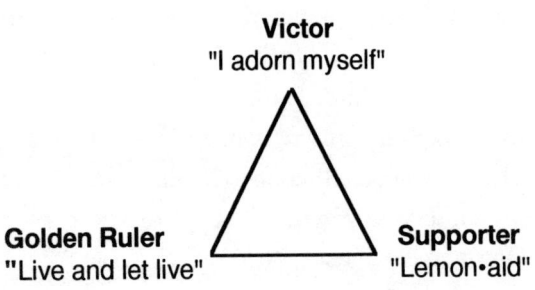

The control games of victim, rescuer, and persecutor keep us little, intensify depression, and hold us from bliss. These patterns of thought are attempts to resolve past pain or make us go home again. But they keep us stuck in past patterns. Each time we reinforce an old imprint the more entrenched and automatic it becomes. To return to joy, you need to stay awake and notice how you act. Then choose new behaviors that are more fun.

People often play victim, rescuer or persecutor at various times. And over a lifetime can "settle in" with a favorite one. Do you have a favorite game? Is it victim, rescuer, or persecutor?

Victim

"How is Mabel anyway?"
"She is, as they say, enjoying ill health."

Is Victim My Dictum?

___"I choose abusive people who (hit, insult, yell, sexually abuse, put me down -Fill in the blank), just like Dear Old _____ did."

___"If I can't find someone else to abuse me, I abuse myself and suffer."

___Help me, poor me. Life is so difficult. I can't get along without you."

If this sounds familiar, you've played victim in an attempt to relive similar situations from the past.

Suggestions For A Victor
Most folks are as happy as they make up their minds to be.
              — Abraham Lincoln

Take a deep breath and put yourself in center, into relaxation, the way you do so well. Good. Now read these ideas slowly so that their meaning sinks in.

I am 100% response·able for everything in my life—my health, my behaviors, my relationships, my success, and my peace of mind.

I allow others to run their own life. I regard others with positive neutrality. I honor others right to make their own choices and learn their own lessons. I lovingly guide children, teaching them to love themselves.

I forgive myself for the past, and at this moment, I adopt a new attitude. I am 100% responsible for my life. Others are just folks I encounter. I choose to be happy; therefore, I take action to be happy. I claim my body, emotions, behaviors, and my life. I am brave. Each day, I learn new ways to love myself. I deserve happiness and peace of mind.

How And Why We Play Victim?

If we were victimized, neglected, or abused as a child, it's likely that we grow up to take on the familiar role of victim as a grown-up. We become an "active" or a "passive" victim. Active victims go public with suffering. "Life is so difficult." "Everything always goes wrong for me." "My mate beats me." "My kids insult me." "My boss is terrible to me." "My health is so poor." The perils of Pauline. Sufferin' succotash. Ain't it awful.

Passive victims know how to bring the house down with a sigh. Walking open wounds, victims control others in subtle, passive ways. Victims require others to consider their problems, while they discount

Zelda's Story
Zelda is a petite black-haired, dark-skinned lady.

"I had the ten zillionth fight with my insensitive husband. He stormed out and slammed the door. 'Don't come back. I hate you,' I said under my breath and lay down on the floor.

Suddenly, Sister Ignacio, my second grade teacher, popped into my mind. She whopped me with a ruler because I laughed and was disruptive.

It was then that I noticed what I was doing. There I was, lying on my back on the floor. One foot was on top of the other, and my arms were outstretched. I almost felt a wreath of thorns upon my brow. Martyr was my game. That was a turning point for me. I got off my cross and stopped my victim game."

others. Victims control with guilt and hold others responsible for their welfare. "I can't take drafts." "You know I can't climb stairs." "Could you please bring me that?" Victim's subconscious desire is to be saved from underlying pain, anger, confusion, and disappointment.

Rescuer
"I've come to collect my dead friend's belongings."
"Why doesn't he pick them up himself?"

Is Mighty Mouse In My House?

____"I am the leader of the casserole brigade."
____"I am the Dolly Do-Good helper to all."
____"I 'fix' others."
____"I choose victims of abuse to rescue (including those I have abused)."

Rescuers, "help" victims, because they want someone to rescue them.

Suggestions For Ex-Rescuers
"I decided long ago, never to walk in anyone's shadow. If I fail, if I succeed, at least I live as I believe."   — Whitney Houston
"The Greatest Love of All"

Take a deep breath and put yourself in center, into relaxation, the way you do so well. Good. Now read these ideas slowly so that their meaning sinks in.

I am 100% response•able for everything in my life—my health, my behaviors, my relationships, my success, and my peace of mind.

I maintain clear boundaries between others and myself. I allow others to run their own life. I regard others with positive neutrality. I honor others right to make their own choices and learn their own lessons. I lovingly guide children, teaching them to love themselves.

I respect others by honoring their innate ability to run their own life, except babies, of course.

I teach children to think for themselves. If I am a helping professional or friend, I only hold the mirror so others may "reflect." I trust that every human being is endowed with profound inner wisdom. I teach myself and others to tap their own strength and trust it. I love others when I honor them. I assist others because I enjoy empowering others just as I enjoy empowering myself.

How and Why We Rescue

As a rescuer, we find every stray dog in the neighborhood, every poor pathetic soul, and every cause. Rescuers often became health professionals nurses, psychologists, psychiatrists, hypnotherapist, flight attendants, or neighborhood do-gooders. They're often at the forefront of club, church and volunteer organizations: white knights in shining armor.

We rescue others because of a subconscious desire to be rescued ourselves. Rescuers attempt to control others by doing for them. Rescuer is the flip side of the victim role. Rescuers are magnetized to victims. This gives them an opportunity to take charge of someone else's life and take the heat off themselves.

Persecutor

Two cannibals eating a dead clown:
"Does this taste funny to you?" — Jim Vogl

Top Banana Quiz

I often think, say, and/or do:
_____ "I _____ (hit, insult, yell, sexually abuse, put down others...), just like Dear Old _____ did."
_____ "I _____ (hurt, insult, abuse, put down ....) myself."

If you play the persecutor in the Victim Triangle game, you usually act out the role of the person who victimized you in the first place.

Ex-Persecutors Affirm Success
"Real gold does not fear even the hottest fire."
Take a deep breath and put yourself in center, into relaxation, the way you do so well. Good. Now read these ideas slowly so that their meaning sinks in.

I maintain clear boundaries between others and myself. And allow others to run their own life. I release anger as energy in positive, non-destructive ways. I don't have the right or permission to attack or insult anyone, including myself.

I clearly express my thoughts and feelings. I ask for what I want and I take responsibility only for myself by asking, 'Whose problem is this?' I get a grip.

How and Why We Persecute
When you play persecutor, you attempt to control others with rage. Your style of expression may sport familiar resemblance to rage directed at you in your childhood or the way you acted out rage then.

Rage can be expressed in blatant tantrums or in quiet ways. Passive-aggressive anger "doesn't get mad, it gets even." Rage can be veiled in put-down humor of snipes: However, if it manifests, it feels ugly, or you go numb or out-of-control in a kind of trauma trance.

Out•rageous

English surgeon, John Hunter' whose research showed that anger and anxiety brought on chest pains, died of a heart attack after he got furious with two other doctors during a staff meeting.

TIARA'S STORY

Tiara is a beautiful, shy 55 year old woman

"My stepmother is a rude lady who always puts me down and insults my son. I call her and my passive father once a week. I guess I call them because I want to feel like a good person. Kids are supposed to call their parents. After I hang up, I feel sorry for myself.

When Shelley, my hypnotherapist, asked me: 'what is a good person?' I said, 'A good person doesn't hurt others and is kind and thoughtful.'

How strange that in order for me to feel like a 'good person,' I phone 'bad people.' I got to make them wrong. In some way, perhaps I'm as angry as they are, or I wouldn't be calling them at all.

When I discovered this game of dominance and submission, I thought it was very sick, and I no longer wanted to play.

If I were to put my life script in a few words, it would have been helpless, hopeless, powerless, and passive. Because I have given up this familiar habit and replaced it with a new life script (called power and control, joy and peace) I feel so much better."

SHELLEY'S STORY

"Before I had children, I vowed I would never yell at my kids like Irma screamed at me. And I didn't. Instead, I put myself down with humor, at my own expense. When I had my son, Bryce, I was well controlled. One day, when stressed out, I heard myself yelling in my mother's voice about his trivial messy room. It was sickening.

I didn't bring Bryce into the world to absorb my rage. I never wanted him to feel like I did when my mother screamed. Now, I tell him what bugs me with a calm voice, and I take charge of my behavior. I know that if I'm stressed, I flip out. So I avoid stress by eating well, getting exercise, telling my truth, and, if need be, having a good cry, or calling a friend."

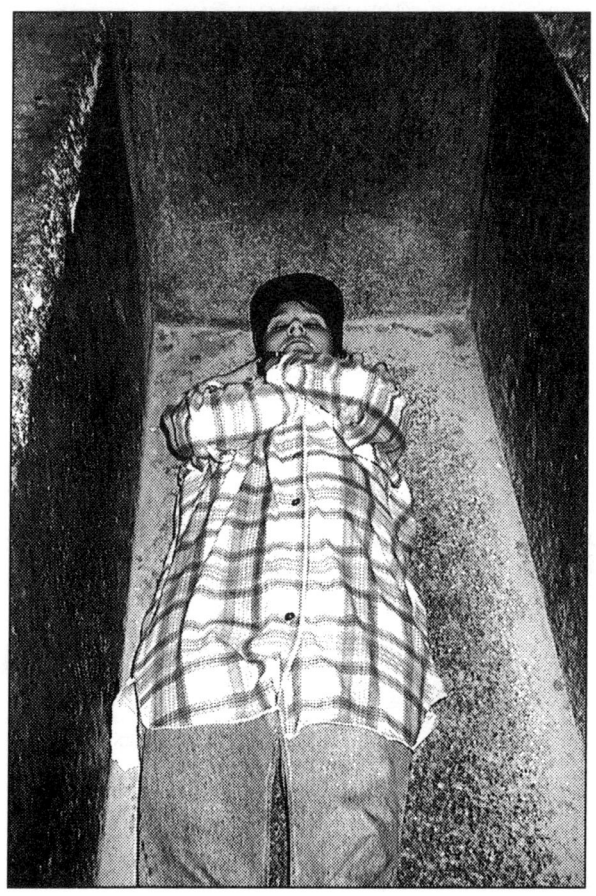

Pharaoh Flyin'

Imagine yourself in a gorgeous sarcophagus (coffin) inside the Great Pyramid. Your name is inscribed in hieroglyphics on a cartouche (a sign with your name) on the side of the coffin. There you are tightly wrapped in bandages—pressed for time.

Peel Take a deep breath and unwrap yourself. As you remove each bandage, one by one, any depression, limiting attitudes, disappointments, and anxiety peel off.

New Footing Stand up, climb out, and stretch. Return to your magnificent body, full of energy and movement.

Pharaoh Thee Well A portal opens. Follow the light and leave this sacred tomb. Your eyes adjust easily to the light. You walk tall. Good-bye mummy. Good-bye daddy. You are now the ruler of yourself.

The Denial Triangle
"Destruction"

"Did you hear about the fountain pen that didn't have an inkling?"

The Denial Triangle begins when we feel sad, awful, and frustrated, with no place to go:

Depression

In an attempt to feel well and forget our problems, we often go numb with self-destructive behaviors:

Addiction/ Compulsion/ Phobia

But these solutions don't work for long, and the very pain we avoid, exaggerates and intensifies. Our inner wisdom cries out, "Stop hurting me." If we respond, "Shut up," we deceive ourselves by ignoring our truth:

Denial

The more we lie to ourselves, the more depressed we get. Our life becomes a never-ending saga of sadness, self-destruction, and deception. We break our own heart in slow-motion suicide. This is no way to live.

Denial

Addiction/Compulsion/Phobia   SUICIDE   Depression

BLAM!!

Smile and Money

The Truth Pyramid
"Reconstruction"

"Reality is a temporary illusion brought on by the absence of beer."

The Truth Pyramid breaks me free from limiting attitudes and behaviors. Freedom begins when I choose to wake up and tell the truth about my life. I get real and heal:

 Expression

Nothing to hide, no need to numb. Positive patterns replace negative ones:

Nourishing Life Style

Awake, I listen, hear, and live my truth:

Truth

I love myself and come back to life:

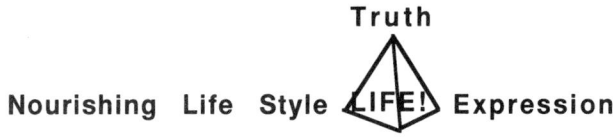
Truth
Nourishing Life Style — LIFE! — Expression

The Stockwell System

Steps For Taking Control Of Your Life

"Baby steps. Take baby steps."   -Bill Murray
What About Bob

Seize control in baby steps.
Take back control, one little step at a time. At work, become orderly. Straighten up your desk, throw away things you don't use, get rid of clutter. Put a sign up saying, DO IT NOW. In your personal life, clean out one drawer, give away clothes you don't wear and write one letter a day, get rid of clutter.

Give yourself a hug.
Remind yourself of your successes. At the end of every day, think of three things you did that day that you feel good about. Count your blessings.

Extinguish worry.
Keep a gripe list. Write down all the things that are bother you and your problems. Prioritize them and then put them away for a month. A month later, when you look at them again, cross off any that you are willing to forgive and put the list away for another month.

Write two forgiveness lists.
List all the things you might consider forgiving someone else for. You don't have to forgive the other person, just consider it. Write a second list of what you need to forgive yourself for. Prioritize both lists in order of biggest to littlest crimes.

Now read them in order of priority and, one by one, ask yourself if you are willing to forgive yourself (or the other person) for this crime. If so, take a deep breath and when you let it out, say, "I forgive you."

Be Positive
The right attitude changes lives.

Make time for relaxation.
Always put time in your schedule to chill out. A simple two minute self hypnosis session can give you an amazing clarity and revive you.

STEP FOUR:

The Stockwell System

Give one your wisdom and they might succeed. Give one tools to tap their own wisdom and they most definitely will succeed.

How can you use hypnosis for yourself to create joy and abundance? How do you let your conscious, subconscious and higher self manifest money, love, wellness, creativity, peace and harmony? And, how do you hypnotize others?

How do you hypnotize others? The Stockwell System is gleaned from experience. I applied each of my techniques in my own life and proved first to myself that they get results. I smile a lot and go to the bank often.

I then was brave enough to try the system on my willing students, clients and friends. Yes, it worked for them too. Many were so impressed they have become professional hypnotists themselves. They tell me that the most rewarding way to practice the Stockwell System is in their own a professional hypnosis practice. Maybe you'll think so too.

Follow each procedure carefully and see for yourself. In a short time, you'll see results and your confidence will grow.

Each method for trance induction, deepening, suggestion and processing information is one I find to be most effective. Experiment, and see how you like them. Then, let your own inner wisdom create new approaches tailor made for you.

Happy trails to you,

Shelley Stockwell

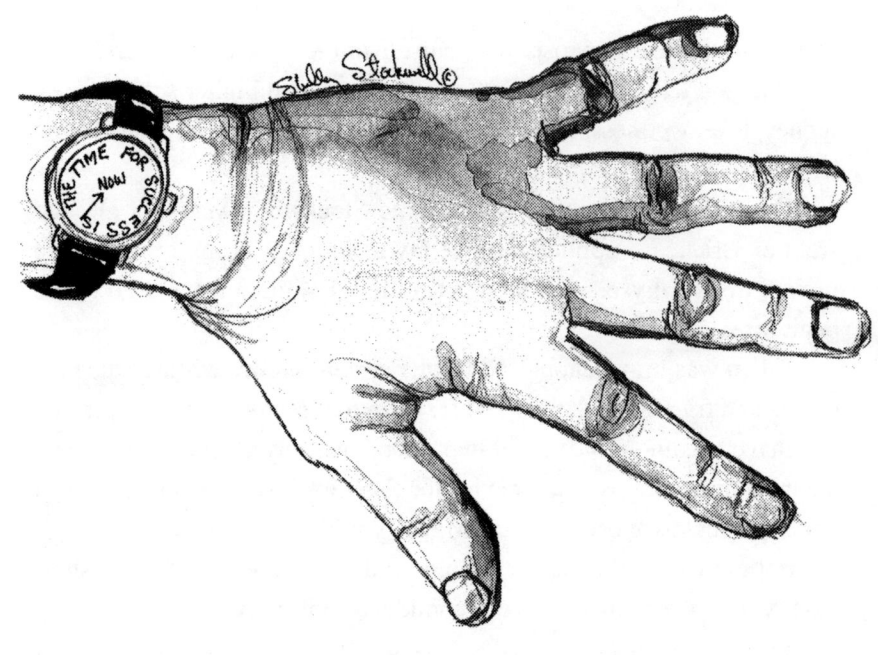

Illustration by Shelley Stockwell

Chapter 16
How To Be A Hypnotist

Love at best is teaching what you need to learn.
Learning what you need to teach.
Giving,
receiving,
a bit of each.
Risking it all in the naked truth.
Love's a timeless dance of maturity and youth.
It's the drive to return to the land of your soul.
Love at best is you.
You are love's goal.   -Shelley Stockwell

AFFIRMATIONS FOR HYPNOTISTS
I am joyous, serene and energized. I now do and become my highest work. I easily attract clients who are light bearers who help heal our planet.

I stand in my client's "moccasins" and speak to them in the language that they hear. I always succeed as a hypnotist. If one induction gets weak results I choose one that gets stronger ones. I hold the mirror steady so that they may reflect upon their inner wisdom. I trust their innate ability to discover their own perfect solutions. I give my clients my full support, wherever they lead me.

I touch the lives of others so that they can experience love, joy, peace and physical, spiritual and mental well being. I see the beauty in each client.

Goals For Hypnotists

"Advice is like snow, the softer it falls, the longer it dwells upon, and the deeper it sinks into the mind."   -Coleridge

The goal of all hypnosis is to bring the subject to joy and self- respect! If you want to hypnotize another, think of yourself as a mirror holder that allows your subject to reflect on their magnificence. It is essential that you like your subject. And that you know that they hold all the answers for their success. Your job is to guide them to the place where their inner wisdom lives. Their personal readiness for change will be an unknown quantity. Your job is to motivate them to evoke their own positive shifts.

To be a great hypnotist you must love yourself and walk your talk. It's almost impossible to convince someone in trance to quit smoking if your own auric field is grayed by cigarettes. A good hypnotist motivates others; sells them positive ideas and attitudes. Hypnotists support clients into positive change.

Remember, entranced people are more keenly aware of truth than someone in a normal frame of mind. Make suggestions colorful and exciting but come from a place of integrity, love and truth.

Make the following your personal goals and your life will work. Plus, you'll be a fine role model for others:

Seek Pride and Joy

I have to live with myself and so
I want to be fit for myself to know.
I want to be able as days go by
always to look myself in the eye.
I don't want to sit with the setting sun
And hate myself for the things I've done.

I see what others may never see.
I know what others may never know.
I have to live with myself and so
whatever happens I want to be
self respecting and conscious free.

            -unknown

When pride and joy are your goals, life becomes fun. Take pride in doing your best. Be sure to give yourself praise for caring and making the effort. If you can't look yourself in the eye, it's time to be honest, forgive yourself and dedicate yourself to behaviors of which you are proud.

Make joy your life goal and you just may wind up happy. Humor helps a lot. When I was a flight attendant with TWA, a captain asked me if I'd like to see a picture of his "pride and joy." He gleefully produced a photo of two detergent bottles (one titled Pride and one Joy) on a kitchen counter. His joke made a big impression on me. Why? It had the element of surprise and it made me laugh. Life taken lightly uplifts the spirit. Hypnosis taken lightly is fun for you and your client and plants vivid impressions on the mind to cleanse the past and sparkle in the present.

Unconditional Love

Before you begin a session say good, kind and nourishing things to yourself. Love yourself; it's contagious. Your client will model your self-esteem. Love each client as a gift God has sent to you. Your job is to be a friend, helper, teacher and of course, builder of independence for your client.

Into-Great Yourself

Physically: Healthy, good diet, exercise, breathing, and no toxins
Mentally: Clear Minded, focused, reach goals and learn
Spiritually: Open, creative
Emotionally: Joyously living in the present.

Manifest Abundance
Affirm; "I deserve to be paid for my work."

It's No Act

Actor Jim Carey upon receiving an Academy Award for the Mask told viewers how as a struggling actor, he stood in the moonlight on a hill in Hollywood and affirmed again and again; "I am the star of a major motion picture and my salary will be $10,000,000.

My mission sentence came as an affirmation "I am Shelley. I am perfect just the way I am. Feeling so glad to be alive. Deeply loving you and deeply loving me."

Achieve Dreams and Goals

"I promise each and every day to share the miracles I have found in this greatest gift called life. Not by changing the world, but by fine tuning it for my children and all children."

>   Ken Vegotsky's life mission statement

Follow your bliss and life works! What do you want? What gives you pleasure? Go to the smorgasbord of life, taste many delicacies and notice what flavors linger. The things that pleasure you become the cobblestones on your life's path.

Embark On A path Imagine a path that calls to you. Sometimes the path unfolds as you go from cobblestone to cobblestone. Each step brings you to something that interests and pleasures you. This path takes you to your very reason for being. When you become involved step by step with your journey, and are satisfied and excited by it, you discover your reason for being.

Now, write the words Mission Statement on the top of a piece of paper or on a computer. And without editing, analyzing or judging, answer the question: "What is my purpose for being?" with the first thoughts that pop into your mind. Or you may want to write the steps that bring you pleasure or self-satisfaction.

Make dreams and goals, remind yourself daily what it is you truly desire and the journey becomes the destination.

Hypnotists Do's and Dont's:

DO's
▲ Make your hypnosis space comfortable and pleasant.
▲ Turn off the telephone, lower lights and play soft music.
▲ Know how long the session will be and stick to that time.
▲ Keep confidentiality.

DON'TS
▼ Don't "lead the witness" active listen instead.
▼ Never label a client as "resistant", "not ready for change" or a "poor subject," it is inaccurate and negatively conditions them for failure.
▼ Don't touch the client without permission and only then in appropriate ways. Absolutely never violate the trust between subject and hypnotist. To do so is unethical and immoral.

Bad News

August 4, 1996 Los Angeles Times Staff writer Ann W. O'Neill reported the tragic story of Licensed Psychologist's aid Michael Lamont Buffington.

Buffington, 46, was ordered to stand trail on six counts of sexually assaulting two female patients after putting them under hypnosis. Both women encountered Buffington at the offices of Some People's Children Medical Group on Cahuenga Blvd in Los Angeles.

According to the article, the center is run by Buffington's wife and specializes in treating victims of sexual abuse.

Hypnotist's Styles

"Help does not consist of solving 'problems' that exist in the real world, but of dis-solving illusions in learned structures of thinking."
-John B. Enright

The style a hypnotist uses can be Authoritarian, Non-directive and Cooperative. Each has its value and place. You may find that one style is more comfortable for you than another. Mix and match and, at all times, remember to honor the inner wisdom of the client. Flexible hypnotists who offer a variety of approaches are often more successful than those who use a "one formula only" approach.

Authoritarian

An exaggerated form of this all-knowing and superior attitude is dramatically portrayed in the movie Network. Drapes close, lights dim, a spotlight comes upon the corporate leader across a vast boardroom table as his booming voice commands his employee to "stop" his rebellious behavior.

Authoritarians take a parental, dominant, invasive posture. Based on their "expertise" an authoritarian interprets the clients' life and problems and gives solutions. The danger in using only this top dog, bottom dog approach is that it fosters co-dependancy. The client plays victim while the hypnotherapist rescues or even worse persecutes. An authoritarian approach does work well in small doses and with the right subject. But use it sparingly.

If you choose this style, make sure to give your subject stroking and empowering remarks as well. When you "lead the witness" or hold the belief that you know more that they about what is best for them, you take on too great a responsibility.

Chewed Out, a true story

A well known California hypnosis teacher tells the story of a boy brought to him by concerned parents who couldn't get their son to stop biting his nails. After the initial family interview, the hypnotist takes the boy into his soundproof office, alone. There, this enormous man with a penetrating voice and used car salesman determination, looks the lad squarely in the face (enough to intimidate a grown man):

"Hear me well: Stop biting your nails." he bellows

"Do you hear me. Stop biting your nails."

The quaking boy nods.

"So what are you doing in school?" and he fills the remaining time with chatting. Problem solved.

Non-directive

A "kinder gentler" approach, the non-directive hypnotherapists sit in the back and puts the client in the drivers seat. A non-directive style requires active listening, empathy, support and an occasional gentle nudge. Suggestions only reinforce the subject's wishes. Psychiatrists, favor this more "neutral" posture and can listen to patients for years. Maybe that's why they're called patients!

Cooperative

Cooperative hypnotherapists form a partnership of growth and learning with the client. This, in my opinion, is the best approach most of the time. Similar to the non-directive style, the cooperative Hypnotherapist honors and encourages the wisdom of the human who sits before them. They then add the element of re-commendations and suggestions. It's understood and communicated that "These are my ideas that you may use or not as you see fit."

How To Be Successful Every Time

You are sure to succeed every time with every client when the deck is stacked in favor of success. The best results come when your client has a readiness for change and you and they expect positive results. Here are positive ingredients for success:

Love your client
If you can't love who they are, refer them out.

Honor your client's readiness for change
Most people demonstrate their readiness for change just by showing up. You might say, "The fact that you came here today is proof that you have a sincere desire to..."

Establish rapport
When someone thinks and feels that you understand and empathize with them, they trust and take on suggestions. Establish rapport by active listening (repeating back words and phrases); model their posture, gestures, voice tones and body language and supportive phrases like:

"I understand."
"Let's see how we can help you."
"You're right." and
"Good."

Hold a positive expectation
Be confident that your client will get the results they want. Value your work and the client will value it too. The belief and expectations of your client heavily influence their results. Expect that each will get what they need in your behavior, tone, manner and attitude.

Be Grateful
Count your blessings.

The Hypnotist/Client Formula
✓**Greet**
✓**Fill Out Forms**
✓**Interview**
✓**Hypnotize**
    Teach Self Hypnosis
    Induction
    Blessing
    Deepening
    Suggestibility Tests
    The Process
    Suggestions
    Wrap up
    Welcome back
✓**Closure**
✓**Payment**
✓**Next Appointment**

Rules of the Road
Know how long the session will be and stick to that time.

✓ Turn off your phone ringer and turn down the sound on the answering machine.
✓ Prepare any music you'll need.
✓ Stay focused on your client.
✓ Get centered.

Greet
When your client arrives, their session has begun. When you open your door, you must establish rapport. Be friendly, kind, warm and professional. Make non-invasive physical contact as soon as possible. I like to shake hands or offer a hug.

    Men, when greeting a woman, be careful that your hug is not misunderstood. Leave no room for misinterpretation. You don't want someone to think that you are coming on to them. A gentle pat on the back is nice as you guide someone to be seated.

Fill Out Forms

Have them fill out a form that gives helpful information and specifically answers the question: "What would you like to achieve with hypnosis." I like to leave the client alone for a minute so that they can get comfortable in their environment.

Name
Address
Phone number
Any health issues
Any medication
How much do you drink per week (be honest)
What do you want to accomplish with hypnosis

Have them write down their favorite color, favorite place in nature, hobbies and what they do for fun. This way you can incorporate these personal symbols into the session.

Interview

The interview allows you to put your subject at ease and as a fact finding mission so you know which way to go in the session. Carefully monitor the words you use for you are already beginning your induction as you talk. You're building trust and showing support as you active listen, smile and model their movements. Note key phrases, they will be used during the hypnotic journey. Actively listen and observe. Noticing the following:

Key phrases and dominant senses

The words used are always clues of ones dominant senses. For example, if the clients say phrases like "If you see what I mean," or they describe vivid visual images, you know they are visually dominant. If their talk describes words spoken and they use phrases like "It didn't sound right to me," they are sound dominant. You'll get the feel of it. (touch). When communicating or hypnotizing another, talk to the subjects using their dominant mode.

It's nice to ask them "What is your favorite color?" or "What do you like to do for fun?"
"Who do you admire?" When you discover their preferences you can

incorporate them into your induction and suggestions and it makes a deeper impression.

Description of problem
Repeat the problem back to them so that they know they've been heard. Then assure them that you can and will help with that problem. Listen and write down in their own word the description of their issue, goal or problem. Or, if they filled out an intake form, make sure you read what they write in response to "What do you want to accomplish with hypnosis?"

Active listen and model gestures
It makes people feel loved and supported when you repeat back to them their own phrases, voice inflection and gestures. This also helps you to empathize with what's going on within them. Make the person feel loved and supported. If you can't love and support them, refer them out to someone who can. Assure them (through active listening) that you can and will help them solve their problems.

Ask if they've been hypnotized before
Ask; "Have you ever been hypnotized?" If so, "Tell me about that experience. What was it like for you? What do you remember about the experience?" This will save extra work when you build on past positive hypnosis experiences. If it was positive, recreate that same induction that was used. If not, educate them as to what hypnosis is, how it benefits them and use another induction.

Structure of The Session:
✓Blessing
✓Teach self-hypnosis
✓Induce Trance
✓Deepening
✓Suggestibility Tests
✓Suggestions
✓Wrap up
✓Welcome back

Blessing

Bless them and your self either out loud or silently. Avoid religious references unless they tell you that they are devoutly something. My favorite blessing is:

Bless (their name) on all levels:
physically with radiant health,
mentally with clear thinking,
and emotionally with unconditional love for themselves and their loved ones.
Let joy be their compass in all that they do.
Bless them spiritually so that they may see the bigger pictures and find beauty in all that is.
Help them release from their consciousness anyone who has harmed them with insensitivity.
Let all of these teachings be for their and my highest good.
And please help me to hold the mirror steady so that they may reflect on their beauty and enjoy their special gifts
(Here you might add their reason for coming. Remember that this blessing is an induction and that you are already planting suggestions).
Thank you.
Amen.
Awomen.
Ah life.

Teach Self-Hypnosis

Teach self-hypnosis to empower your subject. In teaching them something like the Shelley Stockwell's 30 Second Zap (see induction chapter) they go deeper during the induction's that follow.

Induce Trance

Use any of the inductions found in the induction chapter.

Suggestibility Tests

Some hypnotists insist on giving the subject "suggestibility tests." These can be valuable because the subject then convinces themselves that something different is happening. Call these tests "concentration"or "imagination" tests that makes them seem less threatening. Some popular tests suggest:

Hot and Cold
Temperature variation often feels pronounced while in trance

You are feeling very cold, colder and colder. A chill runs through you. You are so cold. You need to rub your hands together they feel so cold.

The sun just came up now. You are getting warmer and warmer. Your temperature is rising.

Arm Levitation
The natural distortion of body sensations makes a lightly lilting hand or arm pleasant and convincing to the subject.

Imagine a gorgeous balloon. It's your favorite color, shape and size. This special balloon is filled with high powered helium and if we were to tie it by a silky ribbon to the wrist of your right hand, you'd discover that it just lifts your arm right up. Your arm is lighter and lighter and it starts to lift and rise and float lighter and lighter. Up. Up. There it comes."

If necessary you can gently get the arm started by lifting the wrist and then releasing. If they are too passive and relaxed they may not want to respond. That's fine.

Very Good. You are so relaxed nothing wants to move, yet that one hand feels light and so relaxed. It continues to lift and rise (if it is). Now focus your attention on your other hand and discover that that hand and arm is so heavy. It's as if that arm and hand is made of 20 tons of lead. As if it is glued where it rests. You can try to lift your other hand now and no matter how hard you try it just won't budge.

Chuckles
Laughter is the best medicine.

Imagine that you are watching a funny movie and you begin to laugh. You smile and laugh and roar. It's hilarious.

Illustration by Shelley Stockwell

Reinduction

Each time you repeat or layer an induction the subject goes deeper into trance.

When I say to you "sleep" your eyes close and you go into the hypnotic state just like that (snap finger).

Eye Lock

The brain engages its energy on relaxation and the eyes just don't feel like opening.

Your eyes are so relaxed they just don't feel like opening them. You can try to open them only to discover that they just don't want to open. Now stop trying and go deeper and deeper.

You and I both know that you could open your eyes at any time. The reason they don't want to open is that you are choosing to enjoy the deeply relaxing and rewarding state of hypnosis.

Suggestions

The way you want to approach the heart of your session is up to you. Trust your instincts. If you are centered you will be quite comfortable. Sometimes new hypnotists feel better using a script and that's fine. As you use a script you are actually memorizing suggestions that will come easily later when you put the script away. Some possibilities for your process are detailed in the next chapter. They are:

- Positive Programming
- Regressions to the source of issues
- Remembering
- Extracting old imprints or programs that aren't working
- Reframing
- Extinguishing pain
- Reinforcing positive programs and attitudes, enhancing their goals
- Re-empowering them

The Process
Positive Programming

Affirm and repeat the reversal of any negative imprints that you noted in your original interview or that have been revealed in trance. Remember to plant these suggestions using their favorite phrases and via their dominant senses.

If you are stuck for positive suggestions, here is an approach that gets the job done very effectively:

I am talking to your higher self, the part of you that is so wise. What does (their name) need to do to make his or her life work (or quit smoking, lose weight, stop stealing...whatever)? What simple steps can they take.

If your subject isn't inclined to speak at this moment say:

As you think of a simple step (their name) can take, let me know with a nod of your head...Very good. If they are willing to take that action step this very day let me know. Excellent.

Affirmations
For Memory Improvement Or To Overcome Amnesia.

The creative intelligence within you knows how to restore your memory to its full potentials. That's what it is doing right now; turning on the memory switch with the help of your profound inner wisdom.

Think about your memory. You may have inaccurately taken on a belief that your memory is limited. In fact, your memory is unlimited. You can remove any old veil from your memory any time you want to. And you want to now. Take a deep breath and let the veil fall away. "I remember." You say, "I remember."

Any traumatic incident no longer affects you in such a large way. Children sometimes avoid responsibility by saying: "I forget." From this moment forward, your memory functions perfectly. The creative use of your mind is restored, just as it was when you were a child.
When it comes to memory, the greater the effort, the less the results. You remember everything with the greatest of ease. If something you wish to recall doesn't just pop into your mind you say "It will come to me," and it will.

Wrap Up

It's important that your client has closure. You want them to leave your office peaceful and complete. Good closing questions are:

> "Is there anything you want to say?"
> "Is there anything you want to say to yourself?"
> "Is there anything you want to say to me?"
> "Who do I remind you of?"
> "How do you feel about _____?"

If positive, say **"Very good"** and bring them back.

If not, you're not done yet. Continue your process on unfinished business so it can be resolved. I sometimes say:

"I have a Native American burden basket here at my entrance. You may put any concerns or unfinished business there and I will recycle them. Just take a deep breath and put them right by my door, right in the basket. Next time you come, if you want, you can take them out and notice how they are perfectly resolved. But for now just leave them here."

Welcome Back

When they return to room awareness or consciousness say;

"You surprised yourself, didn't you?" or

"That was terrific. You did so well."

What if they don't come right back?

If your subject is reluctant to return to room awareness, just let them sleep if time allows. If you need to bring them back, terminate with a simple suggestion. If it doesn't work, try another. Be loving and firm. The reason folk's stay attached to trance is that it feels so good. No one wants to miss out on such a great feeling. If all else fails, you can give them a suggestion that works every time

"If you don't return to room awareness when requested, you will NEVER again enjoy this wonderful experience of hypnosis."

That pops everyone back into conscious awareness.

Payment

Fees for your session should have been settled at the time that they booked their session. I like to collect after the subject returns to room awareness. Some of my colleagues like to collect before they start. I accept check and cash and no insurance.

Next Appointment

Make a determination if your subject needs another visit. If so, say: "I'd like to see you next week. Is this time good for you?"

Photo by Mary Bontempo

Chapter 17

STOCKWELL HYPNOTHERAPY

🏠 Structure Of The Stockwell Session
↑ Extinguish Negative Feelings
🌹 Forgiveness
🐑 The Source Of The Problem
😈😊😈 Subpersonality Work

The Stockwell System of Hypnotherapy is a more intense form of hypnosis that enhances and embellishes your clients goals.

It allows you to explore and release the cause of behaviors that need modification or reframing. Hurt feelings and behaviors positively shift as you extinguish pain, learn from mistakes, forgive, reinforce uplifting thoughts and actions.

🏠 Structure The Stockwell Session

Establish Rapport
Teach Simple Self Hypnosis
Bless
Induce trance
Deepen trance
Trance-formations: regress, reframe, resolve
Reinforce
Return to Room Consciousness

The Source Of The Problem
Trance-formation #1

Problem
What is the problem? Following the induction and deepening phase of trance, focus on the problem so you can reprogram, regress, and extract old imprints.

Problem's Source
Go back to the last time you had that problem. When you discover a life trap or old pattern that isn't working, you help your subject release and reframe it.

Associated Thoughts Or Feeling
A word or phrase to describe the thoughts or feelings you had during that time.

Exaggerate And Intensify Feelings
Exaggerate and intensify those feelings (repeat back their words)

Go To The Source Of Feelings
Go back in time to the source of those feelings "The first time you, consciously or unconsciously, remember having that feeling.

Extinguish and Release Negative Feelings
Forgive if necessary. Reframe hurtful situation: ask what did you learn. Review it as if you were ruler of the universe. Or play the scene again, as you'd like it to be. (A script to help with will follow.)

Bright Failures
Before Thomas Edison invented the light bulb he discovered 1,800 ways not to build one. Radium was one of Madame Curie's errors.

Reparent
Become your own perfect mommy and daddy. Embrace the inner child and let it be safe for them to come home.

Reinforce Affirmations

Repeat the positive highlights about what they learned. Put the past in perspective as only a memory, the future as a fantasy and this moment of choosing joy, peace, success and wellness as reality.
"Is there anything you'd like to say to me?"
"Is there anything you'd like to say to yourself?"
Complete any unfinished business that may be in the answers to these questions and then lovingly, return them to room awareness.

Wrap Up

The hypnotherapist re-empowers the subject to build high self-esteem by pointing out their strengths and beauty.

Welcome Back

"You surprised yourself, didn't you?" and congratulate them on how well they did.

↑ *Extinguish Negative Feelings Script*

The purpose of all life experiences is to gain wisdom. We learn from mistakes. That's why every "mistake" is a blessing. It gives you the chance to find out what doesn't work so that you know what does.

You had to fall many times before you could walk. When little, you didn't know how to walk, so you stood up and leaned to the left and fell to the left. Did you quit? Of course not. After much toppling to the left, you figured out that leaning to the left didn't work so you leaned to the right. Again you tumbled, this time to the right. "Leaning to the right doesn't work" you observed. So you leaned back and fell on your padded behind. Then forward.

Only when you learned all the ways that didn't work did you discover what did and walked. Your success then reinforced further success.

If you judge yourself harshly, and punish yourself beyond belief, that punishment can literally run and ruin your life. Give it up. Forgive and live.

The Stockwell System

Any mistakes were simple opportunities to learn what didn't work so you can learn what does. Mistakes gave you a wonderful chance to try a new approach with a better outcome.

❦ Forgiveness
"I Forgive Myself and Others"

I FORGIVE YOU, MOM
She had done the best she could.
With what she had, she'd done real good.
Held back in joy and stuck in pain
she did what she could to keep her sane.

She followed the rules, as she understood them,
exercised options as she construed them,
gave her kids what she never had:
love and lessons. A house. A dad.

Her youth was a nightmare chasing a dream
wrapped around a primal scream.
She disguised all this in her perfect show,
hoping no one would ever know.

But we know:
She had done the best she could.
With what she had, she'd done real good. — Shelley Stockwell

Affirm Success
I choose to be kind to myself and others. I am now aware of anyone who has harmed me with insensitivity and I forgive them right now. I am aware of anyone who I have harmed with my own insensitivity. I forgive myself.

The process of forgiveness has four steps:
1. I am aware of who and what hurt me.
2. I choose and commit to forgive.
3. If necessary, I grieve for the loss of an old, familiar pattern, and
4. I claim a new pattern and celebrate the growth of my wisdom.

Holding onto resentments is a lot of work. And the longer we lug resentment around, the more work it becomes. Forgiveness is the cornerstone of joy. It leaves childhood trauma and re•creational drama in the past. There are three kinds of forgiveness: Forgiving myself, forgiving someone else, and having someone forgive me. Who do I need to forgive?

Forgive And Forget, but not at the same time. It's OK to get real to heal. Some people begin to forgive by saying, "I forgive you, you dirty SOB." Or "Peace on you." The trick in forgiving is the willingness to start now and keep forgiving until we feel complete.

Diane's Story

"Forgiveness is a double blessing. It blesses the forgiver and the forgiven." James Demirjian

When Shelley, my hypnotherapist asked me, 'Who do you have to forgive to take back your power?' I thought of Dad. I'd always blamed him for limiting and controlling me. When I work for him, he tells me how to run my life and he puts me down; it ticked me off.

When I forgave him, I discovered that I had chosen to let him run my life. It made us close and it was easier. I didn't know how to run my own life. But in giving Dad my power, I felt impotent, angry, frustrated, little and whimpy.

Forgiveness is the key. I've made a new choice to be grown-up and responsible for my own life, and to love Dad in a grown-up way. I forgive him for power tripping me and forgive myself for blaming him, staying juvenile, and not standing up for what I want.

Since I forgave, I no longer depend on him to make my decisions. And I'm not angry any more. He's a separate person too."

To Err is Human, to Forgive Divine

Err·apparent. I write two lists. On the first, I write down anything I've done for which I need to forgive myself. And on the second, I list others who have hurt me and the insensitive things they did.

Royal review. I read each list, and with each offense, I imagine that I am king or queen of the universe. I ask myself, "How did I create or contribute to this situation, hurt, or abuse? What did I learn? And can I create it differently if it happens again?"

Pharaoh the well. One-by-one, I decide if I am willing to forgive each offense on my lists. If I am willing, I say, "I forgive you," as I read the offense, and I cross it off the list.

I Forgive For ME

Are you the judge, the jury, and the prisoner of my your guilt? Haven't you suffered enough? Most people are pretty hard on themselves. The truth is that everything you've ever done in life was an opportunity to clarify who you are and what you want to become.

A Little Pain Never Hurt Anyone

Expressing pain isn't always fun, until it's done. Yet, releasing pain is crucial for positive change. We are punished by our sins, not for them.

Re·cognizing and remembering your true feelings (sadness, anger, guilt, shame) allows you to face and release painful memories. When you remember the past, you may also discover past pleasant memories. These help balance the picture.

Bury the Hatchet
(Try it. It works.)
"And forgive us our trespasses as we forgive those who trespass against us." —The Lord's Prayer

Write A List
Write a list of incidents, actions, or inactions for which I need to forgive myself.
Prioritize Number your "crimes" from biggest to littlest.
One By One Review the list, starting with little transgressions.
Decide Ask: "Am I willing to forgive myself for this?" If so, It will be easy to let it go. If no, still let it go.
Blow It Off Take a deep breath, and on the out-breath say, "I forgive and cross it off your list.

FORGIVENESS JOURNEY

Adapted from the late Reverend Helen Street. Thank you, Helen.

"We've got to forgive just for ourselves, not for the ones who have done us wrong. We must forgive, because if we don't, unforgiveness causes resentment, and resentment causes misery. To forgive someone is to set them free, even if they abuse that freedom beyond exasperation."
                                                                         -Helen Street

I close my eyes, am still for a moment, and take a deep breath. I imagine a holy temple on the top of a mountain. In this place is an altar with all my favorite things. I imagine myself dressed in vestments, for I am the priest of this temple.

Someone I need to forgive knocks. I go to the door and open it. I notice their face and energy. We walk to the altar (if I wish, I take their hand). Behind the altar is a curtain, and behind the curtain is the All-Knowing: the holiest of holies. As we stand together, I address this wise one with my heart, for I am this temple: "I have brought this person before you to vouch for them. This person is innocent. They were born innocent. Along the way they got some misinformation, and they forgot who they were. I vouch for the purity and innocence of this beautiful being."

I take a deep breath, and my visitor vouches for me: "This person is innocent. They were born innocent. Along the way they got some misinformation, and they forgot who they were. I vouch for the purity and innocence of this beautiful being."

The curtain opens revealing a mirror. As we look into the all-knowing eyes, our own eyes reflect back. "I am pure and perfect, and I forgive myself and you. We were born innocent. And although we make mistakes and receive imperfect information, we are learning to return to our purity. Underneath it all, we are each a child of God. We are forgiven. We are innocent."

Deep breath. I take my visitor's hand, walk them away from this sacred place, and let them go. I release them. When they have vanished, I walk back and face the All Knowing: "I am innocent. I am forgiven. I am healed." I open my eyes.

Letter Go

Another powerful healing tool is to write a letter. You don't have to send this letter, but if you choose to send it, you do it for yourself. They probably won't change, no matter what you write. In this letter, allow your inner child full expression. Don't pull any punches. Write the first things that come to mind. They can be bad, nasty or naughty. But, you must tell your truth from the hurt part of yourself. If you feel resistant, do it anyway.

Address this letter to someone (living or dead) who you suspect may have harmed you in some way. Tell that person what they did and how it made you feel. Then how you wished it could have been.

Shelley's Letter

Dear Mom:

Your out-of-control hysteria, depression, and manipulation made my childhood a nightmare. Here's why:

I never knew if I'd get the nice Mommy or the screaming, ranting one. When you screamed, you called me "stupid and mean." You sarcastically called me "Einstein," and said, "What did I do to deserve you stupid kids?" You insulted my splendid artistic abilities by saying, "There she goes, drawing those dumb little pictures again." The way you insulted me was barely offset by the dancing lessons and drama classes you took me to.

I often felt like I was supposed to be your mother and that being a "good girl" was critical to my survival. Did you know, that I silently cried myself to sleep every night? And that when you screamed, I had to stand in the closet and wiggle my fingers in my ears for hours at a time so as not to hear your harangues about my room not being clean?

When my seventh grade teacher, Mr. Papadakis told you that I had a high IQ, you said, "We're amazed." When I was 40, and reminded you about that, you said, "Yes. We were amazed." Because of your insults, it took me 38 years to become real and to recognize that I am intelligent, artistic, and worthwhile.

I know you did the best you could, and that you had some problems, but that was my childhood, and you wrecked it. I want to forgive you and love you. In the past, I've hated and loved you.

Shelley

The Source Of The Problem
Trance-formation #2
Remembering, Reframing and Healing

Identify the problem
You might simply ask, "What is the problem?" Ask in the preliminary interview and, if they're not sure ask again when they're in the trance state. Or you can ask; "If you left here today having accomplish what you really want. What would that be for you? What attitude, behavior did you change to have what you want?"

Go back to the last time you had that problem

Associated thoughts or feeling
A word or phrase to describe the thoughts or feelings you had during that time.

Exaggerate and intensify those feelings
Exaggerate and intensify those feelings (repeat back their words)

Ask the subconscious or higher self to go to the source of the problem. "There is a feeling you get when you 'just have to eat everything in the refrigerator' (use their phrases). That feeling is growing very strong within you. Notice where you feel it. Now a word or phrase to describe that feeling. It doesn't have to make sense, it might not. Let the word or phrase just fall from your lips."

However they respond, repeat it "You'll not get the best of me ...You'll not get the best of me." That feeling grows stronger and stronger within you. "You'll not get the best of me." Do not think analyze edit or judge. How old are you. Are you inside or out. Alone or with somebody? What's going on. Talk to them as if they are there and in that age in time.

Go back to another place in time the first time you had those same feelings
Go back in time to the source of those feelings "The first time you remember having the feeling of ___ (use their phrases)."

Extinguish and release negative feelings
Forgive if necessary. Reframe hurtful situation:
Ask, "What did you learn?"
Review the situation with new eyes as if you were ruler of the universe, or play the scene again as you'd like it to be.

Reparent

Reinforce affirmations

Return to room consciousness

Feedback
The Tin Can Trick
Offers a device for feedback. Scientology uses a lie detector like contraption to "clear" limits and desensitize memory. If a question or a time frame gets a rise out of you, the tin cans in your hand register high on the gauge. Through repetition your reaction looses its punch. In actuality the accuracy of being on the cans is subject to doubt. Their effectiveness is wholly dependent on your belief in their accuracy.

Gestalt
Gestalt Therapy was created by Fritz Perls and helps folks dialogue and resolve inner conflict. You might ask:
"What happened at age ____?"
"Be age_____ and tell me what is going on."
"Where are you?"
"Who is there?"
"What happens next."
The client is then seated facing an empty chair.
"Talk to them. Tell them what it's like for you. Be very honest."

Verbalization heals; you may have your subject complete unfinished sentences;
"When I'm three and sitting all alone in my room I feel_____"

Engrams

The term engram has been used since the early 1900's. In the 1950's dianetics used it to describe their clearing process. Actually, an engram, similar to an imprint, is a constellation of neurons or a neural network. This set of reaction and response to an experience communicates with the brains central processing unit.

When an engram, or a series of imprints, is planted in the brain, it can be reactivated in minutes, days, weeks or years. Engrams can remain dormant, or fade away entirely.

Let's say you had an encounter with a dog when you were small. The smell of his breath, the look in his eye, the texture of the walls in the room you stood, the sound of the train nearby can create a string of engrams. Any piece of an engram can trigger the entire memory. If pleasant, that's terrific. If terrifying, it can be debilitating.

Engram therapy reactivates and desensitizes limiting neural patterns by recalling, in full living color, the entire memory. The client is asked to look at the story form all points of view and in such detail that it loses its energy. Then they are instructed to shut it off, remove, reconstruct and let it go for good.

Psychodrama

Psychodrama involves acting out and role playing real life characters so you may rescript the scenes. I call it "play it again Sam." Dr. Irving Katz calls it "Critical Incident Hypnodrama."

Alex Lessin's Play It Again With Love Process

Dr. Alex Lessin, my wonderful brother, employs regression and psychodrama to resolve current dilemmas. Use this script to guide your client to harmony.

Lie on your back. Close your eyes. Breathe deeply. Relax.

Pick an issue, concern or difficulty you want to resolve that has as its basis an earlier situation involving another person.

Imagine you are standing before an elevator. Its dial shows you're

on a floor whose number's the same as the number of years old you are now. Enter the elevator. Or if you choose, an open place of ascending plateaus.

You are now ready to descend to that time in the past to clear the issue you thought about a moment ago. Push the floor number on the button that takes you to the age you are in that earlier time. Tell me the number you push.
Go down to the floor/age of the button you push and step into a hallway or corridor.

Here there are many doors. One bears your name and the incident, or typical scene critical for you to resolve so you can grow past your problem or concern.

When you're ready and feel it is in your best interest, open the door and go inside. There you can objectively experience or observe the situation. At any time, you can shift to a neutral, witnessing mode, detached from emotion.

See, hear, feel, sense, think and intuit everyone and everything as it was. Tell me when you start to remember an incident or symbolic scene. (pause for the answer) Say what you see, hear, feel, sense, think and intuit. Use the present (the 'is' tense) as though it's happening now. (pause for answer) Notice your breathing. Tell your bodily sensations. (pause for answer)

Now let's act it out; I'll play...[Say the name of the other person in the incident]. As I pretend I'm...[the other person in the incident] and tell me how to play the part. (pause) Tell me this time how you felt and what you would like to express and express it. [You act out the incident and allow emotional expression.]

What decisions did you make as a result of this incident? (pause for response)

What did these decisions do for you? State your pay-off from these decisions. (pause for response)

What would you like to do that you did not do? (pause for response)

Let's redo the scene now, the way you'd like it to have been. How would you like me to play my part? (pause for response)

I'll do it the way you wanted. You can do what you would have liked to. [Re-enact the incident again, following the new scenario. Encourage full expression of feelings.]

Forgive yourself and each of the others involved. (pause). **If you are not ready to forgive, tell me what needs to be completed.** (pause)

Allow an affirmation to come forth which summarizes what you have just learned. (pause for response)
Each time you say the affirmation, it will help you complete your unfinished business from the incident and further heal any wounded feelings. Say your affirmation two more times, loud and clear. (pause)

Imagine and describe a future scene when you live from the affirmation instead of your earlier decision. Use the present tense to describe the scene as you imagine it. (pause)

Return to the elevator or plateaus. Enter. Push the button of the floor to your current age in the building of your life. Go up to the present. If there is anything incomplete, you will be able to complete it in your dreams, which you will remember and use well. Open your eyes and look into mine. Discuss the experience you've just had. (pause for response)

Reverse Speech
Back Talk

You've heard of talking out of two sides of your mouth. Well, in fact, we talk out of two parts of our brain, simultaneously. We deliver two messages at the same time, one forward and one backwards. The conscious mind speaks forward while the subconscious goes in reverse. The conscious forward talk reflects our personality, while the subconscious, goes beyond personality.

When recordings of conversation are carefully slowed (by 30 degrees) and reversed, you discover that in "backtalk," the subconscious, either repeats or expands what the conscious mind is saying. Or, the back talk contradicts the forward message. This binary behavior is our subconscious mind attempting to resolve incongruity.

A reverse speech hypnotist will tape answers to questions like: "How can we resolve your binge eating?" Review of reverse speech may reveal a sentence like:

"Mommy, hungry, help."

From this information a script for resolution is formulated.

This process can be cumbersome and time consuming. To make it even more challenging, the backward messages are often presented as metaphors or archetypes.

The Glickman System

Ph.D. Psychologist, Rosalene Glickman, identifies 12 core beliefs that empower us. The idea is to be strong on each one. During a session, she tests each belief using kinesiology: The subject holds up their arm at shoulder height, as she says the affirmation out loud and then measures arm resistance. If the arm goes down easily, it means weak in that belief. She then devotes a separate session to clear each limiting belief.

In each of these resulting sessions, still using kinesiology, she starts at age zero (birth) and moves to the present time as she repeats the affirmation. Any age where weakness is detected is where hypno-regression and Gestalt therapy are used.

If conversation lulls, give the strength test again. Weakness means more clearing is needed until the subject is desensitized and the emotional charge is gone. Role playing in this way resolves inner

---

Dr. Glickman's Core Beliefs:

I'm OK as I am.
Others are OK as they are.
The world is OK as it is.
I can have what I want.
I deserve the best in life.
I deserve to have what I want. I'm safe with pain.
I'm safe with rejection.
I'm safe with failure.
I'm safe with success.
Life is easiest as I create what I want.
I'm fully responsible for optimizing my life.

conflict. So does sentence completion (to verbalize feelings). Affirmations, or "optimal thinking" is then used to clarify what would work best for the subject.

🎭😊🎭 Subpersonality Work

Who in the world is in here now?
For heavens sake and holy cow
This profound communication
Brings me to illumination   -Shelley Stockwell

Know Thyselves

Within the vastness of yourself are a multitude of "you's" or subpersonalities. You have an angel, a pussy cat, a tiger, a bitch or bastard, a greedy one, a generous one, a shy one, a bold one: The army of "you's" is infinite. Each of your "sub-me's" serves a purpose.

In subpersonality work we "personify" our emotions and attitudes as distinct mini-selves. The goal of this work is to quiet internal conflict and get our many "selves" to form a well functioning interactive team. They "show up" as teachers to enhance our awareness of who we are. We certainly learn more about ourselves when we focus in this way.

This approach is common among tribal peoples who dress, dance and speak the parts of their being. In more recent times there have been many variations of this theme. Fritz Perls called it Gestalt, Carl Jung Archetypes, Roberto Assagioli Psychosynthesis, Hal and Sidra Stone call it Voice Dialogue and Virginia Satir Parts Therapy.

Why Are We Here Anyway?

Subpersonalities are born within you in many ways. Some protect you from hurt so that you can survive a threatening experience. Some show up to expand our awareness in some way. Your subconscious mind manifests each inner voice to help you cope with challenging situations.

Some of your subselves serve you well, while others may interfere with success and joy. Integration requires the taming of the "inner critic" and the empowering of the "master controller."

Multiple personality disorder appears to be the extreme of this natural phenomenon. Multiples however often are unaware of the "others" and find it difficult, if not impossible, to get all facets of self to work together.

Conflict Mediation For Me, Myself and I

Bring your subpersonalities forward and dialog with them. Ask yourself or your subject: "Is there a part of me (you) that blocks unconditional love? Is there a part of me (you), a sub-personality, that is interfering with my (your) financial goals? Happiness goals? Health goals? Is there a critical tyrant that's running the show for all the other selves? That way you'll meet any limiting sub-personalities.

These limiting characters are most challenging voices. If you discover your inner critic or any character that says NO, dialog with them directly. Call them by name. Thank them for coming.

"How do I address you?"
"What do you need (their name)?"
"Are there better ways for you to fill those needs?"
"I understand you want my attention? You've got it now."
"When did you come into my life?"
"What is your job?"
"Do you enjoy your work?"

Reinforce how well they've done their job in the past even if their posture is destructive to your goals (or your subject's). Reframe their work into nourishing ones for the whole being. Help them to establish a more supportive or productive approach.

Ask to meet the "Master Controller," the subpersonality that allows all the personalities to come forth. Interview that voice as well. Ask your master controller to invite all the other selves to a conference table. Place the master controller at the head of the table as the chairperson. Their collective task is to work together so that each has a say but all decide what is best for you.

This is a terrific way to resolve conflicts. It puts all subpersonalities into compatible working relationships. Compromise allows the inner critic and other overbearing subpersonalities to become part of a team effort.

Archetypes

Archetypes are another approach to subpersonality work. Universal human essences are characterized as symbolic "types." You have individual symbols and archetypes that resonate with you. What does a hero look like to you? A heroin? A bad guy? A bad girl? A wizard? The perfect mother? The perfect father? Identifying these symbols helps you talk to your subselves.

Forever Jung

Carl Jung popularized seven stereotype archetypes including; wise person, animus (male), anima (female) and shadow. Ancient Egyptians identified human characteristics with gods, goddesses, and animals, much like the more recent Native American cultures. Greek Pantheons correspond with our, now popular, astrological signs:

Mars, male	Venus, female
Cronos, father	Earth, mother
Pluto, sex	Zues, spirituality
Mercury, mental power	Neptune, mysticism
Apollo, child	Uranus, friendship
Vesta, perfectionism	

Resources:

Time Travel The Do It Your self Past Life Journey Handbook
Denial Is Not A River In Egypt; Unveil Drugs, Denial and Other Wacky Thinking, Stockwell, Shelley
Peace and Calm, Stockwell, Shelley. Audio stress buster
Sleep Beautiful Sleep Audio tape that makes sleeping a dream.
Highten Your Holos, Lessin, Alex Ph.D. Teaches how to get the most out of holotropic breathwork.
Can be ordered from Creativity Unlimited Press
See order form at the back of this book.

Illustration by Shelley Stockwell

Chapter 18

Stockwell Transpersonal Hypnotherapy

"Your Essential Self"

☼ **Enlightenment**

🦅 **Shamanism**

💼 **Time Travel**

✍ **Automatic Writing & Drawing**

⌀ **Psychic and Intuitive Skills**
   Clair Audiant, Empath, Clair Voyant, Trance Channeling

Hypno or Guided Meditation

⚕ **Hypno Yoga**

Transpersonal Hypnotherapy

Transpersonal hypnosis explores the fascinating realm of the superconscious mind. Here we discover an unlimited vista of creativity, expanded consciousness, guidance and peak experiences. Every seasoned hypnotist will tell you that even if your intention is to be a simple reprogrammer, your subjects will spontaneously enter these fascinating places.

If you're doing work as a hypnotist, guaranteed, you're going to be dealing with this expansive and intuitive part of consciousness. Guaranteed. The transpersonal phenomenon is as much a part of you, as the body that you're sitting in right now as we talked about before; body, mind and spirit is the conscious, subconscious and superconscious.

A Real Life Hypno-Tale

I was once speaking to 150 senior citizens at Leisure World (my mother calls it 'seizure world') about how to use hypnosis to deal with stress, when a hand went up in the back of the room and a lovely lady said:

"Is this kind of like knowing something is going to happen before it happens." I said "Well I guess hypnosis is kind of like that" and then asked, "How many of you folks, know that something is going to happen before it happens?"

Over half of them, very reluctantly, raised their hands. "Look around at all those hands." I said. "Just out of curiosity, how many of you feel like a loved one who's passed on, has talked to you," and again over half raised their hands.

"This is amazing," one said. Another said: "I'm so startled. When I had this experience I felt embarrassed to tell anyone for fear that it wouldn't be OK."

☼ Enlightenment

To en•light•en means to give spiritual insight to. Enlightenment was an 18th century philosophical movement that emphasized universal human 1progress and the use of reason. As we alter normal consciousness, your journey may move into the amazing realm of transcendental states of awareness.

The Kundalini

Kundalini is a form of energy associated with the feeling of being alive—filled with freely moving energy—flooded with light, or enlightenment. It is a first-hand experience of the body opening through the central nervous system via the spine and the seven chakras.

The Kundalini releases emotional or karmic "blocks." As the chakras clear and open, releasing freely moving energy, we can flood with a myriad of physical and emotional experiences. Experiencing the Kundalini is an on-going process, lasting from several months to many years. As the energy moves through the body, it clears away blocking impurities or imbalances. It leaves us with an experience of being fully alive, reborn, and reawakened into a full feeling (fulfilling) experience of resonating energy. Joseph Campbell calls it "feeling the rapture of being alive."

The Seven Chakras:

➡ the base of my spine,
➡ sexual organs,
➡ solar plexus,
➡ heart,
➡ throat,
➡ third eye (in the middle of my forehead), and
➡ top of head.

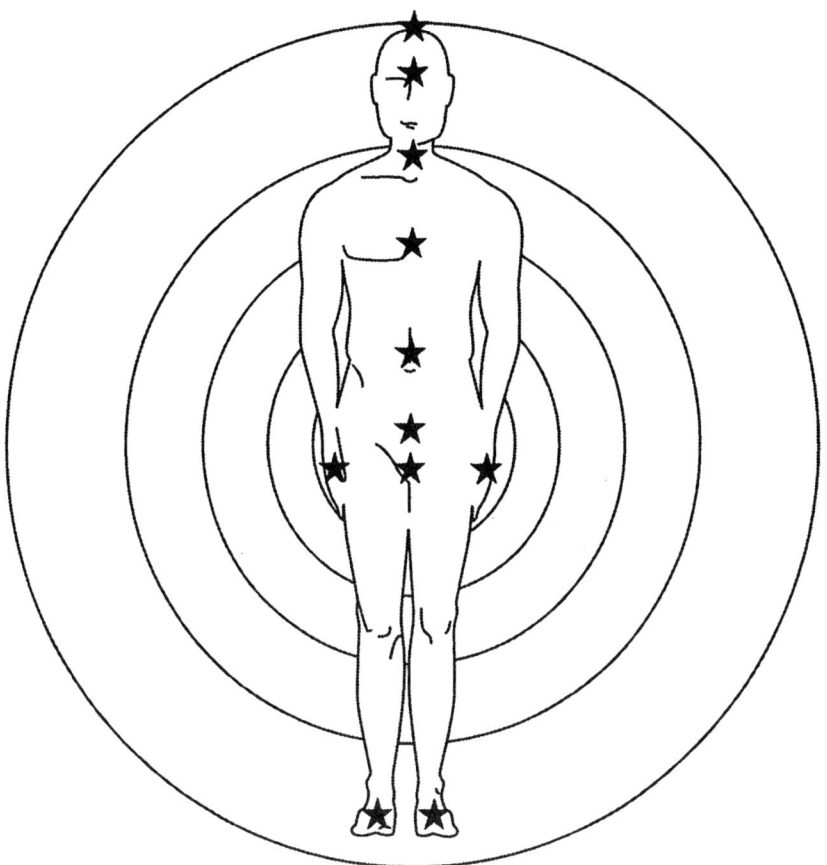

Illustration by Shelley Stockwell

The Sanskrit word "Kundalini" was used by the Yogis as far back as 7000 years ago. They believed that without the kundalini energy, no enlightenment was possible. "The Kundalini," they said, "is the central energy of all life." At death, this "energy cocoon" leaves the body and determines the nature of each reincarnation. The patterns of movement, as energy travels through the body, vary slightly from culture to culture. Yet every pattern corresponds to the central nervous system. All agree that as the different centers are activated, a person's spiritual awakening intensifies.

Signposts of the Kundalini

The following objective or subjectives signposts, mark purification and balancing. The results will be greater emotional stability, enhanced intuition, and a feeling of peace.

Body sensations:
  Deep ecstatic tingling vibration
  Feeling of orgasm
  Feeling hot and cold
  Actually seeing light internally
  Visions of inner light or having an "ah ha!" experience

Hearing sounds
  Hearing strong sounds and voices seemingly from the inside

Feeling discomfort
  Headaches or focused sensations in any region of your body, beginning and ending abruptly

Time distortion
  Thoughts speed up, slow down, or stop

Spontaneous trance states

Visual balancing
  Simultaneously seeing the inner and outer

Detachment
  A feeling of watching yourself

Out of body experience
  Feeling that you are away from your physical body

Intense emotions
  Ecstasy, bliss, cosmic harmony.
  Occasionally fear, anger, depression, or confusion followed by peace, love and contentment

Increased ESP
  Natural psychics are more likely to have a kundalini awakening
  Increased intuitive powers and ability to see auras

Temporary paralysis
  Involuntary positioning of body, limbs, or fingers

Many experience the Kundalini spontaneously, as a result of a key event, such as a near-death experience or childbirth. Spontaneous Kundalini awakening can also be stimulated by hypnosis, acupuncture, energy-balancing, meditation, rolfing, and touch therapies. Learning to contact and express the truth stimulates the kundalini.

The process of enlightenment can be quite dramatic. Those who do not understand might inaccurately label the person having a spiritual emergency as psychotic. This puts a kundalini soul in a peculiar dilemma. Their "spirit body" is being profoundly lifted into the sacred hand of God, while their physical self might be chastised, exorcised, or even committed! Fortunately, today there is a renaissance of truth and introspection, as we collectively embark on the kundalini journey of an awakened world.

If your client demonstrates the following signposts during hypnosis, hang in there and support them. They will come out renewed and truly transformed. If you have to cancel your appointments for the next few hours do so. It will be well worth you time.

Stockwell Shamanism

Please Don't Squeeze The Shaman

A shaman is the world's oldest spiritual healer and awakener. Also known as a medicine man, medicine woman, mundunugu, witch doctor, exorcist, magician, sorcerer, warlock, witch, dowser, oracle and one who does voodoo; a shaman awakens deeper states of consciousness.

The world's first doctors were shamans who understood that physical, emotional, and spiritual energy were inseparable. In deep states of soul searching the voyager releases discomfort and blocks, restores wellness, and becomes enlightened.

There are as many techniques for shamanic work as there are cultures and individuals, but basically, most approaches balance love and power, male and female, light and dark, with the goal invoking inner awareness, harmony and homeostasis.

Shamanism relays heavily upon ceremony and ritual to evoke the desired response. Many rituals use hypnotic tools like smell, smoke, repetition, sound, suggestion, and sleep deprivation. Soul retrieval, psychic surgery, healing touch, energy work and healing suggestions from an enlightened hypnotherapist can and does work miracles.

Accentuate the positive, eliminate the negative

Some cultures use mood altering substances. It's been popular to "go tripping" into the "dream world" with Peruvian Shaman guides after ingesting the psychotropic drug, Ayahuasca. One experimenter told me recently, "A big part of an ayahuasca trip is vomiting. I figure anything that makes me throw up ain't worth it."

Some techniques are fear based and their main thrust is cutting cords of ghosts, goblins and boogiemen. Religious exorcists are masters of this dark approach.

One participant of a tour I led to Egypt years ago went frantically about each sacred sight releasing "evil spirits." She saw them everywhere while the rest of us did not. Her repetitious powerful negative suggestions became a self-fulfilling prophesy for unhappiness. She is a very sad lady.

My Stockwell personal rule of thumb for shamanism, and everything else, is if it's not fun or doesn't manifest fun, don't do it. Instead celebrate co-creation with a higher source and light.

> Aborigines can put the machas or curse on someone and the object of their spell can actually die. Called "boning," the shaman takes a long stick with a bone on the end and stabs the air saying; " I bone So and So and they die."
>
> The cursed one hears of such a psychic attack and stops eating and fades away. The most modern hospital will not bring them back to vitality. The hope of recovery is a powerful shaman who "removes the bone."

I received a call recently from a depressed woman who visited a Manhattan Beach, California psychic named Madame somebody or other. This psychic told her that it would cost hundreds of dollars to rid her of an attached ghost and therefor her depression. A few more visits and some $15,000 later, this gullible woman was really depressed!

All this to say guru, G-U-R-U or, In the words of Swami Beyondananda, "Gee, you are you!" You hold within you profound magic and wisdom. The trick is to find ways to tap this power at will and seek a path that allows you to discover the spiritual dimension of reality.

Wounded Healers

In shamanic society, the holiest healer was the wounded healer. For in the wounding, the gods were summoned for healing to take place. Those who overcame were gifted with their power to heal others.

Soul Retrieval
"I'm Beside Myself"

Affirm Success
I take back my soul, I am whole
I take back my soul, I am holy.

Shamanic Healing

When we are traumatized, our vitality, joy or soul sometimes split from our being. Our ancestors: shamans, healers, hunas, medicine people, and priests knew that during passages and traumas of life, we can lose vitality and joy. They knew that under stress the soul and body could be parted, like a living death. When this happens, according to the Greeks, we are in "ecstasy" or "stand out of" self. Western philosophy says that we disengage or disassociate.

These precious fragments of self are not gone, they are near us in a parallel reality. Shamans voyage to the "Underworld, Middleworld or Upperworld" or the "God space" to recover hidden selves. Hypnotists venture into the superconscious mind. What ever you call it, a visit to this parallel void it is a truly revitalizing experience and an unbelievable relief. Once there, soul retrieval brings you back from the lost lands and invites you home. You return to your self, whole and holy.

A nice way to do soul retrieval is with a friend as your "sitter," or someone who specializes in soul retrieval. Incorporating soul retrieval into a hypnotherapy session is profoundly healing.

How To Do A Soul Retrieval
Play in•chanting music
If you like, you can play in•chanting music, drumming or ohming.

Bless yourself
If you are the guide, both you and your receiver say a prayer or blessing asking that all of these teaching are for the highest good. Instruct your client to relax and, in their minds eye, enter a sacred garden or sacred space as they affirm:

> Bless yourself on all levels:
> Physically with radiant health, energy, vitality;
> Mentally with clear thinking, focus, direction, to find your path and purpose;
> Emotionally with unconditional love, peace, joy, and harmony
> for yourself and others; and
> Spiritually with guidance so that you may truly fulfill your life's purpose.
> Thank You.
> Amen. Awomen

Breathe
Take a deep breath, and let it out. You can shake a rattle, tap a drum, sage the room, chant, tone or spin.

Affirm
Think these words or say them out loud:

I take back my soul I am whole.
I take back my soul I am holy.

Take a shamanic journey
Imagine yourself traveling in the void back to any time in your life where your soul essence, vitality, or energy separated from your being. It could be a little memory, such as skinning your knee, or a big memory, such as being beaten, molested, or abandoned. (pause)

When you find that thought, image, memory, or uneasy feeling, invite that little you out of hiding. "Come home, it's safe now. It's time to come home." Use whatever ploy is necessary to convince this frightened part of yourself to leave this parallel reality and come back home. You can call upon allies, guides, fantasies,

anything you like, to do the convincing. (pause)
When it is done, breathe fully to your heart, and let your heart express itself in its purest form. Know it is safe to come back. Greet all thoughts, feelings and images with, "Welcome home, it's safe now. I love you."

A Shaman Speaks

(Channeled by Shelley Stockwell and excerpted from her book TIME TRAVEL: Do-It-Yourself Past Life Journey Handbook)

"Now listen to me. Eagle feathers on my arms. I stand on the hill. I am wise. And they all come to hear. They think I am powerful because I listen to the sky. And the clouds and the sun and the eagle. I listen well and they ask me. I tell them what they need to know. I am head of the tribe. Broken Cloud is my name. I am very wise Apache. I am as wise as my father, Screaming Eagle. My mother, White Doe, she wore buckskin fringe.
I couldn't do it when I was a boy. I couldn't do it. I had to learn. I doubted I could learn. I had to learn to trust the sky and sun. I didn't believe I could trust the sun again. I was afraid to have a son because of Red Feather. My father said I must be Chief. My father made me go alone in the wilderness for two weeks and I cried for half. I died and woke. And I trusted. I was like the rattlesnake. Sheds his skin. I had to shed Red Feather. His boy was massacred. I carried Red Feather in my heart and gut. He is brown and wrinkled and sad. He has eyes like brown beads and he has white hair.

I send him light and the light comes through his eyes. He is happy. He soaks in the light like Earth soaks rain.

I love Red Feather. Red Feather is my soul. I am always Red Feather. Red Feather loves the light. Has a deep sorrow when the light betrayed him. Worshiped sun, light then they massacred his boy. He went back to the light when he died and kept some sorrow and grief for me.

The sun has always been there emanating truth. Your soul is learning to return fully in light. You must learn to forgive and to not fear. What goes around comes around. I always return to the light. There is a God: dwells in the light, plants, my heart, the light. In the earth, the animals and in all other humans and all other reincarnations.

Trust the light,
Keep looking.
Keep opening.
Keep trusting the light.

🧳 Time Travel
Past life, Future life, Between Life

"The collective unconscious contains the whole spiritual heritage of mankind's evolution, born anew in the brain structure of every individual."   -Carl Jung

Where Will I Travel?

Decide what you'd like to know, explore, or clarify. Will you go back in time (regression)? Will you explore your birth, past lives, or the source of an issue or pain? Are you tracking another to see what your relationship was in another place in time? Are you choosing to go into the future (progression)? How far into the future? Next week? Next month? Five years from now? 100 years? Are you looking to meet an inner guide? Choosing to heal an illness? Alter a pattern of behavior that does not serve you well? Or, do you decide not to decide and go anywhere the journey takes you? Whatever you choose, it will be perfect.

Once you plan your course, begin.

You can easily access:
✓Past Lives (regression)
✓Future Lives (progression)
✓Between lives (ascension)

    A fun way to tap your creative genius is to imagine that you are some famous creative genius that you admire. Imagine that you are E.E. Cummings, Plato, Picasso, Michaelangelo and expand your creativity from their vibration.

Where Do Past and Future Life Images Come From?
How little is known of the mind. Your mind understanding itself is sometimes a heartbeat away from your grasp. That's why time travel is so fascinating. Past life theorists say that other life-time and between life images come from keen imagination, reincarnation or the collective unconscious. Explore powerful scenarios of other people, places and times and judge for yourself.

Are Past Lives A Product Of Genetics?
Roxanne was born with a white streak in the front of her black hair, a striking characteristic that her mother had as well. When her child was born, she too sported that same white lock of hair. What physical characteristics do you reflect from your Ancestors?

Every cell in your body is an identical genetically coded replica of every other cell complete with your family record of eye color, strengths and weaknesses. Does each cell also carry detailed information about the lives of your ancestors?

What Do These Images Do For You?
Time travel brings you into a more intimate harmony with your life's purpose, yourself, and all humankind. You can use it to heal physical and emotional blocks or pain, explore relationships with others, and learn more about what makes you tick. Images of remembered lives are like holograms. You may look at them from various angles and perspectives and they'll change in impact, hue, and intensity.

Each image overlays your life in the present. Each helps you take control of your actions in the "now". When you are unconsciously influenced by an event, you act to recreate it or avoid it. Both of these re-actions determine your action. When you remember the source of a re-action, you empower yourself and no longer need to behave "because of" or "in spite of." Action now is a decision based on your clarity and free will.

How Do You Time Travel?
You can enjoy a singular journey of time travel or you can assist another on their journey.

How To Time Travel On Your Own

✓ Abundance of Paper
✓ Get Comfortable
✓ Bless Yourself
✓ Hypnotize Yourself
✓ Ask For Information
✓ Give auto-suggestions for automatic writing.
✓ Return to here and now awareness

To enjoy a singular journey you may want to record the following suggestions accompanied by soft recorded music. Be sure to leave spaces for you to think and respond to each idea.

Abundance of Paper
Abundance is the word to describe my paper. Make sure you have lots of it.

Get Comfortable
Sit comfortably in a place where you won't be disturbed.

Bless Yourself
Bless me on all levels; physically, mentally, emotionally and spiritually- so I may truly recognize and fulfill my life's purpose. Let all teachings be for the highest good of myself, humanity and the planet.

Help me reconnect with my special gifts as I automatically write words upon my page. And let me lovingly shed any negative messages given by insensitive people. Thank you. Amen. Awomen. Ah Life.

Focus Upon Breath
I become aware of my breathing and notice that I have my own distinct rhythm, energy and vibration. My vibration is unique. In all the history of the entire world there is not another who holds this identical vibration. I might notice any sights, sounds, rhythms, tastes, smells and sensations that come to me now.

Focus Upon Your Destination

I turn my attention now to my past. Do I want to go to another lifetime? Do I want to go back in time to another place in this current lifetime to explore it more fully and remember? Do I want to go into the future? Or discover where I was between lifetimes? Do I want to track a relationship or a physical pain? I decide. Then I take a deep breath and relax.

Give Auto-Suggestions For Automatic Writing

Write down what you receive.

I sit comfortably and bless myself on all levels; physically, mentally, spiritually and emotionally; making sure that all of these teachings are for my highest good.

I take a deep cleansing breath to my body. (pause). Let it out. (pause). One more breath to the mind. (pause) Let it go. Good.

I imagine myself programmed with a solar disc that allows me to flow words upon paper. I know that I can easily let the words move through my right or left hand. I don't think, analyze, edit or judge: just simply let the words put themselves across the page. It may or may not make sense; either is fine. All is well as I write, write, write.

I now imagine myself moving down a corridor of time to the past, the future, or any other specific place in time I'd like to explore. Along the corridor are many doorways; each to another life time where I learned valuable lessons that affect my life now. I find the door that draws me and I enter.

Remember to keep breathing. I put my pen upon the paper as I let the words out. These are called mind scraps. While I write mind scraps, I take full relaxing breaths and let the words flow.

Relaxing my hands, I simply write without censoring or editing. Whatever I write or draw will be perfect. If I like I say the following words as springboards:
    Feet?
    Clothes?
    Senses?

Others?
Location?
Time?
Experience?
Death?
White Light
Learned then?
Learned now?
When I am complete I return to room awareness feeling refreshed, invigorated and so glad to be alive."

How To Time Travel with Another

If you are the hypnotist guide, active listen by repeating back what you hear. Remember to support the time traveler by not leading or changing the meaning of what they report. Scribe on paper their experience and tape it as well.

Induce Trance:
✓Focus On The Destination
✓Ask Important questions and heal any old hurts.
✓Come Back

Induce Trance
Using the relaxation technique that best suits your subject, induce and deepen their trance. I like to begin with the blessing:

Bless you on all levels; physically, mentally, emotionally and spiritually, so you may truly recognize and fulfill your life's purpose. Let all teachings be for your highest good.

We ask that you easily reconnect with your special gifts as you allow yourself to travel your deepest memory.
Thank you.
Amen. Awomen. Ah Life.

Continue with the following induction or any other that you like.

Become aware of your breath and notice that you have my own distinct rhythm, energy and vibration. Your vibration is unique. In

all the history of the entire world there is not another who holds this identical vibration. Notice any sights, sounds, rhythms, tastes, smells and sensations that come to you and breath deeper and deeper.

Focus Upon The Destination

In your preliminary interview you most likely know where they want to go. If not you can offer your subject the following suggestions.

Turn your attention now to the past. Do you want to go to another lifetime? Do you want to go back in time to another place in this current lifetime to explore it more fully and remember? Do you want to go into the future? Or discover where you were between lifetimes? Do you want to track a relationship or a physical pain? Decide and then take a deep breath and relax. You needn't think, analyze, edit or judge, just breathe and answer any questions with the first thing that pops into your mind.

Take yourself now into a corridor of time. Deeper and Deeper. Along the corridor are portals, doorways to other places in time. One calls your attention. Perhaps the way it looks, feels, smells, tastes, sounds and you, with the next breath enter into that entry and discover yourself in another place in time. Answer my questions with the first idea or impulse. Don't worry if it makes sense it probably won't. Just answer.

Ask The Important Questions

Always active listen and support your subject as they respond. Don't back off or quit just keep asking. The best questions during a time travel journey are:

> **Look at your feet, if you have feet, How are they wrapped?**
> **How is your body wrapped? What are you wearing?**
> **Are you inside or out?**
> **Are you alone or with someone?**
> **What's going on?**
> **What happens next?**
> **How old are you?**
> **Where are you?**
> **What's going on?**
> **Where's your Mommy?**

Do you love your Mommy?
Does your Mommy love you?
Where's your Daddy?
Do you love your Daddy?
Does your Daddy love you?
What happens next?

To close the past life regression:
   How did you die?
   Send them the Light.
   What did you learn from this lifetime?
   How is that affecting your life in the present?
   Where do they live in your body right now?
   If there's any healing to do, go back and do it. Release and/or forgive.
   Return to room awareness feeling refreshed, revitalized and so glad to be alive.

Examples of Shelley's Past Life Regression
"Gary Oldsten"

Gary Oldsten of the great greenest of green land. Open to sea, sand, standing alone by the sea, my sea made for me. Seaweed, shells, I like to walk upon the sand. Cold grains in my toes, I will die barefoot of cold before I am old. I am always slightly alone. My right foot gimp, drags sand trails to the sea. Pop the seaweed poppers, that's my music calamity.

My mothers, has yellow hair like pale lemons in the sun, long days in the sun. White walls n my island in Greek lands. Small and tidy, my island. Abraxus is its name. I eat pomegranates and paint my gimp foot red. Octopus and squid are rare delights. My mouth drips with oozo and squid. My father likes to dance in the hall with red-lipped lady of the night. His hair is white and smells of pipe. My dog is gray and stupid and fine. I have a lip tucked tight above and speak tight and my teeth hurt, lowers crushed upon uppers to my nose. I am alone on my sandy beach looking at a million stars. I die on this beach from drinking salt and learn that I have melted sand. I reach a silent beach.

Bison

How do you do this and that? How do you go into and out of awareness and don't care. I am holy holy holy. Jaw tight, throat tight, going in and out of buffalo. Buffalo horns upon my head, my crown for (king to some) buffalo prince in our land of smoke mountains and sage caves. My head hurts. Like the bison I wear. I have to suffer for my food. The bison gave his life. I wear his horns and head upon my own. His life is within me. Food from the great white clouds, food of life runs through the river, the sun. The bison up from now to forever. The bison and man locked like interlaced branches of trees. Like finger on hands. Bison God. Bison Food. Bison Life.

The Girl In The Middle

I am going to die. Oh, why must I die?
I love living clinging upon me
Like spider webs tickling my nose
I want to feel the grass in my toes.

The pollen is strong;
(yellow crumbs of life sprinkled on little bee legs)
I want to be.
I want to stay sprinkled on earth.
I don't want to go or leave you; (you of my heart)
You are my heart.
I have struggled to love this body (where I dwell)
This body which transports my heart and soul and thoughts.
I don't want you to leave me, body,
after we finally got to love again.

If I go (torn from you)
what will become of our dreams?
Our visions of tomorrows?
Our time to laugh
and our deep sorrows?

I have no control and I want to control.

The Stockwell System

I want to choose that I have no choice.
I have no choice.

I want to go back
back to the years of tender corn
(waving in fields, steamy and warm)
back to the earth
(hot, mud parched, dry)
back to mama and apple pie.

Back to the checkered tablecloth
and coffee (black as sin)
back to the swing (the big white swing)
creaky in the hot summer night.
Sweat smells sweet like tea.
And the children in white frocks
skip-the-loop upon the brown grass.

Jonas and Becky come to the fair.
The barker came. The clown is there.
Joelly and Barbara and Cary Ann,
will take you back where everyone can
dance and swing and play the fiddle
and I can love the girl in the middle.

Why do I write this gibber posh pie?
Why am I in this stew?
Tell me what is wrong with me.
What am I to do?
>*So give me a plum cake and apple flap*
>*and I will give you my love back.*

⚡ Psychic and Intuitive Skills
Channel Your Guides

Channeling
A molecule moving in the dark of night
Silently entering beyond my sight
Surging in rhythm with my heart
I am the whole
I am a part.   _Shelley Stockwell

Channeling is the way you express your higher, source self or guides. Healing, intuition, inspiration, creativity, and psychic awareness are all forms of channeling. When you know that something is going to happen before it does or see a bigger picture you are generally channeling. Channeling opens you to information that may not be consciously known to you. It's very rewarding and feels great.

The information that comes from spirit guidance is generally very accurate and psychic. It could however, be inaccurate. Any information that you receive is just more information that you can use for your entertainment, growth and awareness. If it doesn't resonate or vibrate as correct, simply let it go. The purpose of this type of hypnotic journey is to expand awareness and use everything for your highest good.

On Channeling:
A Message From Kendra channeled by Shelley

Spiritual Intercourse
You've got the body
We add the spirit
You experience spirit
We experience body

What is a channeling?
Channeling is an energy exchange between a human (or animal) and spirit. The channel is a portal, a doorway, between dimensions of consciousness. This doorway swings in both directions. For humans, channeling allows them to re-member their essence and ancestry. For

spirits, channeling allows other dimensions or realms of consciousness (spirit) an opportunity to resonate in a physical body. This for us is an all-together enjoyable vibration or interchange.

Why would spirit choose to lower vibration and visit an earthling?

For us, we reflect ourselves and our own history through your physicality. We, of altered dimension, or as we call ourselves, earth connected spirits, are teachers. We believe that for you to know about your essence, origins and structure you must also know your future. We come to you as a fragment of your future, so you may know your essence in the marrow. We think that then, the you of the future and we of spirit, will enjoin in a harmonic exchange. We find our encounters with you joyous, instructive and beautiful. And so do you.

Who are you?

You might think of us as energy freaks. Our bumper sticker would read "Spirit does it with frequency." Just kidding.

Talk to me about ageing

To age is to return to full vibration (full spectrum) and recall ones origins and future. From our point of view, one never ages or loses vibration. Even in your physical plane, even in illness or what you call death, humans are an eternal vibration. Aging may refine your vibration causing a more tightly calibrated energy tonality or it may return you anew to full vibration. Think of your life as tones of a scale, or colors of a spectrum. Your job is to sound each note of natural vibration, or shine each color.

The baby is born in full spectrum or tonality and he resonates full on his own accord because she is newly returned from our dimension. The training and rituals of others often put this fullness of energy and color below raps or stifling units and the child grows to specialize only in certain tones.

As one ripens by age, permission, spirit or guidance, a person often returns to full spectrum or tonality. Artists of life, younger ones and those who have, what you call "near death experiences," those who are restricted in movement, and the aged, often resonate fully.

Is channeling real? Or does the channel make it up?

Are thoughts real? Do you make up the colors you see, the sounds you hear, the tastes you taste, the stirring in your heart or the laughter? Of course not. Each is as natural as breathing. To live is to allow the energy of life's expression to flow through you. Life flowing through you is spirit or channeling.

Focus your attention or perception upon your body and notice how you feel at this moment. Focus upon your mind and notice that you are thinking. This is challenging for you to think about thinking. It is like wrapping a mist about a mist. Now focus your attention upon spirit energy and you will notice its presence (presents) also.

To resonate or dwell simultaneously in the three strata's; body, mind and spirit, is to sing your song in full spectrum. Together you that you are whole-holy.

How to Automatic Write My Guides
- ✓ Abundance of Paper
- ✓ Get Comfortable
- ✓ Blessings
- ✓ Focus Attention On Your Breath
- ✓ Vibrate Your Chakras
- ✓ Ask for Guidance
- ✓ Write

Abundance of Paper
Abundance is the word to describe your paper. Make sure you have lots of it.

Get Comfortable
Sit comfortably in a place where you won't be disturbed.

Blessing:
>Bless me on all levels
>Physically, mentally
>Emotionally and spiritually
>So I may truly
>recognize and fulfill my life's purpose
>and let all teachings be for the highest good

The Stockwell System

of myself and humanity.
Help me reconnect
with my special gifts
and let me lovingly shed any
negative messages given by insensitive people.
Thank you.
Amen. Awomen

Focus Your Attention On Your Breath
Become aware of your breathing and notice that you have your own distinct rhythm, energy and vibration. Your vibration is unique. In all the history of the entire world there is not another who holds this identical vibration. You might notice any colors, sounds, rhythms, tastes and smells that come to you with this awareness.

Vibrate Your Chakras
Close your eyes and become aware of your breathing and breath to the base of the spine and hold it in for a moment. Then, with the out breath "Ohm" vibrate yourself from bottom to top. Any vibration that flows easily is perfect. Or you breathe in with the word "hun" and out with "shah." Whichever you choose.

Imagine that light enters your crown chakra and fills you with bright whiteness. Some folks see flashing lights behind their closed eyes. You may feel a rush, as if you leave your body or you may feel quite normal and think that you make it all up. Each perception is fine.

Ask for Guidance
Summon your guide by a specific name if you know it. Writing the name again and again works well for some. Or simply invite spirit for a message.

Record
Relaxing your hands, simply write without censoring or editing. Whatever you write or draw will be perfect. Or, using a tape recorder, relax the jaw and just let the words come forth. Don't worry if you're making it up or if it's accurate. Just babble.

Sandi Automatic Writes Her Spirit Guide
"I type the name of my spirit guide repeatedly "Aswana, Aswana, Aswana." This gives my rational mind a focus and it turns off. The next thing I know, my hands are typing."

Departed Loved Ones
You can easily contact:
✓ Departed Loved Ones
✓ Guardian Angels
✓ Guiding Spirits
✓ Ascended Masters

Departed ones from the other side are easy to contact and their messages can often be profoundly moving. Decide whom you'd like to contact and what, if anything specific, you'd like to explore. You can decide not to decide and contact anyone who is willing to communicate? If you want to be specific you can contact a departed loved one, one who departed with unfinished business, historical figures or friendly ghosts. Whatever you choose, it will be perfect. Once you plan your course, begin.

How to Automatic Write Deceased Loved Ones
✓ Abundance of Paper
✓ I Get Comfortable
✓ I Bless Myself
✓ I Focus Upon My Breath
✓ I Focus Upon My Loved One
✓ I Ask Them To Communicate
✓ I Write or Speak Without editing, censoring or judging
✓ I Return To Room Awareness And Ground Myself

Turn your Attention to a deceased loved one you want to contact. Notice their energy, vibration, rhythm, colors, textures, sounds tastes and smells. Let your mind and awareness wrap themselves about this departed one. Imagine them in physical body or as a spirit, either is fine. Ask Them To Communicate and then, let it happen.

> ### Sisters Automatic Write
> ### Their Beloved Mother
> ### From The Other Side
>
> Lisa Marie:
>
> "I receive messages from my deceased mother. The first time I felt her presence I said to myself. "Mom if you have something to say, why don't you say it now as I write. I receive her messages in my hand and then my hand is kind of guided along as I write. Now, when I feel her around me, I definitely feel her hand when she's ready to write. I can be thinking about something else and my hand plops down on the page and that's it."
>
> Susan:
>
> "When Lisa Marie showed me her writing, just from the look of it and the way it felt I knew it was my Mom. I immediately started crying just from the look of it. I knew it was no way possible it was anyone else. I knew it was my Mom. A few weeks later I tried and I started to do it too."

How to Use Psychometry

Psychometry is the art of holding or touching a physical object and picking up information about others whom have touched or worn it.

✓ Abundance of Paper
✓ I Get Comfortable
✓ I Bless Myself
✓ I Hold or Touch The Object I Am "Reading"
✓ I Ask My Guides For Information
✓ I Write

Abundance of Paper

Abundance is the word to describe your paper. Make sure you have lots of it.

Get Comfortable
Sit comfortably in a place where you won't be disturbed.

Bless Yourself
    Bless me on all levels
    Physically, mentally, emotionally and spiritually
    So I may truly recognize and fulfill my life's purpose
    and let all teachings be for the highest good
    of myself and humanity.
    Help me reconnect
    with my special gifts
    and let me lovingly shed any
    negative messages given by insensitive people.
    Thank you.
    Amen. Awomen

Hold or Touch The Object You Am "Reading"

Ask Your Guides For Information

Write
Relaxing your hands, simply write without censoring or editing. Whatever you write or draw will be perfect.

Auto Suggestions For Guided Messages
Another way to channel write is to record in your own voice the following set of instructions accompanied by soft recorded music.

I sit comfortably. As I bless myself on all levels physically, mentally, spiritually and emotionally, making sure that all of these teachings are for my highest good. I Take a deep breath and cleanse my body my body. (pause).

Let it out. One more breath to the brain. (pause) Let it go. I Close my eyes and relax my eyelid so much that they just don't feel like opening.

I imagine myself programmed with a solar disc that allows me to flow words from spirit upon paper. I know that I can easily let the words move through my right or left hand. I don't think, analyze, edit or

judge: just simply let the words put themselves across the page. I'm not concerned if what comes to me makes sense; it may not.

I now imagine myself being lifted in wings that guide me to write. I take another deep breath. Let it out. Put my pen upon the paper as I let the words out. This is called mind scraps. While I write mind scraps, I take another full breath."

A Message from Archangel Michael

"Let us not mince the words, it is the seven survival essences you request. All is a process of life and death but it is the survival essences you request. For a human to survive they must:

Fuel with sun (warmth) water, air and rest.

Perpetuate their species with sex and teaching their young.

Release energy with movement, laughter tears and elimination.

Have purpose. Need to be needed (succor). Be part of, be recognized and be productive.

Re•member (all genetic memory) Their origin (spirit), their structure (body) and earth memory (mind)

Contact others, love, touch and companionship.

Evolve, die, grow and expand, rip and kill, love and nurture, live and die (all cells, ideas and body package),"

How to Tap Your Deepest Mind
✓ Abundance Of Paper
✓ Get Comfortable
✓ Blessings
✓ I Focus My Attention On My Breath
✓ I Vibrate My Chakras
✓ I Call Upon My Inner Wisdom And Higher Self
✓ I Write

Abundance of Paper
Abundance is the word to describe your paper. Make sure you have lots of it.

Get Comfortable
Sit comfortably in a place where you won't be disturbed.

Bless Yourself
Bless me on all levels
Physically, mentally, emotionally and spiritually
So I may truly
recognize and fulfill my life's purpose
Let all teachings be for the highest good
for myself, humanity and the planet.
Help me reconnect with my special gifts
and let me lovingly shed any
negative messages given by insensitive people.
Thank you.
Amen. Awomen. Ah life.

Focus your Attention On your Breath
Become aware of your breathing and notice that you have your own distinct rhythm, energy and vibration. Your vibration is unique. In all the history of all the world there is not another who holds this identical vibration. You might notice any colors, sounds, rhythms, tastes and smells that come to you with this awareness.

I Vibrate My Chakras
Close your eyes and become aware of your breathing and breath to the base of your spine and hold it in for a moment. Then, with the out breath "Ohm" vibrating yourself from bottom to top. Any vibration that flows easily is perfect. Or breathe in with the word "hun" and out with "shah". Whichever you choose, imagine that light enters your crown chakra and fills you with bright whiteness.

Think and imagine yourself in a spotlight of light. Within this light is your auric field, your past, present, future, all your experience and guidance. This is your energy. It belongs uniquely to you. And relax.

Call Upon Your Inner Wisdom and Higher Self
Ask for a message from the part of yourself that knows all of your answers: knows exactly what you need to do to make your life work perfectly physically, mentally, emotionally and spiritually.

Write
Relaxing your hands, simply write without censoring or editing. Whatever you write or draw will be perfect.

Time Travel Resources
Time Travel: The Do-It-Yourself Past Life Journey Handbook, Stockwell, Shelley, Automatic Writing and Time Travel audio tapesContains detailed instructions, scripts and chronicles for fascinating journeys.
See order forms at the back of this book.

Illustration by Shelley Stockwell

CHAPTER 19

Stockwell

≋Breath Techniques

- ≋ STOCKWELL BREATHING
- ≋ YOGIC
- ≋ REBIRTHING
- ≋ HOLOTROPIC
- ≋ INFINITY
- ≋ MER-KA-BA

≋STOCKWELL BREATHE

Air, air, a breath affair,
I will hold you if I dare.
Pulling life force energy
feeling you in ecstasy.
Into my cells, into my brain,
if I breathe, I shall remain.   — Shelley Lessin Stockwell

Inspire or Expire

We take some twenty thousand breaths a day. University studies prove that people who breathe fully live longer, and people who do not breathe, die.

Breath too, is a most powerful hypnotic and a good way to get tension and resentment off your chest.

In antiquity air was said to hold the essence of the soul. The word air derives from the sanskrit word atmos, "breath." The Greek God Zeus was also called Air.

Hindus call this becoming one with the infinite and believe that the soul literally leaves the body when you breath your last breath and then it merges with your spiritual Oversoul just as a drop of water merges when entering the sea.

What Kind of Fuel am I?

Oxygen allows each cell to give off steady, gentle heat. Breathing assists your body in burning the food you eat, turning it into fuel for your cells. When you work out, make love, and expend a lot of energy, you need more oxygen. Oxygen allows your cells to work faster, heat up, and you perspire, thereby cooling your body and releasing waste products through your glorious organ: the skin.

When folks stop smoking, it usually takes 12 hours for CO (carbon monoxide) to leave the blood. Breathing more fully speeds up that process. As a matter of fact, everything works better when you breathe.

Prana My House

In ancient India, sacred breathing, or prana, was said to connect our earth-bound mind to expanded consciousness. The yogis found that by varying the length and depth of their breath, they could achieve different levels of conscious and super-conscious awareness.

STOCKWELL FOUR BREATHS

Take a deep breath into your body, through your diaphragm. Take all that your lungs can hold, slowly and easily. Hold your breath to the count of three, then gently let it out, releasing any tension as you do.

Take a second full breath, breathing from the diaphragm and to your mind, the oxygen fuels your thinking. Hold it to the count of three, slowly let it out, clearing your mind.

Take a third breath, imagining white light coming from the bottoms of your feet, to the crown of my head. Hold it in to the count of three. When you let it out, it cleanses you.

With this forth breath, relax and let your breathing breathe you, for you are your breath.

Baloon Breathing

Baloon breathing increases your breathing potential. Each time you do it, you reopen the airflow into your lungs.

As you inhale, fill an imaginary balloon in your stomach. Feel your stomach expand. When you exhale, let the balloon deflate and your stomach contract. If you put your hand on your chest you will notice that it doesn't rise. If you put your hand on the stomach it will expand.

Expand The Baloon

Start with the balloon breath.
Expand your imaginary stomach balloon with the in breath.
When the balloon is full, raise your elbows to shoulder level and continue to inhale.
Lower your elbows as you begin to deflate the balloon.
Your stomach contracts.
Now close your eyes and notice how much more fully you are breathing.

Energy Breathing

This breath improves your concentration and awareness. It recharges the mind and releases carbon monoxide as you empty your lungs.

Inhale five consecutive breaths via the nose. Hold the fifth breath as you count to yourself one-two-three-four-five and then, on six, inhale exhale completely.

After several of these breaths you might feel a tingling sensation. That is the feeling of aliveness. Some feel dizzy or lightheaded. Close your eyes and notice if you do.

When you open your eyes notice that everything is brighter.

Yogic breathing

I breathe golden sunset
Kaleidoscope wonder
I am the sunset.   -Shelley Stockwell

Every 90 minutes one nostril becomes dominant. Yogic breathing through alternative nostrils nourishes both hemispheres of the brain. When the right nostril is dominant, the logical analytical left brain becomes activated. When the left nostril is dominant, we tap the creative hemisphere. The nose is the only part of the body where the brain is in direct contact with the environment.

Yogis focus too on the spaces between breathing in and breathing out. In those microseconds, they say, you experience full death. When you learn to be in the space between life and touch the void, you achieve enlightenment they say.

Breathe The Yogic Way

As you inhale, think and intone the sound of "Ahem," "hun," or the Chinese, "hon" meaning center, essence or origin. Such inspiration brings in the source, the oneness.

As you exhale, intone the sound of "sah" or "sha." In Chinese this means shimmering light.. You might want to think center (hon) as you breath in and Shimmering light (Sha) as you exhale. Together Ahem-Sah, Hun-Sah or Hon-Sha means harm-not.

Rebirthing

"Fathers help but mothers deliver."   -Diane Zimberoff

Rebirthing is a gentle form of breathwork used as a regression technique. Leonard Orr and Sondra Ray have done much to popularize this approach to the subconscious (superconscious) mind. The first phase or "induction" part of the process involves a circular breathing technique followed by inner focus.

Some people fear that deep breathing will cause oxygen deprivation or hyperventilation. The following techniques do quite the opposite: they give you extra oxygen. These "super" ventilation styles use full deep and relaxed exhalations. Hyperventilation is caused by shallow panting exhalations, which stops the oxygen flow. I have never understood why certain birth preparation techniques require limited panting breaths just when mom and baby need oxygen the most!

The Stockwell version of rebirthing can be done with the help of a hypnotist, rebirther, or by yourself. It's, of course, much more fun to have someone to guide you and process and release any confusion or discomfort. Yet, going it alone can be satisfying too.

If You Rebirth Another
If you are assisting a breather, clear your mind, relax and envision a loving, positive session. Stay in your integrity and be lovingly detached. Rebirthing in a Jacuzzi is fabulous. But just lying on the floor and doing this breath work is terrific too.

Some hypnotherapists run their hands about five inches above the breather to feel their energy (aura). Allow your instincts to intuit any physical blocks. Let's say the breather tightens his forehead, go ahead and touch the forehead asking: "What is going on here? If your hands tingle or get very hot or cold above a chakra ask, "What's going on here?"

Of course, if you're going to touch your client get permission first and then be sure any contact is noninvasive and appropriate. I usually say before we begin "Is it all right if I touch your hand, shoulder or forehead during your session." Or "If I notice that you aren't breathing fully I'll tap your hand like this, is that OK?"

HOW TO DO REBIRTHING
Music
Play soothing music without lyrics. Bold rhythms and classical music work well too.

Breath
Breathe in a Circle. Use deep connected relaxed breaths. Link each full-lung inspiration (inhalation) to each cleansing breath (exhalation) without any pauses. Let your breath be easy and relaxed. Choose to breathe either through your nose or through your mouth. Make sure that both your in and out breaths are done through the mouth (my preference) or the nose. In one and out the other is seldom as comfortable.

Blessings
Say a prayer for protection and enlightenment.
> Bless me on all levels
> Physically, mentally, emotionally and spiritually
> So I may truly recognize and fulfill my life's purpose and let all teachings be for the highest good of myself and humanity.
> Help me reconnect with my special gifts

and let me lovingly shed any negative messages given by insensitive people.
Thank you.
Amen. Ah Women. Ah Life!"

Keep Breathing

Keep breathing fully for at least ten minutes. Don't quit. Let your breath weave into the music. Imagine that the breath is breathing you. Experience whatever comes up. As with all enlightenment techniques, do not think, analyze, or judge this material. Just let it be. If the images are scary...keep breathing. If you experience bodily sensations or tightness...keep breathing. No matter what, keep it up until you experience a feeling of surrender, ecstasy, or as the scientist call it...integration.

Let It Happen

Express any feelings and release energy by kicking your feet, moving your head from side to side, letting out sounds or words, hitting a pillow with your fists or a bataka (cloth bat) or a rubber pipe. Let out any sound that wants to emerge.

Ask Questions
This life

If you are using rebirthing to recall your birth in this life time. Ask questions like:
"What is the reaction of your mother as you are born?"
"How about the others? Are they happy to see you?"
and so on.

Past Life

To explore a past life, ask past life questions:
What is on your feet?
Clothes?
Senses?
Are others present in this moment in time and space?
Where is this place?
What is the time frame?
What's going on?
How did you die?

Send white light to the deceased that was you and notice what happens. And most importantly, what did you learn in this lifetime?

Welcome Back

How do you know when a rebirthing is complete? You'll know. There will be release and peace. It's like knowing when an orgasm is done. You know.

To complete your journey, draw a mandala or write down your experiences. If you are with a hypnotist share your experience out loud.

After that, get grounded; take a walk, take a bath, pull weeds, scrub a floor or eat something. In general, ground yourself.

TWO PAST LIFE REGRESSIONS USING REBIRTHING

Before this regression, I had chosen to explore a vague irrational fear I had of dying. I also wanted to understand my strong sugar cravings. As I breathed, I reported my feelings as they came through. I noticed my jaw was tight. What was I holding back? I reported my feelings. An onlooker reported the experience like this: She began to talk in an old woman's voice as if she had no teeth. She said she hated cooking and breathing all the smoke inside the round place covered in skins. She wanted to be outside with the others, with the children.

She began hitting the ground with the hose, said she had arthritis in her hands and legs, couldn't hit hard. Said she was hitting with the big spoon, getting food all over. Said Big Bear died and she wants to die too, but they would not let her. (This session was guided and videotaped by Diane Zimberoff. Here are the transcripts.)

INDIAN LADY (Deep Breathing)

I have to make lots of food. Not enough food for everybody. Not enough food for me. I don't have enough to eat. I'm hungry. I look fat but I'm not, I'm hungry. I have to cook all this food and I can't eat. I don't have any teeth. I don't know why, they all fell out.

(Putting the feelings in motion I tried to kick my feet) Not enough. I'm hungry. I need more. I don't have any teeth. I can't eat. I am very old lady. I am starving to death. I can't kick arthritis in my legs.

They always leave me here to cook. That makes me angry. This is a round place. Got skins over the roof. Have to breathe this smoke. I don't like it. They all get to go out and be with the children and the animals and I have to be here and cook. It really makes me mad!" (Using a rubber hose, I hit the floor to release new energy) "Food all over. My spoon it will break. So angry. Big Bear will be mad. Big Bear died. I have arthritis. I'm hungry. I want to eat something. Arthritis in my hands and legs came when my teeth fell out. I must stir the pot of corn and venison." (my guide, Diane asks, "Where did the arthritis come from?") "Big Bear died. I died too but I can't die now. I have to cook the food. They won't let me die. He goT to die but not me. (I let out a large sigh and relaxed which is generally the sign of a reliving phase of a regression). "Poor lady: she wasn't very bright.

I then went on to recall in vivid detail my own birth, my feelings of disappointment of being removed from my mother, and most Importantly, my feelings of being debilitated by my mother's taking drugs during the pregnancy and at the birth. When my mother took drugs, so did I. I felt paralyzed. I felt like I was dead. My first bonding with my mother came the next day after my birth and my mother held me lovingly and fed me very sweet drink that tasted exactly like the candies I have been craving my whole life.

HAREM GIRL (Example of a past life regression using rebirthing breathwork.)

I have a veil over my nose. I am hidden. I am a harem girl. I dance. I'm too skinny to be a harem girl, but I dance anyway. I try to get fat but I can't. I'm not hungry and the other girls try to feed me. Not hungry enough.

Eight girls: Sylvie, Gloria (her name's not Gloria but its Gloria), Munchee. A man Gregory is in the harem. He's a eunuch and takes care of us and protect us. He has a hearing problem. Doesn't hear very well.

I like to dance to please the master and his friends. They always laugh 'cause I am so skinny. I'm skinny when all others are fat. I like to make love with master. He likes to make love with me, too. We make love lots and lots. They always try to make me fat. Master says when he makes me fat with baby; I'll be fatter. He has a beard, a big beard, a big long beard and blue eyes with one brown spot in one. One eye is very blue - he is blind in that eye.

Bugs brought blindness. I have beautiful, black eyes. Shiny eyes. Master smells good. Master born to family where he is master to harem. He lets me be master when we make love. Smiles when he sees me. He has pretty teeth. He has many camels. Many friends, much food. Many harem girls. He likes women best. He lounges in the middle and we all cuddle him. He is a good man. An honorable man.

I like to dance. I can't get fatter, I don't know why. I'm older, I got fatter. I was his favorite. I run the whole house now. He spends most of his time with me. He's getting very old now. We are good friends. I love him. He loves me. We are all his wives. He dies before me. I am very sad. I want to go with him now. I will will myself to go with him. I will stop eating. Funny, I always wanted to be fatter. I will die skinny. I will die with my master. My heart is broken. I will die of a broken heart. I will die because my heart is broken. I will talk to no one.

      She died of a broken heart. It took her a long time to die. She was in great pain. She spoke to no one; not even the eunuch. He stood by her bedside. The others didn't understand. She was happy and solid and a little too skinny. (He was Steve from Shelley's lifetime) I learned love - real love. And devotion - conviction. A good one. He loved, he was the teacher. I was very young. He was very wise and a good human. I was loyal and devoted and joyous and trusting and loving. It was a really good lifetime. I'm proud of it. I haven't changed much from that one. I learned the lessons well. I know how to love from then. The ape didn't know how to love that's why I had that one. Mainly the loving. That's my specialty.

Holotropic Breathing

Deep sustained breathing was dubbed Holotropic (moving toward wholeness) by Stan and Christina Grof. Grof wanted to recreate the enlightenment experiences that he had recorded during twenty-five years of LSD research and he found breathing to be the ticket.

    All of his subjects, whether healthy, psychiatric patients, terminally ill, or criminals, reported almost identical experiences. They accessed and resolved inner conflicts and reported feeling deeply healed and more peaceful. Many described it as a spiritual rebirthing process. Stan and Christina found that breathing deeply to provocative music paralleled the LSD enlightenment studies. Oxygen released the nervous system into a powerful spiritual emotional awakening (or reawakening perhaps). Thus, holotropic breath work was born!

    To do this process; breathe fully and rapidly to provocative music. A breath worker, hypnotist or friend may assist with comforting touch or hand-holding or you may choose to take my Shelley Stockwell approach on your own.

BIRTH PHASES AND LIFE DECISIONS

An interesting aspect of Stan's approach is his theory of birth phases. Stan sees birth as having four distinct categories and emotional influences. Decisions you make at birth about the meaning of life, he believes, are aligned to the where you unconsciously place the most energy.

His four phases of attention are:

PHASE OF BIRTH	LIFE ATTITUDES
Floating, Womb With Room	-Peaceful, Joyous, Free Relaxation, Mellow, Bliss
Compression, No Exit, Crammed In Womb	-Helpless/ Hopeless/ Trapped +Feeling Your Limits
Labor, Birth Canal, Cervix opening	-Life is Struggle/ Rage +Strive To Succeed, Cooperation, Hope
Delivery Nirvana	-Sacrifice, Lonely, Hurt, +Win, Succeed, Intense Joy, Triumph

How To Do Holotropic Breathing

Music

To take this style of breath journey on your own, put on provocative, stirring music, chanting or rhythms. Make sure that the music is long enough to last the time you choose for your experience and that it ends on a peaceful note. A breathwork session can be fifteen minutes to three hours long. For your first session, I recommend sixty minutes one day followed by another breath session the next day for an hour and a half. Extend your breathing longer if marvelous things are happening and you have the time.

Breath

Breath is more rapid and deeper than normal breathing. My preference is to breathe in through the nostrils and out through the mouth, but you decide how you would like to do it.

It is very important that the breathing remain full, as though you were breathing down to the tips of your toes, full deep breaths in. Full cleansing breaths out, rapidly, one right after the other. Ask your sitter (if you have one) to encourage this full and rapid breathing.

Think of your breath as a deep internal bath of oxygen. Occasionally people experience a feeling like bands around their foreheads, at their wrists or ankles. A few people might experience an uncomfortable "heady" feeling. Just keep breathing. These feelings will deepen, give you information and evaporate into the oxygen and the music, opening and cleansing you.

Visions

As you are breathing, unresolved sequences from childhood may emerge. You might confront death or birth. And, of course, you may access visions and experiences from other places and other times. (In Stan Grof's words "Anything biographical, parental, or transpersonal may emerge.")

There are no rights or wrongs in this or any of your processes. Each person can experience things through images, physical sensations, and any of their senses. The results, however, are always the same; a wonderful feeling of awareness and clarity about your life and your life's purpose. Respect whatever comes up, it is your process for now.

TWINS
Shelley's Holotropic Breathing Experience
When I was 33 years old I became pregnant and was elated. Four months into a queasy pregnancy, I began "spotting" and apparently was experiencing a miscarriage. I was sent for ultrasound testing. The ultrasound technician said, "I see a septum separating the egg sac and two little fetuses deteriorating. Shelley, you miscarried twins."

Upset, I decided to go up to Esalan Institute in Big Sur, California before I was required to return to my job as a TWA flight attendant. I called Esalan and asked what classes they were offering the following week. They gave me a list of classes including one called "Death and rebirth" with Stan and Christina Grof. I signed up. During the course of the week, I learned about holotropic breathing and during an hour to two-hour breath work session, I had the following experience. Since this was a nonverbal experience, it is a little difficult to share it in words but I will do my best.

I felt bands of pressure around my forehead and wrists. The pressure mounted. Then suddenly it was as if I had burst through into another world, more magnificent, stunning, and more glorious than anything I had ever heard or read about. I was flying upward to an orb of white light. My flying was done by a sensation behind each of my "wing bones." As I moved upward toward the orb, I felt an unknown level of ecstasy. Imagine the biggest orgasm of your life multiplied by 100. That is how it felt.

Up, up I flew moving toward that brilliant orb of light. I felt detached from my physical body except for an occasional feeling or sensation of someone gently sliding me sideways. I was told later that I was sliding across the floor and that my hands were floating upward.

I saw a ring of white garbed "souls" holding hands in a large circle as I ascended. They were magnificent. Each radiating peace and beauty. They were neither male nor female. Radiant light beings I didn't know. All I knew, in those moments without words, were that these white robed visions were all of mankind. Loving and peaceful. I rose above them, flying in my ecstasy and then I saw her. The wisest most knowing of all. I had to smile and a thought came to me at that moment. The "all knowing" was a woman who looked like the Statue of Liberty. I flew about her swooning in the rapture. After some time or else a year (you totally lose track of all time when you are in this consciousness) I had my second thought. "What about the twins?" I extended my right hand and magically there was a small person on it. I extended my left hand and another small person alighted. I flew, giddy and joyous, with my two small friends who suddenly grew larger and larger. They flew to me and one extended their hand and the other extended their hand below and together they lifted me upon their hands and flew me into forever. Bliss.

My awareness was that my miscarriage was no accident but a perfectly timed and planned step to bring me here to learn techniques and to open the door to my spirituality, enlightenment, and understanding. In the hours after this experience I had a strong desire to sit in the sun. I spontaneously moved into one yoga posture after another (I never studied yoga). I understood why earlier cultures worshiped the sun. From that moment forward, I could see auras around people (something I had never seen before). I understood why pictures in Christianity and Buddhism often show halos around the heads of special people. Perhaps there was a time when we all saw auras. Religions of all sorts never had made sense to me before and suddenly I felt the underlying truth that is the foundation of all religions.

I had undergone a powerful and moving transformation. So this is what was meant by an enlightenment experience! Since those moments I have never been the same.

Shelley Stockwell's
Mer Ka Ba
Ascension To The Forth Dimension

Thoth taught the truth of creation
as the sacred flower of life.
This mandala of circles entwine,
and generate perfection divine:
Laws of physics, language and light,
math, geometry and genetics ignite.

Here is the key to creation;
a portal that opens the way
to a tree of life everlasting.
and the source that made it that way.

-Shelley Stockwell

Mer Ka Ba breathing was created as a sacred initiation ritual by the Ancient Egyptians. They said it opened you to enlightenment, and enhanced your creativity, stimulation and elation.

Known as the breath of the sun or the flower of life, it is a portal to the Godhead. Try it and achieve Mer Ka Ba or enlightenment. Eighteen spherical breaths move you from your own light and love to spiritual light and love.

History
Salutations to you, you Five Great Gods,
Who come out of the City of Eight,
You who are not yet in heaven,
You who are not yet upon the earth,
You who are not yet illuminated by the sun.
    -poem about creation from an ancient Egyptian papyrus

The Mer-Ka-Ba originated thirteen thousand to twenty thousand year's ago. It is called by the Ancient Mystery School "The Right Eye Of Horus."

This Ancient Egyptian initiation uses the most sacred geometric form "The Flower Of Life" which is said to be the same geometric structure as our genetic code (44+2). The flower of life can be seen on carvings of six thousand-year-old temple walls.

This Book Of The Breathing was said to be scribed by Thoth, the god symbolizing wisdom and truth.

Priests were taught to charm nature and gain magic to control the world of the dead. The Mer Ka Ba was the key to all teachings that "enabled souls to breathe forever. "

Mer

Mer or mar in current Egyptian means to "walk before" or "proceed movement." The mer in MerKaBa means a vehicle to carry us through time and space. That vehicle is the spinning star tetrahedron.

The ancient Egyptians built and hid huge solar boats to carry the ba to the heavens. In the modern Egyptian language merkaba means boat. In this breathing technique think of the word mer as counter- rotating light.

Ka and Ba

Ancient Egyptians believed that you have three souls the ka and ba represent two of those. Ka meant double or soul mirror and was symbolized by the hieroglyphic of two arms. The ka was said to reflect your physical body much as a statue might, but is made of finer matter than mere flesh. Yogis refer to this as the subtle body. You might think of it as the vital force of life.

Ba meant the soul in heaven or the projection soul and is symbolized by the hieroscript of a bird, the soul bird.

Over four thousand years ago, Imhotep (the father of modern medicine) designed the famous "step pyramid" of Sakqaara, Egypt. When I visited there, I found pottery chards used to bake loaves of bread shaped. They were shaped like the "beehive" pyramid itself. Bread and bulls blood was offered to the statue of King Djoser to feed his Ka or soul. Both bread and slaughtered beef were left for several hours, and were blessed in return by Djoser. When eaten mortals could receive the blessings of his King Djoser's heavenly Ba.

In the time of Djoser (or Zoser), some four thousand years ago, the builder of the step pyramid, the oldest known pyramid in Egypt, the Mer Ka Ba was considered sacred and only practiced by the high priests.

The purpose of spherical breathing is feel limitless love and to radiate energy outward like the sun (who radiates out life force energy to us). As you breathe you envision counter rotating field of light that join heaven and earth. Here's how it is done:

This information came to you through my channels, daughter of Pharaoh, and Kendra. You may make contact with your own guidance and enlightenment using this technique. It is easy to learn and becomes more powerful each time you do it.

Let your profound wisdom and angels guide you on your journey. As you breathes, image a star tetrahedron. This image and your focused breaths will transform your personal energy into the vitality of all life.

Sit comfortably, touching your thumbs to your forefingers. Picture and imagine a double or star tetrahedron or two pyramids overlapping and interlinking.

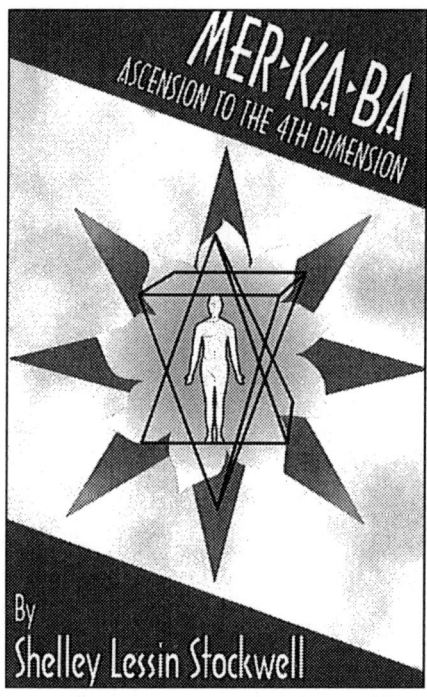

Illustration by Sandi Madearis

Affirm
I am ready and willing to heighten and expand my consciousness in every way. I open and expand my consciousness in every way. I open and expand my consciousness in every way.

Breath	Affirm	Posture	Thought
one balancing exhale slowly	"I open my heart to love." Open heart to the love of life	thumb to forefinger	inhale look 3" above 3rd eye, exhale down
two balancing exhale slowly	"I open my heart to love." Let negativity go as white light into the earth's center	thumb to forefinger	inhale look up (3rd eye may tingle) exhale down
three balancing exhale slowly	"I open my heart to love." Negativity vanishes.	thumb to middle finger	inhale look up exhale down
four balancing exhale slowly	"I open my heart to love."	thumb to ring finger	inhale look up exhale down
five balancing exhale slowly	"I open my heart to love."	thumb to little finger	inhale look up exhale down
six balancing exhale slowly	"I open my heart to love."	thumb to fore and middle finger	inhale look up exhale look down
seven prahnic flow	"I bring in the light." Light tubes meet at your navel and form a sphere of light the size of a grapefruit.	thumb to fore and middle finger	Two white light tubes (the thickness of your thumb) meet at navel. Up from the base and down from the top of at same time
eight prahnic flow	"I bring in the light." Sphere of light grows large, bright, concentrated, until it ignites into the sun.	thumb to fore and middle finger	Continue light moving up and down and meet at navel. To keep sun brilliant. Gently blow excess energy out small hole of lips. If sun bulges, rapidly release air
nine prahnic flow	"I bring in the light." Sphere of light grow larger, brighter and more concentrated until it ignites into the sun.	thumb to fore and middle finger	The sun shines Tubes of white light continue simultaneously up and down meeting at navel.
ten prahnic flow	"I bring in, expand and let the light shine"	thumb to fore and middle finger	The sphere grows larger

eleven	"I expand the light" The sun shines out as a large sphere.	Females right hand on top of left. Males left hand on right.	Feel the flow let the prahna flow from the two poles meeting in the sun.
twelve prahna flow	"I expand the light."		Relax and let the prahnic flow from the two poles meeting in the sun. The sun shines out as a large sphere.
thirteen prahnic flow	"I expand the light. I am the sun"		Large sun shines and moves up slightly. Relax and let the prahna flow.
fourteen	"I feel the flow" Breath between navel and sternum The large sun (which contains the original small one) moves here.	Males, place left palm on top of right palm Females, Place right palm on top of left palm	Star tetrahedron rotates clockwise to the right.
fifteen	"Equal speed."	Hands remain the same.	Rotate the tetrahedrons in opposite directions (1/3 the light speed at their outer tips)
sixteen	As you exhale "34-21." (your code for spinning)	Hands remain the same.	Tetrahedrons spin in opposite directions Tetrahedron of your mind left 34 x light speed, tetrahedron of emotions right 21x light speed
seventeen	"I am filled with Unconditional Love."	Hands remain the same.	Rotate in opposite directions. Reduce speed of every atom and electron to 9/10th light speed.
eighteen normal breath	"My higher self takes me to the 4th dimension and beyond."	Hands remain the same.	Normal breath Disappear from this world and reappear in 4th and 5th dimensional worlds.

Breath

While breathing, imagine that you are standing in the middle of a double tetrahedron (two interlinking pyramids that looks like a three dimensional Star of David) and opening yourself to unconditonal love. During this process, the two pyramids rotate in opposite directions. This is the thought form for the energy and structure of everything that exists.

Imagine that each of the eighteen spherical breaths combine with the energy of the sun. For both sun and breath gives life. Each breath opens you to your vitality as you create, radiate and stimulate your own personal energy and transform it into the source of all life.

When you feel the love in your heart, you open to spirit. Without love there can be no Mer Ka Ba. You know that you are doing the breathing correctly when your love flows fully. Each of the seventeen breaths of the Mer Ka Ba are separate and unique. As you breathe, open myself to the feelings of love. That feeling you get when you give and receive love and are open to Spirit or God.

Breaths one through six, balance

Breaths one through six balance and cleanse you as you open your heart to love. When you feel the love in your heart, you open to spirit. With out love there can be no Mer Ka Ba. This cleansing balances your polarities and opens you to the journey.

Breaths seven through thirteen increase energy

Breaths seven through thirteen increases your prahnic or energy flow as you bring in light and radiate and become the sun.

Breath fourteen

Feel the flow

Breaths fifteen through seventeen, rotating energy fields

During breaths fifteen through seventeen, imagine counter rotation of energy surrounding you. You create rotating spiraling energy fields in and around your body.

Breath eighteen, ascention

This forth dimensional shift lets you ascend from the third dimension into the forth dimension and beyond.

Let your eyelids close down as you breathe. Be aware of life itself, for your breath is life. The sun is upon you. The sun is the giver of life, without breath or the sun we would cease to exist in physical body.

Each of the eighteen breaths of the sun opens you to your radiance and vitality as you create radiate and stimulate your own personal energy and transform it to the energy of all life.

Let the light which lives within each and every cell of your being expand and radiate. As you breathe open yourself to the feeling of love. Let your breath be deep and relaxed. Breathe from the stomach into the diaphragm and then the chest. Then without pausing, exhale.

Relax for five seconds and take your next breath. Imagine yourself now surrounded by a double tetrahedron or two pyramids one upside down and the other superimposed upon it right side up and you are in the middle of this star tetrahedron. The top of the point above your head is about one hand length and the bottom point is below your feet is about one hand length. Females will imagine the mid point facing back and males of course would imagine it facing forward.

Take a deep breath, deep and flowing and open your heart to love. 'I open my heart to love.'

Breathe in, opening your heart to the love of life and exhale slowly, feeling the love in your heart opening. You are opening to spirit from which all love comes; Mer Ka Ba.

With the next breath, open your heart to love. Touch your thumb to your forefinger and breathe in. As you do, look up at an imaginary place about three inches above your third eye. As you exhale look down and see and imagine myself releasing any negative energy as white light, right into the center of the earth, just sending it down in a triangle pointed down. Let any negative energy vanish.

The next breath opens your heart to love, this time touching your thumb to your middle finger. As you breathe in, look up at an imaginary place about three inches above your third eye and as you exhale, look down. 'I open my hear to love.'

Touch your thumb to your ring finger and breath in, looking up at an imaginary place above your third eye and as you exhale, look down. 'I open my heart to love' as you touch your thumb to your little finger breathing in and looking up exhaling and looking down.

With the next inspiration 'I open my heart to love' as you touch your thumb to your forefinger and little finger. Inspiration; looking up and release and cleansing; looking down.

Now start to increase your prahnic energy flow as you bring in the light keeping your thumb and fore and middle finger together. Think, imagine or visualize a tube of white light about the thickness of a thumb moving up from the base of my tetrahedron and down from the top of my tetrahedron, the tube of light meets at your navel. When it does it forms a sphere of light about the size of a grapefruit.

Bring in the light with the next breath 'I bring in the light.' The tube continues moving up and down. The sphere of light begins to grow larger more concentrated for it is beginning now to ignite into the sun.

As it becomes more brilliant you can blow any excess energy out of a small hole in your lips. If the sphere bulges, let the air out rapidly as you bring in the light with the next breath. Light continues moving up and down meeting at my navel. The sphere of light grows larger brighter more concentrated until it ignites into the sun. As you bring in the light. 'I bring in the light.'

The next breath lets the sun shine brightly. Bringing in the light, relax and let the prahnic energy flow from the two poles and meet in the sun. The sun shines out as a large sphere and as you breathe now.

With the next breath expand the light. Expand the light and the prahnic flow meets in the sun and the sun shines out as a large sphere. 'I expand the light.' Relax and let the prahnic flow meet in the sun. The sun is a large radiant sphere. 'I am the sun.'

With the next breath, feel the flow. Females place the right hand on top of the left; males place your left hand on top of right.

Breathe between your navel and sternum and let the large sun that contains the original smaller sphere, let it move up slightly as you 'I feel the flow' and let your star tetrahedron start to spin clockwise to your right. As you rotate the tetrahedron say to yourself 'equal speed.' The tetrahedrons spin in opposite directions. Rotating in the opposite directions, one-third the speed of light at their outer tips. The next breath rotates the tetrahedrons in the opposite directions. As you exhale say 'thirty four, twenty one.' The tetrahedron of your mind spins at thirty four times the speed of light. The tetrahedron of your emotions spins right twenty one times the speed of light.

As they continue to rotate, with the next breath you are filled with unconditional love. Reduce the spinning speed of every atom and every electron to 9 tenths the speed of light and you are filled with unconditional love.

The next breath is easy, normal breathing. It takes you from the third to the fourth dimension. Ask yourself now to take you to the forth dimension and your higher self lets you disappear now from this world and reappear in the forth dimensional world.

Resources

For a pre-recorded version of the Shelley Stockwell's Mer Ka Ba with background toning music by Wayne Perry, see order forms at the back of the book.

For more information on holotropic breathing, Heighten Your Holos by Dr. Alex Lessin, send $15 to Creativity Unlimited Press, 30819 Casilina, Rancho Palos Verdes, Ca. 90275

Gods and Myths of Ancient Egypt by Robert Armour 1993 American University in Cairo

Nothing in this Book Is True, But It's Exactly How Things Are Frog Limited, Berkeley California, 1994 Bob Frissell

Graduating Hypnotist Deanne Whitley Receives Certificate From Instructor Shelley Stockwell

Photo by Jon Nicholas

Chapter 20

The Business Of Hypnosis

Suggestions For Hypnotists

Take a deep breath and put yourself in center, into relaxation, the way you do so well. Good. When you are ready begin reading these suggestions:

I easily attract clients who are light bearers who help heal our planet. I touch other's lives so they can experience love, joy, peace and physical, spiritual and mental well being. I am joyous, serene and energized. I am doing and being my highest work.

I see beauty in each client. I trust their innate ability to discover their own perfect solutions. I always succeed as a hypnotist. If one induction gets weak results, I choose one that gets stronger ones.

My work is my play. My play is my work. I am a terrific hypnotist: always learning better and better ways to bring my client and myself positive results.

Building A Practice

Creating and running a successful hypnosis practice is easy and fun.

Success starts with wrapping your mind around these ideas easy, fun and action. In other words, commit to do whatever it takes to make your hypnosis practice happen. This determination, coupled with professionalism, public relations and marketing, make you a winner.

Business Cards

Have business cards made with your name and the title you want people to identify you with; "Hypnotist", "Master Hypnotist," "Hypnotherapist", "Hypnocounselor," "Certified Clinical Hypnotherapist," "Past Life Regression Therapist," "Sports Hypnosis." Make sure the words are big and that the phone number is huge. Generously give your business cards away. They are your best marketing tools. Remember that everyone you meet is a potential client. Let folks know what you do and hand them a card.

Your picture on the card is a nice touch. Make sure that your picture is positive and reinforces your message. I saw one photo card with the caption "Hypnosis and Hope" with the saddest face beneath. It did not evoke confidence. If you look depressed, stressed or obnoxious, get a better photo taken. If your specialty is weight reduction, a chubby face will only make people laugh.

Hypnotist Jerry Valley has created a card that really gets attention:

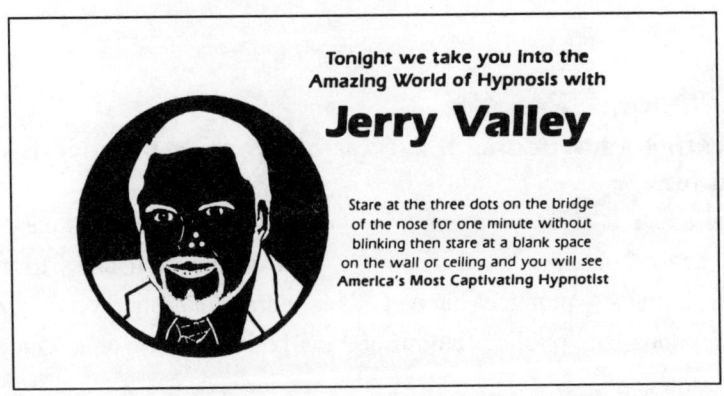

Business Brochures

A simple one-page flier is a great advertising tool. I like to use an 1/2" x 11" sheet written on both sides and then folded in thirds. It looks professional. Use a large font on the part that shows that says something like.

"HYPNOSIS WILL CHANGE YOUR LIFE,"
"FOCUS ON SOLUTIONS,"
"HYPNOSIS GETS RESULTS," or
"MAKE YOUR MIND WORK FOR YOU."

The inside of the brochure should sell the benefits of hypnosis and answer the question "What's in it for me?"

Build Confidence
Eliminate Undesirable Behaviors
Reduce Stress
Improve Relationships
Raise Self Esteem
Perform Better At School, On Stage, At Work, In Sports
Lose Weight
Quit Smoking
Improve Medical Conditions

Of course, all advertising needs your name and phone number prominently displayed. Some of my students like a brochure with a rolodex tear out. You can order the paper stock for this and many brochures from paper mail order companies.

Distribute fliers and business cards on library bulletin boards and all local stores or markets. Mail fliers to gyms or chiropractors or doctors who might refer you. Give them to friends to post at work.

Target your market with a letter and include your brochure. Inform your client about your professional qualifications. Your brochure must answer "Who?" "What?" "Where?" "When"; "What's in it for me?" It must let them know that you have invested the additional time and energy necessary to teach an important seminar.

A corporate hypnosis brochure would be formatted something like this:

Front flap: what?
Inner flap #1 and 2: sell yourself and details
Back flap: Mailing info and interesting caption

Front flap tells what you are offering:

On Sight Stress Management Training

A Highly Effective

STRESS MANAGEMENT TRAINING

*That Gets Results
with*
SHELLEY STOCKWELL

A Two-Day Intensive Training For
Employees, Managers and Executives

YOU WILL LEARN

*How to effectively manage stress
*Ten simple tools that instantly
 unload overload
*How to cope with difficult people
*How to be centered and cool when
 the heat's on
*To replace self-defeat with positive
 motivation

YOU WILL RECEIVE

*Dr. Stockwell's powerful cassette
 Peace & Calm
*Certification of Completion that
can be used for continuing education credit

*"I'll show you how to keep your focus even
when those around you are losing theirs. The
positive results of these hands on tools
will startle and delight you."*

Inner flap #1

Hello, my name is Shelley Lessin Stockwell and I am a Certified Stress Management Consultant. I am also a Certified Clinical Hypnotherapist, a Hypnotherapy Instructor for the National Guild of Hypnotists, Director of The Creativity Learning Institute and Founder of the Global Creativity Foundation. As a professional seminar leader, and an active member of Toastmasters International and the National Speakers Association, I've conducted workshops in the United States, Japan, Australia, New Zealand, Indonesia and Egypt. My cable television program "The Shelley Show" received the coveted Angel Award of Excellence. My sixteen motivational hypnosis tapes are popular here and abroad.

Because I make sure that my course is exciting, educational and entertaining, I have been blessed to teach and interface with thousands who say:
THIS SYSTEM WORKS!
I think you'll agree. The stress management skills you'll learn are so successful, you'll forget that tension was ever an issue.

My books include;

The Stockwell System For Success

Hypnosis, Smile On Your Face, & Money In Your Pocket

Time Travel, Do-It-Yourself Past Life Journey Handbook

Inner flap #2

Fact:	1/3 of Americans say they experience "great stress" several days a week.
Fact:	Eighty percent of on-the-job accidents are stress related.
Fact:	Seventy-eight percent of employed Americans surveyed gave their job as the major source of their stress.
Fact:	The fiscal consequences of job stress, results in losses of more than 200 billion dollars annually. This amount is higher than the after-tax profits of all Fortune 500 companies combined.

As a business manager, owner or corporate officer, you don't need surveys to tell you that tension related problems directly correlate to workers compensation claims, low employee morale and poor performance. You, of course, are keenly aware of the big bite stress takes out of your bottom line profits and you yourself may be "stressed out" trying to do something about it.

That's where Shelley Stockwell Seminars come in. Our Stress Management Training generates tangible results. One company says that their workers' compensation costs dropped 64% after taking this program. Because our program is based on the unique concepts of harnessing the power of the mind, results are always far beyond the temporary motivational pep talks of other seminars.

This is your opportunity to cash in on the results of this remarkable training while providing a tremendous service to yourself and others.

CALL TODAY
(310) 541-4844

Telephone Technique

Hypnosis begins from the initial "Hello, how can I help you" telephone conversation to your "good-bye" at the door after your session. While on the phone establish rapport by saying, "Yes" and "I understand," as much as possible. Give your caller time to share a bit with you about how they feel and think, but avoid doing free phone counseling. Your purpose is to get them into your office so that you can help them with hypnosis and teach them tools so that they can help themselves.

Set a definite time and place for your meeting and write down their full name and phone number. Some like to ask, "How did you hear about me?" so that they can verify which advertisement worked the best or thank and acknowledge the one who referred you to them. Before saying "good bye," give them directions to your office.

I tell my clients what my fees are on the phone. What you set as your fee is up to you. A hypnosis session is usually somewhere from $65 to $200 an hour. If you are a medical doctor practicing hypnosis, of course, your fees will be higher. I usually say something like; "I charge a hundred dollars an hour and your first session will be an hour to an hour and a half so it will be either one hundred or one hundred and fifty dollars depending on how long we need to go."

Close with "Great! I'm looking forward to meeting you tomorrow at 4:00 here in my office."

Some hypnotists call their clients the day before the scheduled appointment as a reminder saying "Hello (their name) I'm looking forward to your session tomorrow at 4:00."

Publicity

A little effort and people flock to your office. Ads in a local newspaper, newsletter, shopping guide or new age magazine get results. Statistically, people call after they see an ad more than 3 times. So, if you advertise, do it continuously for several weeks. You can spend as little as $50 a month in the right periodical. And you'll get that back in short order.

If price allows, include a good picture of yourself; a nice face draws the eye. Keep your ad simple; if it's cluttered many won't read it. If you're using a display ad, have it designed with an exciting bold border and a big headline like: "HYPNOSIS WORKS"

Free! Free! Free!

Notice how that word affects your reading right now. A free consultation, or a discount coupon works well for some. An expiration date for one month can be a call to action that puts your coupon on a refrigerator magnet, purse or list.

There are many golden opportunities for free advertising, too. That's right, I said free. Write a news release. A simple article neatly typed on one or two sheets of paper with your name and address and "For more information call:_____." and "NEWS RELEASE," written across the top. Include a good photo of yourself and mail this to all the papers in your area the same day.

The first paragraph of a news release should answer the question who, what, where, when and how. The rest of the paragraphs can talk about hypnosis and blow your own horn. Remember, folks want to know about you, so give them information. Always include address and phone number and a photo of yourself. Inviting the public to an event is also a good plan. Most newspapers will print a well-written release word for word.

NEWS RELEASE (date):
FOR IMMEDIATE RELEASE:
For More Information Call (310) 541-4844

Local Hypnotist To Open New Office

On Friday, October 6th at 4 pm, local hypnotherapist, Shelley Stockwell, will open her new office on Casilina Drive in Rancho Palos Verdes. Stockwell, who specializes in pain management, senior citizens and wellness using the power of the mind, has been in practice for twenty two years.

"I decided to move to Palos Verdes so that I could be closer to local hospital and senior citizen communities." Stockwell says...

If you also plan on advertising in that paper, tell the editor that you'd like to advertise your new business and maybe they can help with a story about you. Let him know that you're sending a news release or would be happy to write an article or a weekly column about how hypnosis works or a current noteworthy accomplishment. Say that they can run your article if they mention you and your phone and location in the article. If you spark an editor's interest many will send a reporter and photographer and do a story about you.

NEWS ARTICLE
For More Information
Call (310)541-4844

Famous Hypnotist Trains Others

Hypnotherapist and author Shelley Lessin Stockwell will offer certification courses in hypnosis. Presented at the Creativity Learning Center, in Rancho Palos Verdes, California. "Each fifty hour segment teaches a different aspect and application for harnessing the power of the mind," Stockwell says. "You'll learn how to use hypnosis as a powerful tool for yourself, your family and for clients."

The first fifty hours answers the most commonly asked questions about how the brain and mind work, as students explore induction, deepening and programming techniques, and how to run a successful hypnosis practice. Advanced classes offer hands on experience for using hypnosis for success, test taking, habit breaking, trauma recovery, pain management, past life regression and honing sports skills and psychic abilities.

An expert on transpersonal hypnosis, Stockwell says that everyone can be hypnotized. "It's not a magic act but sometimes the results seem magical..."

Submit articles about interesting case studies (change the names and details to maintain confidentiality) to professional journals and magazines. Then you can collect them and maybe write a book. With a book, you are selling a product (your book) as well as a service (your sessions and seminars). Speaking of seminars, that's where you'll sell a lot of your books.

Media Blitz

Calls to local TV and radio shows are also terrific. Many talk shows need interesting topics and guests. Be one of them. When talking to the producers of shows, be confident. Hypnotize them to have you on their show. When it's time to appear, type up an introduction, a biography and include a photograph and business card. You might even write a list of questions that you can answer.

Once you appear on one show others will call you. I appeared three times on NBC's The Other Side when a producer from the Phil Donahue Show put me on their program. National shows pay for your transportation, hotel accommodations and meals and often pay a small amount for your appearance. If you belong to the union, your pay will be in the thousands of dollars. But it costs that much to join the union. If you are invited to go on any show, ask how much they pay. It never hurts to ask. Of course, for that much publicity, you might want to do it for free.

Speeches and Public Demonstrations

If you get a chance, tell everyone about your career. Stand up and announce it at church or in club meetings. Some of my students like to hype their career in networking or marketing clubs. Here you're expected to stand up and advertise for business.

Or arrange to give a ten-minute demonstration or a mini class. The more you "go public," the more business you'll attract. If public speaking is a challenge for you, join Toastmasters, Platform or the National Speakers Association. Or, sign up for a speech class at the local college. Or, make yourself a self hypnosis tape to build your confidence.

If you decide to give a talk follow this simple formula:

➡ Tell everyone what you're going to tell them.
"In the next 10 minutes I'm going tell you about hypnosis, what it is and how you can use it as a powerful tool for your self, your family and your friends. When I'm done you can ask me questions."

➡ Tell them. Make three points and briefly underscore each one. Be interested in your message and your audience will be interested too. If you use visual aids make them BIG

➡ Tell them what you told them.
"So now you've learned what hypnosis is and you now have a simple tool that you can use every morning to listen to your inner wisdom.. Any questions?"

If you have time to plan your speech, take a moment and think about what you want to tell them. Put your statement of purpose into one or two sentences.

If it interests you, it's sure to interest the audience. You don't have to have an earth-shattering theme. Talk about the things that interest you. A chat about hypnosis, like you might have with your mate at breakfast, can make a fascinating talk.

After you've written down your central theme, write down an outline. This roughs out the structure of your talk and clarifies for yourself where you're going. If you take a trip it's a good idea to look at the map first:

✓Introduction
✓Two or three basic points
✓Any related "stories" that go with these points
✓Conclusion

Now you can decide what points you want to cover under each category.

Rehearsals are a great way to hear yourself. It helps you to be sensitive to your audience. Use a tape recorder and capture your speech on cassette so you can decide if your talk is going where you want to go. Notice if the points you make are well balanced and in a sequence. Do they make sense to someone who knows nothing about hypnosis? If you're talking to a group of hypnotists, does your talk offer new insights and in a logical progression?

Be sensitive to time frames. You'll need to know how much time you'll be given for this talk. Stay within the time limit.

When it's time to give your talk, make sure you arrive early to check out the sound system and room logistics. The best speech in the world will be meaningless if no one can hear you or your volume hurts the ears.

Public Events

Group sessions can be very rewarding. Schools, church, hospital or bank meeting rooms, hotel conference rooms, libraries or a volunteered living room can be excellent meeting spots. If you must pay for the facility always ask for a discounted rate. A simple "Is that your best price?" always brings down the price. If the price is still too much say "Thank you but that's too much, I guess I'll go _____ (your competitor down the road)." This often drops the fee. If not, down the road you go.

An exciting way to build your practice is to stage a public event like "The Great American Smoke Out." Or a "Lose Weight Clinic." Often you can get support from large organizations like the American Cancer Society or The American Heart Association. In the next chapter Hypnotherapist Charlene Ackerman offers pointers on how to set up such an events. And, I give you The Stockwell System of smoking cessation.

Hypnotherapy Settings

Make your environment conducive for relaxation: Remember that everything is hypnosis and the subject is taking on suggestions from the first conversation on the phone to what they experience when they walk into your office. What you say, how you look, the temperature, color, sound, light and smell of your space all have a profound influence on your success. Create a physical environment that is warm, nourishing, friendly and clean. You're part of the environment too. Make sure that you also are warm, nourishing, and friendly and clean. Let people feel safe and trusting here.

Certifiably Good
It helps to put your diplomas and certificates on the wall. Any art should be positive, soothing and uplifting. It's lovely to have a book of "thank you" notes from clients that you have helped for other clients to read. Remember that much of success is built on expectation and belief.

Temperature
Make your room slightly on the warm end (73°-75° Fahrenheit)

Colors
Soft colors evoke relaxation, Studies show that gray is the best color for clear thinking and productivity. Blues and greens work well too. Screaming yellow and black (the color of bumblebees), reds and oranges tend to signal danger and elicit the adrenal glands to be on guard for fight, fright, flight or excite. Avoid these or use only in moderation. Fresh flowers or plants are a nice touch. But keep them healthy, a vital plant makes a healthy statement a dead plant doesn't.

Style
Keep the style simple and gender balanced. If your decor is overwhelmingly fuufuu feminine or macho male it can distract.

Light
Soft lighting is lovely. Full spectrum light bulbs make people feel more secure and eliminates depression. Natural sunlight is terrific for this too. Reduced lighting evokes trance. Dimmer switches are good.

Fan-to-see
It's fun to discover new ways of trancing. One day I wasteaching an hypnosis training in my office and the sun shining throughthe skylight was thrown askew by my ceiling fan. The strobe light effect was phenomenal. Now when the sun is right I position myself, or my client, with eyes closed below my sun strobe. It puts me away."

Look The Part

Look presentable. Dress for success. It is a mark of respect that you make an effort to be well groomed for your client. Blue and soft colors sooth the eye. To establish rapport you can dress similarly to your clients or, better yet, a little better than your client. Look like a true business professional. Avoid extreme jewelry and makeup so that you come across as a warm, well adjusted helper.

Comfort Is Calming

Chairs are important. I use simple director's chairs for first visits and initial interviews. Many use recliners or futons. A comfy sofa can be very inviting. A lot of my work is done on the floor. My clients soon learn to take off their shoes at the door and make a nest in my pillow pile. If you use pillows make sure you have slipcovers that can be taken off and washed. You won't believe the tearstains! Speaking of tears, always have tissue handy. You'll need it!

Silence Is Golden

If you have a quiet place in your home to begin your practice, it's a good way to start. The space needs to be private, without invasion from pets or other family members. Telephones and telephone answering devices can be very distracting and even unsettling. Turn off ringers and see if you can find an answering machine that doesn't click loudly (mine drives me nuts). Soft music, a metronome, or a gentle whirring fan can enhance the hypnotic mood.

Sweet Smell Of Success

Since sensory perception is heightened during trance, remember to smell good. Avoid eating in your office. Incense, though mind altering, can be off setting to a heightened sense of smell.

When stimulated by aroma the olfactory membrane in the nose notifies the olfactory nerve in the limbic brain where emotions live. Specific aromas stimulate specific primal emotions, relaxation, memory, hunger, thirst, and sexuality. Shamans have used incense and sage. Priests fill the air with smoke. All to alter consciousness. In modern Japan, hundreds of companies emit lemon odor into the air to influence their employees' work habits. They say it increases productivity by 54%. Unpleasant odors like trash, garlic, cigarette smoke, some strong perfumes or bad breath can get in the way of a successful session.

Your clients skin, too, has the ability to "smell." That's why some hypnotists use essential oils to induce trance. Oils pass their "aroma" into the blood where they affect body response. Everyone's odors and odor receptors are as unique as fingerprints.

The Lovely Scent Willy Sent Millicent
Essential Oils and Aroma therapy

"You need to take aroma therapy with a grain of salt,"

-Environmental Psychologist, Susan Knasko

Environmental fragrance researchers and aroma therapists put in their two cents about the sense of scents:

Antidepressant: Lavender, sage, bergamot, neroli, orange, geranium

Aphrodisiac: Clove, sandalwood, rose, jasmine

Aphrodisiac for men: Hot baked cinnamon buns

Banish appetite: Banana, green apple, peppermint

Burn calories: Strawberry

Energy: Juniper, peppermint

Euphoria: Grapefruit and orange

Combat fear: Sage

Fight aggression: Cedar

Focused/alert/vital: Lemon, rosemary, eucalyptus, peppermint, floral

Heal: Pine

Love: Myrtle

Memory: Geranium, lavender, eucalyptus

Refresh: Lime, peppermint, basil, clove

Relax: Chamomile, lavender, nutmeg, vanilla

Relieve anxiety: Juniper

Relieve claustrophobia: Cucumber

Spiritual Awakening: Lotus oil (available through Creativity Unlimited Press)

Pheromones

Smell has a role in attraction, they say,
but it isn't the Brut or the Listerine spray.
It isn't ma's bacon or strawberry pop or
incense or love balms I've found
It's the fragrance undefined
as you waft through my mind
that keeps me just sniffin' around.

— Shelley Stockwell

Pheromones are the chemicals from odors that "turn us on." This sexy sense develops around puberty. Pheromones may be responsible for "love at first sight." Scientists have actually identified pheromones only in animals; proof of their existence in humans hasn't been proven it yet. Perhaps that's why the Balinese people "kiss" by sniffing each cheek.

Cleopatra understood the power of aroma, seduced Mark Anthony in knee-deep rose petals, as they sipped pearls dissolved in vinegar. Her make-up was scented with cedar wood. She even had the sails of her barge soaked with perfume so that the breezes would let folks know that she was on her way.

Mummies were cedar-scented, too, for eternal bliss. Ancient Egyptians wafted Sandalwood to the gods to turn them on. Ylang-ylang turns Malaysians and Filipinos on.

An Office Makes You Official

If you don't have money to open your own office, there are psychologists, message therapists, acupuncturists, chiropractors And other hypnotists who will give you room in theirs. You can pay them a percentage of what you take in. And, they often give you referrals.

If you're renting a separate office, consider a building complex or an office suite that houses doctors, psychologists, and psychiatrists. Have An "office warming" and invite your neighboring professionals. Offer them the opportunity to come and watch your sessions or have a session themself. Referrals are nice.

Remember that in any business it's location, location, location. Is this a convenient place for your clients to get to?

Fees

Hypnotists charge anywhere from $25 per hour to $250 the average price in the United States at this time is about $75 an hour. Charge what is consistent with other professionals in your town. Some offer sliding scales based upon the client's income. If you're not accustomed to asking for money, you'll need to get over it. People will be thrilled to pay you for your services. Remember, people value more what they pay for. By not charging, you may be doing them a serious disservice!

When a person calls to ask for an appointment tell them on the phone how much it will cost: "My charge is $100 an hour and your first session might go about an hour and half so expect that your first session will be $150."

Some hypnotherapists charge in blocks of time. "If you pay for five sessions now I'll be able to give you a discount. Usually five sessions, based on $80 an hour, are $400 so if you want to pay for the five sessions now the fee is $375." Before you offer long term discounts, make sure that they realistically require them. Weight loss and addictions often require repetitive visits. Remember that your goal is to get your client in and out as soon as possible so that they can successfully live their life with the tools and insights they've received from their visits. A great deal of work can be done in one hour and the results will astound even you.

If you choose to conduct corporate seminars, your fees will be much greater. The average charge for a three-hour seminar, presented to a group of less than fifty people, is around $900 to $2,500!

A four session Weight Loss, Quit Smoking, Sports Clinic and Prepared Child Birth Seminar goes for anywhere from $100 to $400 and usually requires a pre registration fee of $100.

Sample Seminar Contract:

Shelley Stockwell Seminars
Creativity Unlimited Learning Institute
Quit Smoking Program
30819 Casilina,
Rancho Palos Verdes, CA 90275
(310) 541-4844

(Name) agrees to pay ($ amount of fee) for the QUIT SMOKING™ (WEIGHT RELEASE™) PROGRAM that begins on (Date seminar begins). To satisfy the financial arrangement between myself and Shelley Stockwell Seminars I will pay the pre registration fee of one hundred dollars ($100) and the balance of two hundred and fifty ($250) at the first class session. I am aware that the one hundred dollar ($100) deposit is non-refundable.

Pre-registration fee $100
Balance first class date $250
Total class fee $350

Amount of this payment $____

NAME_____
ADDRESS_____
CITY_____ STATE____ ZIP CODE_____
PHONE NUMBER (home)_____ (work)_____
FAX_____ E-MAIL_____

Write on the receipt that this fee is non-refundable. Payment schedules can be arranged for those who want to pay a little each month. This go now pay later approach can be risky business. It is always better to have the money up front. If you have credit card capability that's a better way to go.

Insurance

There is a move afoot by a few small insurance companies to cover hypnosis. Some policies will pay for your council if doctor referred. I recommend that you receive payment at the time of your session and then, by all means, fill out the forms for your client if requested. Insurance is often made available through hypnosis organizations.

Debts To Society

Be sensitive to the laws for home or other based businesses in your community. Most cities' want you to have a business license so that they can take their slice of your pie. Find out what your city requires first and then decide. Some folks find it beneficial to get certified as a minister in order to offer hypnosis as "pastoral counseling." Give yourself a title that satisfies the requirements of your state and community; "hypnocounselor," "hypnotist," "Success Trainer," "Life Coach" or "Meditation Instructor." Do whatever your local laws require for you to help local citizens. They need you. Don't let legislation get in the way, work with it.

Teaching Hypnosis

Another rewarding career in hypnosis is to become an instructor. When you are confident that you know the ins and outs of induction, deepening techniques, and suggestion, you may discover that passing on your wisdom is fun and profitable.

Training other hypnotists in advanced techniques can be profitable. I recently received a flier to learn stage hypnosis training. A four-day class costs $577 if paid in advance or $890 at the door!

Here's a description of the certification courses that I offer at the Creativity Learning Institute in California. I also teach a shortened version this course at local colleges:

Entertainment

Entertainment never goes out of style, nor does the publics curiosity about hypnosis. Stage hypnosis is popular, profitable and lots of fun; you're the star at meetings, conventions, trade shows, night clubs, NACA colleges, proms, grad nights, parties or top-notch casinos.

Imagine yourself walking into a corporation or college building in

Now You Can BECOME A HYPNOTIST.

Add Power To Your Practice And Your Life

Learn how to hypnotize yourself and others instantly. Hypnosis is as easy as breathing: Inspiring healing and releasing limiting attitudes and patterns. All classes taught by Shelley Lessin Stockwell, Transpersonal Hypnotherapist and author of the book Hypnosis: Smile On Your Face and Money In Your Pocket.

Hypnosis Certification Courses

Certification programs are structured for anyone who is interested in harnessing the power of the mind for themselves, their family, their friends, to enhance other professions or as a career path. Therapists, counselors, hypnotherapists, health workers, dentists, doctors and those considering hypnosis as a career. They contain powerful, practical, up-to-the-minute skills and information.

Professional Hypnotherapist Training provides direct supervised instruction in the practice of hypnosis and self-hypnosis. You'll learn simple tools that bring about positive change. Many say that each five-day certification course not only gave an opportunity to practice hypnosis but truly transformed their life. Maybe that's because hypnosis reframes imprints that hold us back and limit joy into proactive and uplifting messages. Additionally, hypnosis allows us to tap the super-conscious part of ourselves that knows exactly what we need to do to have what we want.

Who Should Attend?

All certification programs are structured for counselors, therapists, health professionals, hypnotherapists, and personal researchers. Each transformational training gives tools to start or advance your own hypnosis practice.

Educators receive powerful motivational tools for students
Parents learn to motivate their children
Everyone learns to be pro-active in life
Managers empower and motivate
Advertisers who want to sell and call buyers to action
Professionals who can use hypnosis in their work: psycho-therapists, ministers, healers, dentists, doctors, hypnotists and other health practitioners.

Professional Hypnotism Training

Fundamentals of Hypnosis Course A fifty hour course in the fundamentals of hypnosis teaches what hypnosis is and how you can use it for yourself, family, friends, and as a professional hypnotist. This includes how to run a successful hypnosis practice, induction techniques (and the famous thirty second zap), how to deepen trance, replace limits, give suggestions and move ahead.

Master Hypnosis Course Explore the laws of the brain and mind. Course offers specialized techniques that include power learning, dealing with addictions, compulsions and phobias, wellness work, sports techniques, how to work with children and NLP (Neurolinguistic programming).

Hypnotherapy Training The latest of advanced techniques explores rebirthing, reparenting, and past life regression.

Transpersonal Hypnotherapy Training Explore shamanism, trance channeling, soul retrieval and higher self-communication.

What Will I Learn?
The fundamentals of hypnosis
What hypnosis is and how to use it
How to run a successful hypnosis practice.
Traditional, rapid, and non-verbal inductions
Suggestions and deepening techniques.

What Is Different About Our Training?
We teach you to be a complete hypnotherapist. From the nuts and bolts of inductions, deepening and suggestions to crisis intervention, healing work and spiritual emergencies. How to work with athletes, children, and the elderly. How to bust addictions, compulsions, phobias and replace them with emotional and habitual well being.

How Much Does It Cost?
Certificate and cassette are included in each powerful experiential seminar. The fifty-hour class includes workbook and cassette tape and costs $500. Graduates will be allowed to join the National Guild of Hypnotists as a professional hypnotist as Shelley Stockwell is qualified as a Guild Instructor. Enrollment for each class is limited. To register for our upcoming classes, call the Creativity Learning Institute.

541-4844

Illustration Compliments of Sandi Madearis

your business attire and an hour and a half later you walk out $500 to $1000 richer! Of course, that amount doesn't include the money you receive from your "back of the room" sales (books and tapes and even a video of the show itself for the participants). And, as a bonus, you'll receive referrals for future gigs and yield new clients for your clinical hypnosis practice. Stage hypnosis is a wonderful and profitable thing to add to your repertoire.

The challenge in performing hypnosis for an audience is that you are performing two shows at the same time: one for the subjects and one to entertain the audience.

For the subjects, the trance state is divided into five parts:

Blessing
Getting Subjects
Induction
Entertaining Suggestions
Return to regular awareness

Blessing

Your blessing can sound more like an introduction or invocation. Remember that you are beginning the show by your introduction and the first words that you utter. A powerful way to get things moving is to tell the audience (and, of course, your soon to be subjects among them) what is going to happen here tonight, i.e. "Tonight you are going to witness and experience the remarkable power of hypnosis." Or, "I am about to show you some very scientific demonstrations of the power of suggestion." And you continue; "As you listen carefully, you will learn how you can use the power of your mind to focus on exactly what you want for yourself. For those of you who have the opportunity to come up on this stage you will learn simple tools that will permanently enhance your life and you'll have a terrific time doing it!"

Getting Subjects

We're assuming now that this show takes place with subjects on the stage in front of an audience. I often just hypnotize the entire audience at the same time. Here are some enticing ways to get the most active and willing ones up front that the show has pizzazz.

Psychic Volunteers And Telepathy
(adopted from Hypnotherapist, Ernie Tecklemiere, Thank you Ernie for this great idea.)

How many of you have known something was gong to happen before it did? Maybe you've had a dream that came true? Or you knew someone was going to call before the phone rang? What I'm trying to discover is, how many of you are psychic? I'd like to know because I'd like three volunteers with psychic abilities to come up here and help me demonstrate the power of telepathy and the mind. (after volunteers are seated, continue)

You're about to experience hypnosis using the telepathic power of your mind. Wait 'til you see how easy this is.

going to imagine a neon sign. Like a bright sign you might see in front of a store. This sign is flashing out 'Relax. Relax. Relax.' in your favorite colors. You'll vividly picture and imagine this sign. As soon as you allow your mind to relax you will imagine or see it too.

When that sign is projected on the screen of your mind, it will come as light, sound, energy or color. You'll find yourself deeply relaxing and your head will just droop right down. Of course you can resist if you choose to or you can just go right into deeper and deeper into a beautiful state of hypnotic relaxation.

In a moment, I'm going to go to the back of the room and will mentally transmit and concentrate on the word "sleep." Because my volunteers here on the stage are very psychic they will instantly fall asleep.

Arm Levitation Volunteers
Everybody stand up and put both hands forward. Turn your right hand up and slightly curl your fingers. Good. Now turn your left hand down and slightly curl your fingers. Now close your eyes.

Imagine that I am putting a bucket filled with 20 pounds of glowing phosphorescent sand in your left hand. This makes your arm and hand grow heavier and heavier, heavier, heavier, so heavy. Let the weight of it start to pull your arm down, down, down. Good.

Imagine also that I gently tie a balloon, your favorite color and size, on to your right wrist. The balloon is filled with helium. Your arm and hand become lighter and lighter and begin to lift and rise. Lifting, rising and floating. (Repeat these suggestions until you notice results and then say)

Freeze. Now open your eyes and look around the room and evaluate the suggestible response in this room at this moment. Some people may seem more responsive to these suggestions than others because some were enjoying the relaxation so much they just didn't want to budge.

Chair Demonstration
Those of you with any back problems don't do this exercise.
Stand with your legs touching your chair. Close your eyes. Feel a magnet on your back. Let that magnet pull you back against the chair. As I count from five to one you become aware of this strong pull. You'll notice it immediately. By the time I reach one, you will feel yourself being drawn to your chair almost as if you were pushed into it. Five, the magnetic attraction is strong; pulling you. You fall into your chair. Four. Back, back into the chair. Three. Two. And One into the chair you go.

Every time you experience a hypnotic trance, you go deeper than you've ever gone before.

Induction
The induction opens the door to the trance state. There are as many ways to induce a trance as there are people in the universe. Choose one of your favorites and then make your show entertaining and educational.

The Show
"You are watching the funniest movie you've ever seen."
"A huge helium balloon is pulling your arm up, up, up, lifting you up off your chair, up, up, up."

The Stockwell System

"It's the hottest day of your life. Oops a blizzard just rolled into town."
"You're seven years old and you and your best friends sitting next to you have a case of the sillies."
"You can speak moon talk. And this guy here next to you will translate for us."

References and Resources

PROFESSIONAL HYPNOTHERAPY TRAINING
Stockwell, Shelley, c/o Creativity Unlimited
Learning Institute Casilina, Rancho Palos Verdes,
CA 90275 (310) 541-4844
HOW TO CONDUCT A SMOKE OUT
Ackerman, Charlene, C.Ht. A.C.I.
S. Main Street #24 Janesville, WI 53545
phone (608) 757-0716 fax (608) 757-0945
THE COMPLETE ENCYCLOPEDIA OF STAGE HYPNOSIS,
McGill, Ormond.
A must-read resource for anyone who wants to do a great job in front of an audience. 1997, Anglo-American Book Company, London England (Available from Creativity Unlimited Press, See address at the back of this book.

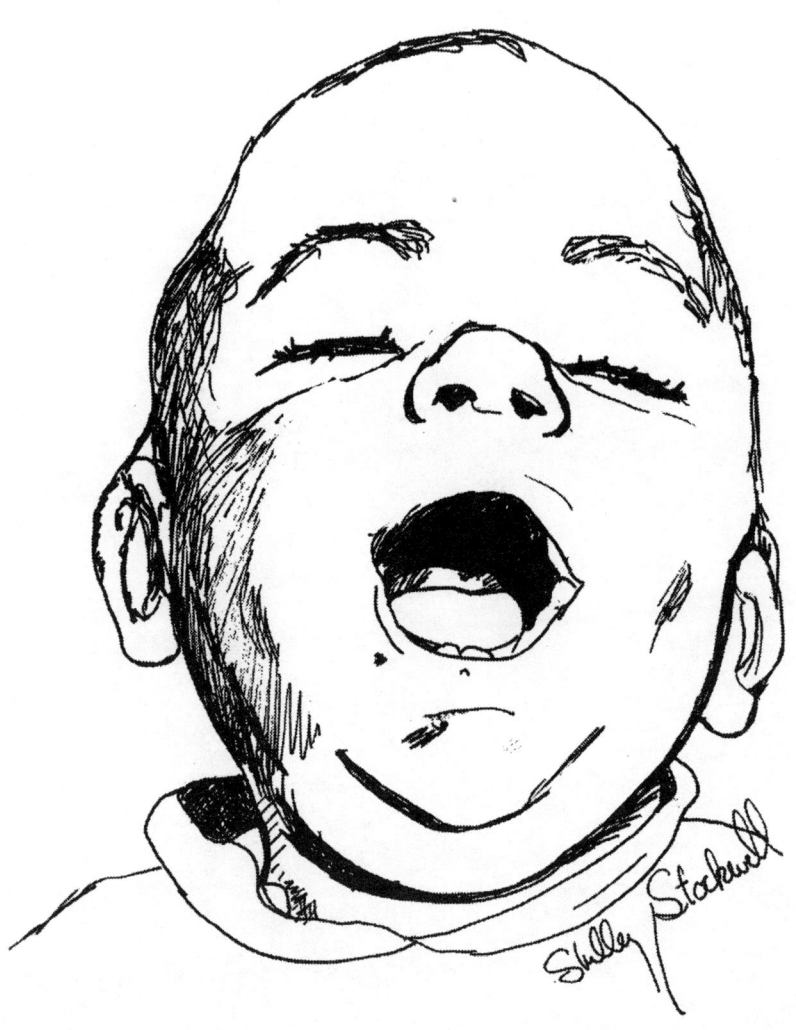

Illustration by Shelley Stockwell

CHAPTER 21

Quit Smoking

"I smoked a pack and a half a day for 25 years, and thanks to Shelley, I don't smoke any more, except after sex. And then, I'm not sure, 'cause I've never looked."
— Jon Nicholas

How To Run A "Quit Smoking" Seminar
Suggestions For Quitting
Busting the "Smoking" Myths

How To Put On a Quit Smoking Clinic
By Charlene Ackerman, Hypnotherapist

We Can Make A Difference!
In the Great American Smoke Out, you donate your time to those who donate to a good cause. And you create clients who have a good feeling about you and your integrity.

If you have spoken before groups and given demonstrations on hypnosis, this will come easily to you. You'll never have a more receptive and eager audience. If you have not given a presentation before, this will be perhaps the best way possible to "Break In." You have before you a group of people who share a common interest, the desire to quit smoking. They are not going to feel the least bit intimidated. They are participating in a fund-raiser and see you as a catalyst. You represent someone that can help them with their addiction and at the same time feel good about making a donation to The American Cancer Society (ACS).

Make it clear to the participants that the entire sum of money raised will be sent to the ACS. There are no costs deducted from the total. Let everyone know that hypnotists throughout the country collect money as a joint effort.

One year, 3 people came together from the same office and all three quit. The next few weeks three more from the same office came to see me privately. I have had people come back months later that had quit for a long period of time and had gone back to their habit. They knew that the hypnosis worked. These clients will come in for other areas of improvement as well. Each is a wonderful source of referrals, better than any single advertising effort I've ever done.

Where Will I Conduct It?

You can use hotels, motels, office buildings with training facilities, bookstores, libraries, industries, clubs and organizations, churches. If you are a member of a Medical facility this would be ideal. (Everyone I have contacted requesting a room has been completely cooperative. Even hotels & motels quickly agree to furnish a room free of charge. Don't be afraid to ask.)

When doing a group event, I often suggest that guests bring a pillow and blanket so that they can lie down. If that's the case does the room lend itself to floor nesting?

Advertising Tips

Contact your local newspaper to donate an ad. The best results I have experienced however, have been an announcement in the "Health & Medical News" and "Calendar of Events" in the local newspaper. Check with "Free" shoppers in your area. These are excellent sources for advertising your Clinic and every one of them that I have contacted cooperated. Contact clubs and churches you visit. Ask that they mention it in their bulletins.

Contact local cable television and radio stations in your area. Request an interview and/or advertising. The cable stations' Calendar of Events was very effective.

Ask your local newspaper to do an article on your "Free Clinic" to print in conjunction with the Great American Smoke Out. The first year I received over a half page in the newspapers; colored pictures and all. If you have asked for reservations in your advertising, it will give you a good idea as to how many to expect.

Make up flyers to post anywhere and everywhere you can think of. Ask friends to place then where they work. Post them in malls, businesses, grocery stores, etc. This was the only expense that I incurred.

About one month in advance, send fliers to local physicians in your area. You can find their names in the Yellow Pages. This gives the doctor a chance to help their patients and it also lets them become aware of you and your work for future referrals.

Getting Ready For The Event

Several hypnotists have had someone from the ACS be there to collect the money. This is an excellent idea, and then everyone knows exactly where the money is going. Most of the people will write a check, but for the cash that is collected, get a certified check made out to the ACS. Have receipts for their donation. (This is a tax deduction for them.) You need someone to assist you with this.

Hand out "$20 Off Coupons" to those who donate. This increases the percent of donations made. I make it clear to the participants that the entire sum of money raised will be sent to the American Cancer Society. There are no costs deducted from the total. Most of the people will write a check but for the cash that is collected, get a certified check made out to the ACS. Again let them know with a sign or verbally that the money was collected as a joint effort by hypnotists throughout the USA.

Be sure to have plenty of brochures to hand out. Let them know you are available for follow-up or reinforcement sessions if they feel it is necessary. I usually charge more for the first private session I have with a client due to the time needed to explain hypnosis and gain rapport. Therefore, I let them know I will see them at the lesser fee charged for the first second session.

Some of you may have tapes for sale. May I suggest if you do sell tapes, to donate the profit or at least a percentage to ACS.

During And After The Event
Have a sign up sheet as they come in. Be sure to indicate a place for their name, address and telephone number. This can prove to be very valuable for your mailing list and you can offer attendees a follow-up call. They will LOVE hearing from you and will be tickled that you have taken time to call. When you do, remind them to come in for a follow up session. If they have gone back to smoking, remind them of the coupon. If not, suggest other ways that hypnosis can benefit them. This is a good time to ask for referrals as well.

When the client calls for an appointment in the future, you save the explanation of how hypnosis works and you already have rapport with them. You could offer a discount coupon equal to the amount that they have donated at the smoke out. The gratification of helping and the exposure you receive makes this quite worthwhile.

How To Lead The Event
Introduce yourself
Give a brief background as to your credentials.

Explain hypnosis
Talk about hypnosis as you would any new client that came to you privately. Answer any questions they may have.

Do a few suggestibility tests
Arms raising and falling, fingers locked together.

Do a group induction
Progressive relaxation induction's work best for groups. Explain this is the first of two hypnotic sessions they will experience today. While in hypnosis you may lead them through a few suggestibility tests. Be on the alert for the ones that are the most suggestible. Before awakening, give a post-hypnotic suggestion to re-hypnotize them. For example, when I count from ten down to one you will go into hypnosis...when I touch your shoulder and say relax...when I tell you to touch your thumb and forefinger etc. Then bring them up, at the point you may do a

demonstration using participants that were the most responsive. This can be a lot of fun and a good way to convince everyone of the power.

Make and follow an agenda

Make an agenda of the event and be sure to take regular breaks. Let them have their last cigarette break. After everyone returns and a brief discussion, have them prepare for hypnosis. Some people have preferred lying on the floor. Let them! Now do your thing!

Agenda Of The Event
Based on an all day 8:30 to 4:00 class

- ✓ Introduce Yourself and Your Credentials. Sharing. Announce Your Agenda
- ✓ Last Roundup Break
- ✓ Explain Hypnosis. Dispel Concerns. Suggestibility Tests, leading to Demonstration (suggestibility tests can be skipped if less time is available)
- ✓ Lunch
- ✓ Group Induction
- ✓ Break
- ✓ Discussion

Note From Shelley:

I always make sure that everyone who attends my seminar leaves with an audiocassette tape to reinforce the class. I instruct attendees to "Go to sleep using my *Quit Smoking* Tape for the next two weeks or anytime they feel off center. They are also told not to drive a car while listening because they need to close there eyes to get the best results.

Information Form

Have attendees fill out a form that helps you support them and bring in more people to help.

QUIT SMOKING INFORMATION FORM

Congratulations you are breaking free!
Date_____
Referred by_____
Name_____
Address_____
Home Phone_____
Work_____

Reasons for wanting to take this program:

Questions or comments:

How long have you used tobacco?_____
What brand do you use?_____
How much do you spend on tobacco per month?_____
Have you quit before?_____
If so for how long?_____

Doctor / Health Care Provider_____
Address_____
Phone_____

Friends or relatives interested in the Quit Smoking Seminar
Phone_____
Phone_____
Phone_____

Letters To Doctors

An introductory or follow up letter to a doctors is another business booster. Since your INFORMATION FORM (above) includes the name of the client's physician and where they are located, you can send a letter like this:

Suggestions That Help Me Decide to Quit

> Shelley Stockwell
> Creativity Learning Institute
> 30819 Casilina
> Rancho Palos Verdes, Ca 90275
> (310) 541-4844
>
> Dear Dr. (doctor's name),
> My name is Shelley Stockwell, your patient (patient's name), recently contacted me to enroll in my QUIT SMOKING™ (WEIGHT RELEASE™) wellness clinic. This national smoke ending (weight loss) program uses hypnosis to permanently change behavior patterns and habits so people can quit smoking (lose weight) safely and effectively.
>
> I would appreciate a letter of referral so that we can work together to assist (patient's name) to achieve their goal.
>
> Enclosed are my brochures and cards. I'd enjoy meeting you in person or on the phone to share with you how my program helps people to bust addictions and compulsionswhile reducing stress. I hope you will share these brochures with any of your patients I might assist.
>
> Sincerely,
>
> *Shelley Stockwell*
> Shelley Stockwell
> Clinical Hypnotherapist
> Ph.D. Psychology

I choose to quit. If I've quit before, this time will be easier because my body has already cleansed and released some toxins. Tobacco grabs us by the throat, emotions, and clear thinking. I am breaking free.

My fresh start begins this moment. The most effective way to overcome this (or any other) powerful addiction is to heal myself on the levels of body, mind, and spirit. It is actually a simple proposition. I release old habit patterns that no longer serve me well, and I replace them with comfortable new patterns that let me feel terrific. Since change can sometimes be uncomfortable, some people are challenged for as long as two weeks. If I am one of those folks, I take one day at a time, one hour at a time. I distract myself. What's two weeks when I have a whole lifetime of feeling great ahead of me?

I'm doing something terrific for myself, my friends and my family. I'm protecting them from deadly second hand smoke. I become a positive role model for my children, friends and co-workers. Cleaning up my act makes me more delectable as a mate and lover. I choose to live. I choose happiness. I choose wellness. I choose to feel terrific.

Certifiably Committed

I (print name) _____
hereby promise not to smoke, chew, or snort tobacco again from (today's date)_____ on.

I am fully responsible for this decision and aware that my commitment to this change is of primary importance to me.

Signed   _____

Co-signed   _____

Myths To Die For

Myth:"I need a smoke to relax"
Truth:"A smoke adds to stress"
Some tobacco users believe that tobacco or marijuana calms the nerves. But in fact, they cause the brain to release epinephrine, a hormone that creates stress, not relaxation. This additional stress makes tobacco users think they need more tobacco to calm down.

Tobacco is a stimulant and a depressant. It raises blood pressure that causes insomnia. Its addictive nature also disrupts sleep when cravings cause us to awaken. It causes the heart to beat faster and irregularly which causes us stress especially if we have resulting angina (heart pain) or a heart attack.

As a matter of fact, there isn't one single problem that is not intensified by drugs and especially the drugs in cigarettes. "I think I'll get some fresh air and a cigarette," is quite an amusing statement when you think about it.

Myth:"I can't possibly go without my fix"
Truth:"I go for long stretches each day without tobacco"
If you are a one-and-a-half-pack-a-day smoker, you light up every 35 to 40 minutes. Yet, when you are asleep, you comfortably go without a fix for some six to eight hours at a time. It's natural for you to be a nonsmoker. You may be born with a little butt at the end of your spine, not with a butt in your mouth.

Myth: "It's impossible to quit"
Truth: "It's done every day"
Though quitting is an amazing feat and worthy of a gold medal, some 40 million men and women, just like me, quit for good each year. You need just to look around you at all the people you know who have quit. They are living proof that you can too. If they can do it, so can you.

Myth: "Withdrawal is terrible"
Truth: "Withdrawal is deliciously cleansing"
You may be one of those folks that don't have any withdrawal symptoms. But, if not, it helps to know what to expect. Symptoms, if they

show up, are a sign that you are detoxifying and that the worst is over.

If you do experience withdrawal it may last only a few days and will definitely disappear within two to three weeks. There are many pro-active steps that you can take to speed up the cleansing process. Drinking lots of water, taking certain vitamins and stubbornly committing to become a pleasure seeker dramatically speeds up the process.

Quitting is like being bathed from the inside. For some, the first two to four days are challenging because the body, which has been poisoned for a long time, says: "Oh good! No more poison. Let's clean house."

The resulting detoxification process is actually a wellness crisis that offers a brand new start physically. Just hang in there. A healing crisis is short lived and, when over, an amazing relief.

Think of any cravings as birth contractions that come and go as you birth a whole new you, free of tobacco. If you distract yourself, with exercise, relaxation, breath or self-hypnosis, these cravings leave.

So what are withdrawal symptoms? For some, it's a little like having the flu. Others report being jumpy, touchy or moody, have difficulty concentrating or feel bored. Some report changes in body temperature, heart rate, sleep patterns and muscle tone. Others, headaches, queasiness, cravings, fatigue, dizziness, or offensive body odor. For others, digestive disturbances, increased cough or phlegm, hunger, or a bad taste in the mouth show up before they detoxify.

If you have any of these symptoms, just let it happen. And know it's just a temporary state with permanent reward. Health, beauty, pride, cleanliness, energy, sex appeal and social approval.

Myth: "I've quit before and it didn't last"
Truth: "Prior cleansing prepare me to quit for good"

Every release is different and every releaser is different. Some folk's style is to take two steps forward and one step back until they get into forward gear. If you've quit before, that "old you" may be different than the you that quits now. That's because at this moment you're not the same person you were then. Your cells and attitudes have changed and matured as you've moved through the seasons of your life.

Each time you detoxify you release poison from the body and that makes it easier the next time.

Myth: "I'd quit but I'm afraid I'll gain weight"
Truth: "Not everyone gains weight when they quit and, if they do, it's only temporary"
One excuse some give for not quitting is, "I don't want to gain weight." The truth is that the average weight gain is only five to seven pounds. The reason being that nicotine absorbed through the mucous lining of the mouth and lungs, passes into the blood and then the brain and effects the hypothalamus which controls appetite.

Any weight gain usually falls away easily within the first few months. Many don't gain an ounce. If you think about it, five extra pounds for a short while is worth the eight more years of healthy life you add to your life span. If you don't want to gain weight, drink lots of water and eat low calorie foods. Sugar, fat, caffeine, and alcohol make withdrawal symptoms last longer and cause weight gain.

Because nicotine artificially ups the body metabolism it may also suppress the appetite. When you stop using you may feel slightly hungrier. The kind of food choices you make while detoxifying determines your weight. Consciously choose fresh fruits and vegetables and drink copious amounts of water and your weight will do just fine. Another cause of temporary bloating is water retention. Interestingly, drinking more water helps shed water.

Some try to fill in the old smoking spaces with food. If you used to unwind with a cancer stick after dinner why not choose to unwind with a carrot stick instead. Some suck on a tooth pick or take an evening walk. This is terrific because exercise ups metabolism that of course suppresses the appetite. Nicotine is also found in potatoes, eggplant, and peppers, members of the deadly nightshade family. It may be in your best interest to avoid these foods for a while. Some simply switch nicotine or other chemicals to sugar or caffeine.

Myth: "Tobacco helps me concentrate"
Truth: "Tobacco kills brain cells and destroys memory"
Nicotine actually lowers the level of brain chemical necessary for short-term memory. Studies show that smokers have a shorter attention span than non-smokers. Tobacco and alcohol destroys brain cells. Another study of 288 smokers confirmed that they had cloudier memories and shorter attention spans than non-smokers.

Decide How to Quit

You can quit little by little, or you can quit cold turkey. You can quit on your own, or can quit with some help. You are in charge. It's up to you. You may quit with a friend, a support group, or the help of a professional hypnotherapist and/or acupuncturist. Hypnosis tapes work.

Steps to Stop

- Decide to quit
- Decide how I quit (If I choose, get assistance)
- Readjust the mind
- Change habit patterns
- Drink lots of water (to bathe my body, inside and out)
- Move the body
- Eat good food
- Write six things I get to do instead
- Create fun for myself
- Enjoy nature
- Tell everyone that I stopped

Readjust Your Mind

You can readjust your mind at the deepest level by reading the following power script out loud or into a tape recorder that you play for yourself daily.

Affirmations For Success

POWER SCRIPT

I make myself comfortable in a place where I will not be disturbed. I take a deep breath, let it out, and read the following words slowly, thinking the words as I read them:

I choose to live. I take control of my body, mind, energy, and life. I take control of myself. I acknowledge that my potential is unlimited! I am strong.

I take charge and spring into action. I easily achieve my dreams and goals. I no longer trick or deceive myself. If I blamed others, felt like a victim, or played "poor me," I stop it, now. I honestly take responsibility for everything in my life. If there is something I don't like, I change it.

I take a deep, full breath, get into center, and let it out.
Today, I begin a fresh, clean, new life. Free of toxins and tobacco, and full of health, strength, energy, and joy. I'm no longer a slave to deadly poison. I feel so glad to be alive.

I remember the first time I used poisonous tobacco. It repulsed me and gagged me. Yet I persisted. Now, I realize that tobacco is a nasty, ugly, scorpion that strikes to kill each time it touches my mouth or nose. It's deadly venom travels to each and every cell in my body. I taste the bitter poison, and it's terrible. I want nothing more to do with this rancid, venomous, vermin.

I could smoke or chew tobacco any time I choose. I just don't want to any more. Carbon monoxide, hydrogen cyanide, strychnine, tar, nicotine, salt peter, all a chemical nightmare and are what I want in my body.

I am my body. My body is me. I love my body, unconditionally. My body is a loyal and devoted friend of mine. It works for me 24-hours-a-day since I first began life. My body deserves respect. I love my body. I no longer put anything into it that harms me in any way.
I enjoy another deep breath, taking in as much oxygen as my lungs can hold to the count of five. I let it out slowly. I notice the wonderful feeling of my inspiration, breath, and cleansing. I now take a moment to thank my lungs for doing such a fine job.

Each day the cilia in my lungs filter better and better. These microscopic hairs in my breathing passage sweep away dirt and germs, and protect me from toxins. I breathe fully, deeply, and completely.

If ever I feel stressed, I simply take three full breaths, and with each exhalation, I say the words "relaxed and free." The stress passes. I am free to get on with my many talents and interests. I practice my breathing right now by taking three deep breaths. "Relaxed and free." "Relaxed and free." "Relaxed and free."

If I see someone else use tobacco, I feel sorry for them. For I know how they are damaging and abusing themselves. I feel a tremendous sense of pride in the respectful way I treat myself. I choose to be healthy, to enjoy life, in a free and happy way. I am attractive. I am healthy. I choose to live my life completely.

My commitment to honor and not poison my body is permanent. I deal with it on a moment-to-moment basis. Others do not tempt me. I find tobacco taste repulsive and the smell disgusting. I am not turned on by poisonous chemicals and gases going down my lungs and polluting my body.

If someone offers me chemical-soaked leaves to smoke or chew, I say, "No thank you." I avoid others who are self-destructive and I avoid any habit, place, or situation that triggers self-destructive urges in me.

For the two weeks while I am detoxifying, I drink six to eight glasses of water a day and avoid toxic substances like refined sugar, caffeine, numbing alcohol, and any other depressants and poisons.

I always remember why I quit in the first place and how I did it my way, easing off or cold turkey quitting. I enjoy being totally free of tobacco. I'm proud of myself. I see myself in my mind's eye thinking, feeling, and behaving the way I do when I am successful.

I love the fresh taste in my mouth. I love to smell beautiful smells. My skin becomes softer and loses some of its wrinkles. I feel sexier and more accepting of love and affection. I sleep deeply and soundly, with perfect relaxation. I no longer do anything that harms my body in any way. I am free, calm, peaceful, clear-minded, and healthy from head to toe. I feel terrific. I love myself.

I Change My Habit Patterns

"Never smoke alone in bed"
Were the last words he ever said. —Shelley Stockwell

Remove tobacco (cigarettes, cigars, snuff, matches, lighters, ashtrays, and related paraphernalia) from your home, car, and work place. Stay conscious of when you smoke; even keep a log. Then you change your routine to break those patterns. Take up some new activities. Sit at a new seat at the table. Wash your curtains, walls, and clothes. Clean your home. Get rid of the smell.

Since all tobacco junkies are hypoglycemic, stop drinking caffeine (coffee, colas, tea, and chocolate) and eating sugar, so your body can get back into balance. This keeps you from trading one addiction for another. And because you replace these behaviors with eating complex carbohydrates, such as brown rice, beans, and whole grain breads, you won't gain weight.

Avoiding others who smoke makes it easier to quit. Sit in non-smoking areas. Choose to make life full of health and vitality once and for good.

A client of Shelley's once said, "I'd like to stop smoking cigarettes, but I don't want to lose my taste for marijuana." That kind of thinking just doesn't work.

Purge The Urge.

Cravings are real, yet soon they turn to just thoughts. Cravings last only a few days, so you need to commit to distracting yourself for a short period of time. Here are some things to do if cravings come.

Most importantly, remember that even the most intense cravings last only a few minutes. Five to ten minutes at most. And these urges pass, whether you smoke or not.

✓Think of the reasons you quit in the first place
✓Think of all the benefits you get now that you quit
✓Breathe deeply
✓Call a friend, someone who is not self-destructive
✓Munch on something crunchy: carrots, celery, apples, gum
✓Drink water (at least 8 glasses a day)

- ✓ Exercise (stretch, go for a walk, work out)
- ✓ Shower or bathe, take a sauna
- ✓ Brush your teeth (keep a toothbrush in the car)
- ✓ Avoid alcohol, caffeine, and sugar and others who hurt themselves.
- ✓ Hang out where you can't smoke (Malls, theaters, libraries, churches; most places now days)

Trigger Happy

Use the following news strategies if you encounter these old triggers.

Old Triggers	New Strategy
After a meal	Brush your teeth
Drinking coffee	Chew gum
On the phone	Become a deep breather
Tension	Stretch
Something to do with hands	Doodle, fondle a rock or straw
Boredom	Take a bath or shower
Cocktail party	Drink water or juice
Driving	Snack on celery or carrots
Reward accomplishment	Reward in another way
Crisis or problems	Reaffirm & review your reasons for quitting
After sex	Sing a love song
Own trigger	Give myself a pep talk
To begin the day	Brisk walk
Pleasurable feelings	Find new ways to pleasure yourself
Unconscious smoking	Wrap cigarettes in noisy paper and ask yourself if you really want it
Feel your craving	Distract yourself with a new task For most people, cravings last no more than 7-10 days when they distract themselves. Even if they last longer, they get easier every day.

🛁 Bathe Your Body
Inside and Out With Lots of Water

Drink lots of water, 8-10 glasses a day, because fluids wash nicotine from your system. Water in leads to urine, perspiration, and crying, cleansing nicotine out. Drinking water and exercise also help prevent weight gain. Brush your teeth often. Keep a toothbrush in your car. Wash your hands. Use fragrant perfumes or colognes. Take one or more baths or showers a day. A warm bath before bed is a really wonderful idea. Steam baths, exercise, and showers make detoxification process less painful.

Move Your Body

The main functions of my heart and circulatory system are to carry oxygen to my muscles and organs. Exercise opens blood vessels, increasing blood flow that makes more oxygen available to my muscles and mind. If you use tobacco, carbon monoxide sticks to your blood cells and prevents them from carrying oxygen. Nicotine constricts blood vessels. Exercise puts you back in the flow.

Stretching gets things moving throughout your body. You breathe deeply. If you get a craving, take three deep, slow breaths and release completely after each one. Dance naked, and laugh a lot. Get massages and acupuncture. Massage realigns your body by giving you more energy and releasing stored toxins. It allows the communication system in your body to work better, because it releases tightness in your muscles, thereby releasing the blockages that hinder body/mind communication. Acupuncture realigns the body's meridians and gets the chi (life force energy) flowing. It helps release the stored toxins, and generally makes you feel better.

INTO•GREAT POWER
EXERCISE

Genie in a Box

- ➡ Buy a fancy bottle of designer water.
- ➡ Hold it in my hands.
- ➡ Picture and imagine that this bottle is the final cure for my old habit.
- ➡ Drink all the water in the bottle, and, just like Alice in Wonderland, become bigger than any old pattern.

Heal Yourself with Nutrition
Eat well-balanced meals every day, with lots of fresh fruits and vegetables. Eliminate fats, oils, greases, alcohol, sugar, caffeine, and other drugs. As the nicotine leaves your nerve endings, it takes calcium with it; therefore, take a supplement of calcium and magnesium. You need vitamin C as well. Make sure your multiple vitamins contains a B complex, because that helps you deal with stress. If not, get a separate B complex vitamin. You also need Vitamin E.

Taking up yoga really helps, I Get to Do Instead:
I avoid stress.
I become a pleasure seeker.
I get plenty of rest.
I breath
Breathing well cleanses tar from the bottom of the lungs.

Create Fun
This is your time to pamper and spoil yourself. Use the money you save from not buying cigarettes to get a massage, buy a hammock, go bowling, get a manicure, or something else wonderful just for me. Sleep in late on the weekend, get a new haircut or some new clothes.

Let others reward you, too. Ask someone else to do the dishes, wash your smelly curtain, shampoo the rug, or run an errand for you (while you lay in your new hammock).

Tell Everyone That You Stopped
Use peer pressure to your advantage. When you tell others how you have taken charge of your life, their expectations can help motivate you to hang tough. Your writing also helps them take charge of their self destructive behaviors.

EXERCISE

Wood Chopper, Cough Stopper

If you cough, do the following:
△ I stand tall with both arms above my head.
△ I take a full inspiration. As if chopping wood, I bring my hands down, bend forward, and exhale with a forceful "Haa."

EXERCISE

Write Six Things

Since you now have more time to devote to joyous pursuits, I write down things you get to do instead of spinning your wheels on Tobacco Road. For example, I breathe better, feel more energetic, smell better, and enjoy your many talents, interests, and hobbies. Transform ash to cash, and buy yourself a present.

1. _____
2. _____
3. _____
4. _____
5. _____
6. _____

Enjoy Nature

Discover the pleasure of breathing clean air, of smelling flowers. Mother Earth recharges your batteries. A homeopathic herbal remedy that detoxifies, eliminates cravings, and supports the immune system. Contains ginseng, licorice, ephedra and burdock.

Get Assistance

You may enjoy quitting with the help of a friend, a hypnotherapist, an acupuncturist, or a support group. Some wonderful support groups are offered by the American Cancer Society, the American Lung Association, and the National Cancer Institute.

> **Resources:**
> *Quit Smoking*, audio cassette,
> Shelley Lessin Stockwell, Creativity Unlimited, 30819 Casilina, Rancho Palos Verdes, CA 90275, $12. This is a closed-eye hypnosis tape that dispels cravings and lets you feel terrific.
>
> *Quit Tobacco Easily*, a book you may have been dying to read
> Shelley Lessin Stockwell, Creativity Unlimited, 30819 Casilina, Rancho Palos Verdes, CA 90275, $12.

You are now on your way to success!

Photo by Liane Dyson

Shelley Lessin Stockwell

Internationally renowned motivational speaker. Shelley has lectured extensively here and abroad. In Japan her workshop "Smile On Your Face And Yen In Your Pocket" attracted hundreds of CEO's in both Tokyo and Osaka.

Shelley is a Transpersonal Hypnotherapist, newspaper columnist and the author of many books including "Time Travel: The Do-It-Yourself Past Life Journey Handbook" and "Everything You Ever Wanted To Know About Everything" which she wrote with the Dean Of American Hypnosis, Ormond McGill.

Her talk show appearances include Phil Donahue, Strange Universe, The Other Side, Mike and Maddy and many others. Shelley stars in her own cable television program "The Shelley Show." Her house overlooks the Pacific Ocean. Shelley collects turtles and likes to laugh.

The **Stockwell System** Seminar will give your business the boost it needs.

Shelley's topics include:
Tap Your Creativity.
How to Fight Fair
How to Deal with Difficult People.
Passing The Test Being Your Best
Less Stress For Success
How To Spark Up Your Love Life
The One With The Biggest Aura Wins
Achieving Goals
Self Hypnosis In A Snap
You Don't Get A Second Chance To Make a Great First Impression
How To Be An Urban Shaman
How To Be A Great Communicator
Effective Public Speaking
and many more..

Definitions of Hypnosis Terms

Accidental Hypnosis
Spontaneous trance brought on by trauma, shock, illness or infancy, which causes us to bypass our objective thinking and take on suggestion .

Age Progression
Subject accesses future "memories."

Age Regression
Reliving or revivifying past experiences of this life time, past lifetimes and between life times. Subjects who explore current life times often re-member their own conception, womb and birth experience. Many report memory before conception. Where were you before you were born?

Altered State
Mental shifting of gears from conscious awareness to trance states

Archetypes
Universal human essence characterized as a symbolic "type". Carl Jung popularized seven major ones; including the "wise person", "animus" (male), "anima" (female), and "shadow". The ancient Pantheons of the gods identified them with our now popular astrological signs as "Mars" (male), "Venus" (female), and "Cronos" (father). "Gaea" (mother). "Vulcan" (financial wizard), "Pluto" (sexual), "Mercury" (mental), "Zues" (spiritual), "Apollo" (child), "Uranus" (friendship), "Vesta" (perfectionist) and "Neptune" (mystic).

Artificial Somnambulism Marquis de Puysegur (1781-1825) expanded on Mesmer's approach by inducing the trance state while communing with trees.

Conscious Mind
Earth and Body Self, Room Awareness. The conscious mind makes decisions based upon information it receives from the sub and superconscious mind. And it impresses the subconscious with its sensory observations.

Catatonic Trance
The body is so relaxed that the subject doesn't move a muscle. In this state there is complete anesthesia to pain

Catalepsy
Limb rigidity without flexing a muscle. Arms or legs moved by into different positions remain in that position for indefinite time frames. Subjects "suspended" (neck on one chair back, heel on another chair back) between two chairs enjoy complete comfort and ease.

Unconscious
Forces that exist beyond our personal unconscious. Created by collective energies of all living beings.
Color Therapy
The use of color for deepening, programming and healing.
Emotional Discharge
Emotional release to relieve inner pressure attached to continuing a limiting behavior or attitude.
Ericksonian Hypnosis
A hypnotic art form created by Milton H. Erickson, psychiatrist and M.D. Uses indirect inductions, suggestions and metaphor so the subject will come their own conclusions and attach their own meaning to the words spoken by the hypnotist. A slow, complicated and indirect backdoor approach in my opinion.
Free Association
A Freudian technique that has the client say everything that comes into his mind. The idea is to bring subconscious information into conscious awareness. Free association is often used while the client is in trance.
Freudian Slip
One that comes off easily
Gestalt Therapy
Based on the work of Fritz Perls. The client acts out scenes from dreams or life taking on the roles of each human, inanimate object and subpersonality. "My approach is an integrative one. We make real people out of plastic ones."
Hypnoanalysis
Coined by Hadfield in working with shell shocked war veterans. A combination of hypnosis and Sigmund Freud's psychoanalysis. Hypnoanalysis says that forgotten or repressed childhood memories are the underlying cause of present pain and distress. This approach includes dream interpretation and the use of free association.
Hypnogogic
The transition or twilight state between trance and wakefulness. Characterized by relaxation.
Hypnos
meaning "sleep" from the Sleep Temples and Healing Shrines where folks went for R and R in Ancient Egypt and Greece.
Hypnotic Catharsis
A process used by Sigmond Freud to release emotions while entranced.
Hypnotism, Neurypnology and Neuro-Hypnosis
Names given to "suggestions that became permanent during the sleep of

the nervous system." Or "nervous sleep" by Dr. James Braid from Scotland (1795-1860).

Hypnotherapy
Applying hypnosis for positive therapeutic change

Lucid Sleep or Lucid Dreams
Dubbed by Jose Custodio de Faria (1755-1819), lucid dreaming is the act of being aware of dreaming while dreaming.

Mesmerized
Franz Anton Mesmer (1734-1815) perpetuated a theory he called Animal Magnetism.

Self Conscious
Intense awareness of self.

Somnabulism
An open eye deep hypnotic state where the subject is completely engrossed in the reality of suggestions given in trance.

Sub-personality work "Know Thyselves"
The process of personifying emotional patterns and attitudes as distinct mini- selves. Quieting internal conflict and getting our many "selves" to get along and form a team. Integration usually requires the taming of the "inner critic" and the empowering of the "master controller". Multiple personality disorder appears to be the extreme of this natural phenomenon. Multiples however often are unaware of the "others". Popularized by Roberto Assagioli Psychosynthesis and Hal and Sidra Stone as Voice Dialogue.

Subconscious Mind
Internal Self. The subconscious self makes up the majority of my brain functioning. These mental archives remember all tidbits of uncritically accepted information about myself and life and from these memories draws conclusions. Mental activity here is just below and not immediately known to the conscious mind.

Super-Conscious Mind
Higher Self, Expanded Consciousness. The super conscious mind encompasses and permeates all levels of consciousness. It oversees the conscious and subconscious and it remembers all my experiences within and beyond my individual personality.

Unconscious
The parts of the body/mind that are hidden from our awareness. The unconscious controls our autonomic nervous system. When we are unconscious we are not aware of conscious thought, sensation or feeling.

References

Must Read
The New Encyclcopedia Of Stage Hypnosis by Ormond McGill is one the best "how to" books on hypnosis. It offers an amazingly detailed description, illustrations, and techniques

What, How and Why
Cheek, David B. and Leslie M. LeCron, *Clinical Hypnotherapy* Grune and Stratton, New York, 1968

Follas, Ph.D., Lawrence, author of *Hypnosis and Higher Self* "Are You Happy In Your Dream?" National Guild Hypnotists Annual, New Hampshire, 1995

Leonard, George "Mental Material Interface: Consciousness Transform The Flesh?" Conference Recording Service, Berkeley, CA., 1995

Mutke, Peter, *Selective Awareness*

Sobel, M.D., David, "Mind/Body Medicine Can Save Money" Mental health Update, Cambridge MA, 1996

Stockwell, Shelley, *Trans-formations Video,* 1995 Creativity Unlimited Press, Rancho Palos Verdes, CA., 90275

Wells, C.Ht., Phil, Unlimited Human Magazine

History
Bryan, William J, JR.M.D., *A Histoy of Hypnosis* The Journal, Los Angeles CA 1962

The Brain
Fischbach, Gerald (Chair Dept. of Neurobiology, Harvard Medical School and Mass. Gen. Hospital)

Gober, Joel, PhD. Biophysics, brain researcher.

Goleman, PhD., Daniel, Psychology (Harvard)

Heinz, Melissa (UCLA) "Genetic Female Cells Exposed To Male Hormones"

McLean, M.D., Paul, (Neurologist and former director of the Brain Laboratory, National Institute of Mental Health)

Restak, M.D., Richard, *The Brain Has A Mind Of its Own* Crown Trade Paper books, NY 1991 This 210 page book is folksy, informative and thought provoking. Highly recommended. Also *The Modular Brain* Touchstone Books, N.Y.1994, 200 pgs.

Sperry, Roger (California Institute of Technology)

Vincent, Sally. "Equal Opportunities" Issue Magazine. May 96.

Prado, Lilia Dr. O.D.

The Mind

Bloomfield, Harold H & McWilliams, Peter *How to Heal Depression,* Prelude Press 1994

Fischbach, Gerald Dr., Mind and Brain, Scientific American, September 1992 pages 48-57

Flores, Deborah, "Boosting Your Brain Power", Toastmaster, May 1995

Gibbs, Nancy, "The EQ Factor", Time Magazine, October 2, 1995 pages 61-68

Goleman, Daniel, Ph.D, "Emotional Intelligence", Bantam Press, 1995

Lemonick, Michael D. "Glimpses of the Mind", Time magazine, July 31, 1995

Powell, Cherith and Forde Greg, *The Self Hypnosis Book,* Penguin Studio 1995

Stockwell, Shelley, *Denial Is Not A River In Egypt: Dump Drugs and Crazy Thinking!* Creativity Unlimited, Palos Verdes, CA, 1997

Stokes, Terry, *Understanding Hypnosis and Self Hypnosis,* PDQ Printing 1991

Durbin, Paul G. *Kissing Frogs: Practical Uses of Hypnosis* and "Alfred Adler and Viktor Frankl", Subconsciously Speaking, 1996.

Hypnosis

Ansari, Masud, *Modern Hypnosis; Theory and Practice,* MasPress, Washington D.C. 1991

How To Release Limits

Stockwell, Shelley *"Denial Is Not A River In Egypt: Dump Drugs and Crazy Thinking!"* Creativity Unlimited Press, 30819 Casilina, Rancho Palos Verdes, CA 90275

Cohen, Alan, *Joy Is My Compass: Take the Risk to Follow Your Bliss.*

de Mello, Anthony, *One Minute Wisdom,* Doubleday, NY 1988

Kaufman, Margo, "Psychic Vampires" Redbook, March 1995, pp. 94, 118.

Piorkowski, Geraldine, Ph.D, "Too Close for Comfort: Exploring the Risks of Intimacy",

PEPI Trail Study on Estrogen

Sanders, Pete, A. Jr., P.O. Box 1762, Sedona, AZ 86339.

Sources, Sally, "Health," Woman's Day, July 1995.

Young, Jeffrey and Janet Klosko, *Reinventing Your Life,* Plume Printing, 1994

Zimberoff, Diane, *Breaking Free from the Victim Trap,* Wanatchee, Washington

Sleep
Stokes, Terry, *Understanding Hypnosis and Self Hypnosis,* 1991 PDQ Print, Fort Walton Beach, FL

Resources
"Peace and Calm" and *"Sleep beautiful Sleep"* two tapes that make sleeping a dream. These and others can be ordered from Creativity Unlimited Press, at 30817 Casilina, Rancho Palos Verdes, CA 90275 for $10 each. See order forms at the back of this book.

Dreaming
Garfield, Patricia, *Creative Dreaming* An excellent book that studies the shamanistic Senoi culture and how to conquer dreams. A must read.

Stockwell, Shelley, Hypnosis cassette: *Sleep Beautiful Sleep* Creativity Unlimited Press—order form at back of this book

Ann W. O'Neill, Los Angeles Times Staff Writer. *Therapist is Accused Of Sex Assaults* Sunday, August 4, 1996 page A17

Wellness
Chopra, Deepak, *Quantum Healing*

Kiecolt-Glaser JK, Marucha PT, Malarkey WB, Mercado AM, Glaser R.: "Slowing Wound Healing By Psychological Stress." *Lancet 346: 1194-96, 1995*

LaVelle Steven, "Adventures In Alternative Healing" Unlimited Human Magazine, Florida 1993

National Institute of Health, *Health* Office Of Alternative Medicine

Siegel, Bernie S., M.D., *Love Medicine and Miracles.* Arrow books

Simonton, Matthews-Simonton and Creighton, *Getting Well Again* Bantam Books

Wells, Phil, Hypnotherapist, "Hypnodontics" Unlimited Human Magazine, Florida 1993

White, Ken, healer and graphic artist. This letter first appeared in The Beam Newsletter, Rancho Palos Verdes August 1996

Money
Resources:

The Money Tape by Dr. Joan Lessin and Shelley Lessin Stockwell, with music by Ed Sakota can be ordered from Creativity Unlimited Press, at 30817 Casilina, Rancho Palos Verdes, CA 90275 for $10 each. See order forms at the back of this book.

These affirmations and more are available on cassette. See order form at the back of the book.

Hypnotherapy

Oates, David John, "Reverse Speech: Hidden Messages In Human Communication", San Diego, CA.

Enright, John B, "Help Other People Effectively" The Enright Network, Tiburon, CA 1988

Vegotsky, Ken, *The Ultimate Power: How To Unlock Your Mind-Body-Soul Potential* Toronto Ontario Canada. and The ToastMaster Magazine January 1997

Business of Hypnosis

Griffin, Julie,C.Ht., "Setting Up & Building A Successful Practice" 1996 Journal of The National Guild Of Hypnotists, N.H.(508) 251-1737

Ackerman, Charlene The Great American Smoke Out"

Quit Smoking

Los Angeles County, Department of Health Services, Tobacco Control Program.

"The Human Cost of Tobacco Use: A Compilation of 114 Studies," New England Journal of Medicine, 1994.

"Smoking, Tobacco, and Health," US Department of Health and Human Services, Publication No. CDC 87-8397, revised October, 1989.

"The Surprising Years: Understanding Your Changing Adolescent," *Lions Quest,* Quest International, Granville, Ohio, 1992, 72 pages.

Speech by Don Johnson, Torrance, California, for the National Cancer Association, 1991.

Nic•o•teen magazine, published by Scholastic Inc. and Facts Magazine, NY, NY, 1992.

Kirchheimer, Sid, and the Editors of Prevention Magazine, *The Doctor's Book of Home Remedies II*, Bantam Books, 1995.

"The Surprising Years: Understanding Your Changing Adolescent," Lions Quest, Quest International, Granville, Ohio, 1992, 72 pages.

Young, Lawrence, Linda Young, Marjorie and Donald Klein, and Dorean Bayer, Recreational Drugs, Berkeley Books, NY, 1982,

Wilkinson, Peter, "A new generation, an old danger," *Rolling Stone* magazine, May 5, 1994.

Recommended Reference Books

* Starred books get a two thumbs up.

Acupressure Hypnosis
McGill Ormond, 1990
Anatomy of An Illness
Cousins, Norman, Bantam Book, 1981,167 pages
* Automatic Writing and Hieroscripting
Stockwell, Shelley, Creativity Unlimited, 30819 Casilina, RPV, Ca
* Breaking Free Of The Victim Trap and *Trim Life*
Zimberoff, Diane, MA, Wellness Press, WA 331pgs
Creative Visualization
Gawain, Shakti, Bantam Book, N.Y.127 pages
Crystal Enlightenment Raphaell, Katrina, Arora Press, NY 1985, 171 pages
Crystal, Gem and Metal Magic, Encyclopedia of
Cunningham, Scott, Llewellyn Publications, St. Paul, MN, 1988, 221 pages
Color and Edgar Cayce
Lewis, Roger A.R.E. 1973, 48 pages
Control Of The Mind
Farber, Seymour M. and Wilson, Roger H.L. U of Cal Medical School
McGraw and Hill, 1961, 40 pages
* Consumers Guide to Hypnosis
Kirtley, Christine, National Guild of Hypnotists 1991, 95 pages
Designing Hypnosis Scripts for Relief Of Multiple Sclerosis
Palinsky, Constance, NGH 35 pages
* Doctors Book Of Home Remedies 1 and 2
Kirchheimer, Sid, Prevention Magazine Press and Bantam 1995, 663 pages
Facts About Fat
Finnegan, John, Elysian Arts Book Berkeley 1993, 131 pages
* Frogs Into Princes
Bandler, Richard and Grinder, John,
Real People Press, Moab, Utah 1979, 194 pages
Gestalt Is
Many, Real People Press, Moab Utah 1975, 274 pages
* Gestalt Self Therapy
Schiffman, Muriel Wingbow Press Ca 1971, 221 pages
Get Happy
Wright, Helen D. Price, Stern and Sloan 1983, 92 pages
* Habits of The Wealthy
Byrne, Bill Berkeley Books, NY, 1993, 300 pages
Handbook For The Integrity Tone Scale
Black, Vern, Ph.D. Vern Black 1983, 80 pages

Heal Your Body
Hay, Louise, Hay House, Solana Beach, Ca, 1988
Healing Through Meditation and Prayer
Puryear, Meredith Ann, ARE Press Virginia Beach, Fl 1978, 108 pages
Healing Visualization: Health Through Imagery
Epstein, Gerald, M.D. Bantam Books NY 226 pages
Human Encounter With Death
Grof, Stan and Halifax, Joan, EF Dutton, New York 1977, 223 pages
Hypnosis And Pastoral Counseling
Morton, Richard, B. Ph.D., Westwood, 1980, 93 pages
Hypnosis and Psychosomatics
Dr. Theodore X. Barber, Proseminar Institute, 1978 , 125 pages
** *Hypnosis For Change*
Hadley, Josie/ Staudecher, Carol, New Harbinger Pub, 1989, 265 pages
Hypnosis- Gil Boyne Teaching and Demonstrating
Boyne, Gil, Westwood Press, Glendale 1986, 47 pages
Hypnosis Its Nature and Therapeutic Uses
Gibson, H.B. Taplinger Publishing New York 1980, 187 pages
Hypnotism and Meditation
McGill, Ormond, Westwood Publishing, 1981, 100 pages
Hypnotism Made Easy
Wynn, Ralph, Ph.D. Wilshire Book Co, 1978 N. Hollywood, CA, 167 pages
Hypnosis Theory,Practice and Application
Rhodes, Raphael H., Citadel Press, N.Y, 1965, 175 pages
* *Hypnotism And Mysticism of India*
McGill, Ormond ,Wilshire Book Company, 1979, 167 pages
* *Holographic Universe, The*
Talbot, Michael Harper Perennial 1991,338 pages
Instantaneous Hypnosis Techniques McGill, NGH 1991, 25 pages
Instead of Therapy
Rusk, Tom, M.D. Hay House, Carson CA., 1991, 260 pages
Journal of Humanistic Psychology
Association for Humanistic Psychology AHP 1985- 1987 issues a year includes the latest articles a research in our field, @ 130 pages,
Joy: Expanding Human Awareness
Will Schutz, Grove Press 1967
Life Style
Eckstein, Daniel 1975, 58 pages
Living in The Light
Gawain, Shakti Whatever Publishing, Mill Valley, CA, 1986, 192 pages
Letting Go
Boerstler, Richard W., Thanatology Press, 1985 49 pages
* *Many Lives, Many Masters*
Weiss, Brian, M.D. Simon and Schuster, NY 219 pages

Many Lives Of Alan Lee, The
McGill, Ormond, National Guild of Hypnotists, 1988, 37 pages
Meeting Yourself Half Way
Simon, Sidney, Argus Press, U Of Mass 1974, 100 pages
Mind Over Platter
Lindner, Peter M.D., Wilshire Book Co. 1963, 136 pages
Modern Hypnosis
Ansari, Masud, Ph.D.,Mas-Press, Washington D.C. 1991, 235 pages
On Motivation
Fabun, Don Glencoe Press, Beverly Hills, CA 1986 40 pages
*** Professional Stage Hypnotism**
McGill, Ormond Wilshire Book Company, 1977, 204 pages
Psychological Perspective
C.G Jung Institute of LA, 1989-1990 Reflexology 220 pages
* ***ReFraming NLP***
Bandler, Richard and Grinder, John, Real People Press, 1982, 205 pages
*** Reinventing Your Life**
Young, Jeffrey Ph.D. and Klosko, Janet Ph.D., Plume Press NY 1993, 365 Pgs
Secrets of Stage Hypnotism
Leonidas, Prof.Newcastel Publishing, Hollywood ,CA1975, 149 pages
Sedona: Psychic Energy Vortexes
Sutphen, Dick, Valley of the Sun Publishing, 1986, 169 pages
**Self Hypnosis: Smile On Your Face Money In Your Pocket Stockwell, Shelley, Creativity Unlimited, 30819 Casilina, RPV, CA 90275
*Self Hypnosis
Tebbetts, Charles, Westwood Publishing Co.1977, 129 pages
Self Hypnosis
LeCron Leslie, Signet Books 1964, 204 pages
Selective Awareness
Mutke, Peter, M.D, Westwood Press 1977, 193 pages
* *Sleep At Last*
James, Paul Rutledge Press, 1980, 192 pages
Structured Exercises in Stress Management 2 Volumes
Tubesing, Nancy and Donald, Whole Person Handbook 270 pages
The Modular Brain
Restak, Richard M., M.D., A well written explanation of the brains specialized functions, 200 pages
**Time Travel: Do It Yourself Past Life Journey Handbook
Stockwell, Shelley, Creativity Unlimited, 30819 Casilina, CA 90275 200pgs
Total Mind Power
Wilson, Donald, M.D. Camaro Publishing L.A.,CA 1976, 253 pages
* *Trance-formations NLP*
Bandler, Richard and Grinder, John, Real People Press, 1981, 252 pages
Transactional Analysis: I'm OK You're OK
Freed, Alvyn Dr. Jalmar Press

Transpersonal Hypnotherapy
Maynard, James, Transpersonal Press, Seattle Washington 1989, 58 pages
* *Understanding Hypnosis and Self Hypnosis*
Stokes, Terry PDQ Press, Fort Walton Beach, FL 1991
Unlock Your Mind And Be Free; Practical Hypnotherapy
Barnett, Edgar A. M.D., Westwood Publishing, Glendale, Ca 153 pages
Visualization: Directing movies of the Mind
Bry, Adelaide Barnes and Noble Books, N.Y 1972, 174 pages
* *What Color Is Your Parachute?*
Bolles, Richard Ten Speed Press 1979, 295 pages
Wishcraft: How To Get What You Really Want
Sher, Barbara, Ballantine Books, New York, 1979, 278 pages
How to Heal Depression
Bloomfield, Harold and McWilliams, Peter, Prelude Press, 1994, 228 pages
How to Survive The Loss Of A Love
McWilliams, Peter, Prelude Press
* *Life 101 and Do It! Get Off Your Buts.*
McWilliams, Peter and Rogers John Prelude press
* * *The Portable Therapist*
Stewart, Judith K., Bywood Publishing Company, NY 1991, 320 pages
50 simple Things You Can Do To Save The Planet

Books by Shelley Stockwell
Automatic Writing & Hieroscripting: *Tap Unlimited Creativity and Guidance*
Channeling: You Conduit!
Denial Is Not a River in Egypt: *Unveil Bazaar Behavior and Feel Terrific*
Hypnosis: *How To Put A Smile On Your Face and Money In Your Pocket*
Insides Out
Sex and Other Touchy Subjects
Slim and Sexy
Time Travel: *Do-It-Yourself Past Life Journey Handbook*

Audio Tapes by Ormond McGill
Yoga Nidra
The Violet Flame
Hypnomeditation
Controlling Your Mind and How The Mind Works
Mastering Cosmic Consciousness
Universal Abundance
The Fountain Of Youth
Yoga Nidra: Hypno Yoga

Audio Tapes by Shelley Stockwell
Peace and Calm
Yes I Can!
Time Travel
Sleep Beautiful Sleep
No More Sugar Junkie
Lose Weight
Great Golf
Great Tennis
Kundalini Rising
Meet Your Angel
Sex And Other Touchy Subjects
The Wellness Tape (with Dr. Lilia Prado)
The Money Tape (with Dr. Joan Lessin)
Mer•Ka•Ba: Ascension To The Forth Dimension

I Love To Exercise!
Yes I Can Quit Smoking
No More Alcohol
Flight Attendant Well Being
Mommy Bunny's Going To Work
U R What U Eat

Also by Ormond McGill and Shelley Stockwell
Everything -card game
Out of Your Mind: Hypnosis and Creative Writing
Hypnotically Yours, Ormond McGill- video
Kundalini Rising- audio tape
I Feel Terrific!- audio tape
Have A Great Nights Sleep- audio tape

Books by Ormond McGill
Grieve No More Beloved: The Book Of Delight
Hypnotism and Meditation
Power Hypnosis and Hypnotherapy
The Art of Stage Hypnotism
The Encyclopedia of Stage Hypnosis
The New Encyclopedia of Stage Hypnosis
Atomic Magic
Balancing Magic and Other Tricks
Chalk Talk
Entertaining with Magic
Magic With Soap Bubbles
Paper Magic
Psychic Magic
Real Mental Magic
Science Magic: 101 Tricks You Can Do
21 Gems Of Magic
The Encyclopedia of Stage Illusions
The Mysticism and Magic of India
The Magic and Illusion of Lee Grabel
Voice Magic
How to Produce Miracles
Religious Mysteries of the Orient
The Secret World of Witchcraft
Seeing The Unseen

 **CREATIVITY UNLIMITED PRESS®** is proud to offer the following items for you and your loved ones...

TIME TRAVEL
Do-It-Yourself Past Life Journey Handbook

by
Shelley Stockwell, Ph.D.

This book takes the mystery out of past life regression, future life progression & spiritual journeys. Shelley gives you 14 easy tools for self awareness. Explore the fascinating world that lives behind your eyes, your mind and within your heart.

Learn:
- holotropic breathing
- guided visualization
- your purpose in this lifetime
- retrieve recorded memories
- heightened sensory awareness
- journey past, future & between lives

"More people give me more things to read than I can keep up with but when I received your manuscript, I sat down and read it in 2 days. You have very good suggestions & formulas. I'll recommend it to clients & friends." – Dr. Hazel M. Denning, founder of the Association of Past Life Research & Therapy

$19.95
157 Pages – 5.5 x 8.5"
ISBN #0-912559-19-5

THE ART OF CHANNELLING: BETWEEN LIVES
(video tape)

by
Shelley Stockwell, Ph.D.

Discover the art of channelling in this candid interview. Stockwell shares her remarkable personal journey of awareness and examines ways you can use to communicate with "spirit guides".

Includes:
- ★ An Actual Channeling Session
- ★ No Nonsense Exercises

$19.95
Video Tape
Gateways Inc.

TRANCE-FORMATIONS

Hypnosis, Channeling & Past Life Regressions
(video tape)

by
Shelley Stockwell, Ph.D.

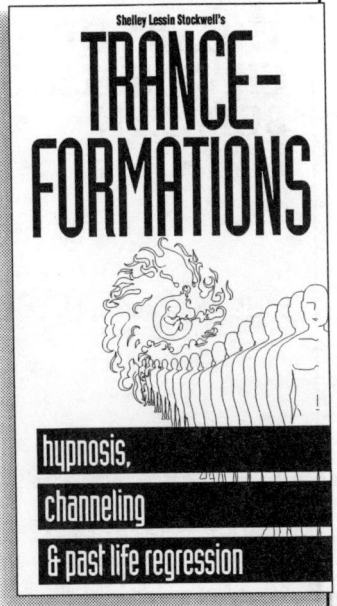

This video will transform the way you see yourself once and for your highest good!

Shelley Lessin Stockwell's Trance-Formations is a riveting opportunity to explore the deepest regions of your mind through hypnosis, channeling and past life regression.

Demonstrates:
- ★ Channeling
- ★ Hypnosis
- ★ Regressions
- ★ Progressions
- ★ Automatic Writing
- ★ Behavior Modification

Available in Japanese too!
$19.95
Video Tape
ISBN #0-912559-23-3

HYPNOTICALLY YOURS

Shelley Stockwell interviews Ormond McGill, America's most beloved hypnotist
(video tape)

Ormond McGill, Ph.D., The Dean of American Hypnosis, shares his secrets of consciousness, hypnosis and the mind. An amazing master teacher, Ormond has been studying and using hypnosis for over seventy years.

In this candid interview with Hypnotherapist, Shelley Stockwell, Ph.D., McGill discusses the functions of the mind and how you can harness its power.

Includes:
- ★ Step by step demonstrations of Hypnosis Techniques
- ★ How to Mesmerize another
- ★ Eye function
- ★ Deepening Skills
- ★ Ideomotor Impulses and much more...

"profound wisdom"
"like spending the evening with fascinating friends"
"I tried several techniques and they worked perfectly! Thank you..."

$19.95
Video Tape
ISBN #0-912559-33-0

AUTOMATIC WRITING & HIERO-SCRIPTING
Tap Unlimited Creativity and Guidance

By Shelley Stockwell, Ph.D.

AS SEEN ON THE PHIL DONOHUE SHOW

Anyone who can draw, write or type can automatic write and hiero-script – learn how!

"...drop your veil of fear and let our words move upon your page, overflow beauty, guidance and creativity. We, your guiding angels serve and love you."
— Arch Angel Michael, written through Shelley

$9.95
Book - 5.5 x 8.5"
ISBN #0-912559-25-X

INSIDES OUT

by Shelley Stockwell, Ph.D.

Plain talk poetry guaranteed to speak to you where you really live. If you want to awaken your vitality and truly enjoy yourself, this is your book!

"...Sprinkled throughout are short thoughts and quippy asides – amusing and anecdotal"
– Focus on Books

"A beautiful, heart touching book. I urge you all to read it."
– Toni Grant, KABC Talk Radio

"There is a lot of humor in this book, but you can learn a lot too. There is wisdom along with the humor... it's really a fantastic book."
– Madelyn Camrud, WDAZ ABC-TV

"Shows how poetry can help see inside yourself. Maybe you'll like what you see."
– Bill Smith, Channel 11 News

$6.95
Book - 156 pages
ISBN #0-912559-00-4
LCN #83-710-30

DENIAL IS NOT A RIVER IN EGYPT:
Unveil Bazaar Behaviors & Feel Terrific!

By Shelley Stockwell, Ph.D.

Guides you out of the depths of denial, depression, addiction or compulsion and into the heights of self love & joy.

"My experience affirms that depression underlies all drug/alcohol dependency. I applaud your contributions to sufferers of this crippling condition."
– J. Nicholas Graves, Counselor, Gerontologist

$19.95
Book
ISBN # 0-912559-22-5

HYPNOSIS
How To Put A Smile On Your Face, And Money In Your Pocket

By Shelley Stockwell, Ph.D.

Learn what hypnosis is and how to use it as a powerful tool for yourself, your family and friends. Teaches you to use the untapped power of your mind to make your dreams a reality!

Learn:
- ★ The 30 Second Tap
- ★ How to vanish "loser" attitudes
- ★ 42 Personal Affirmations
- ★ Hypnosis Script
- ★ Dream Charting
- ★ How to be a Money Manager

$19.95
Book
ISBN #0-912559-17-9

SEX & OTHER TOUCHY SUBJECTS
(The Book)

by Shelley Stockwell, Ph.D.
INCLUDES FREE "BOOK ON CASSETTE" OFFER!

This "Gift Of The Year" award winning poetry book tackles love, money, sex, drugs, religion, Mom, Dad, apple pie and death. Hilariously funny; profoundly sensitive.

"Shelley has an eerie talent for writing MY very thoughts... To enjoy this book is to truly enjoy myself." – Kris Blake, Magic Mirrors

$14.95
Book - 340 Pages
ISBN #0-912559-12-8
LCN #88-71940

SEX & OTHER TOUCHY SUBJECTS
(The Audio Tape)

A most unusual book on tape from the best seller of the same title.

Shelley Stockwell's songs & words are guaranteed to make you laugh, sing and celebrate the rites of Spring. Features the popular singles: *"Static Grit On My CB"*, *"The Dating Game Reject"*, *"Yes, I'm Positive"* and *"Frustration is the 'F' Word"*.

Each song is brilliantly arranged by Frank Unzuata and performed by Shelley, Frank and Betsy Cowen.

$10.00
Audio Tape - 60 min.
ISBN #0-912559-13-6

U R WHAT U EAT & THE DINOSAUR RAP

Created By
Shelley Stockwell, Ph.D., Hypnotherapist
Kathy Felker, Registered Dietitian & famous puppeteer
Betsy Moreland, Special Education Teacher
Frank Unzuata, "The Magic Music Man"
Spike, your basic dinosaur

"*Teaches children an important nutritional message, while providing catchy refrains. Reggae inspired embellishments make pleasant listening for adults as well. Weightwatchers could use this book for positive auto-suggestion*"
– Focus on Books

$10.00
AudioTape
ISBN #0-912559-14-4

MOMMY BUNNY'S GOING TO WORK

By Shelley Stockwell, Ph.D.

"*A simple, reassuring song & story that can help parents enormously in dealing with their children's abandonment anxiety*"
– Ellen Hokanson, Focus on Books

"*Before MOMMY BUNNY, Ryan threw a fit when I went to work. Now, he's happy and I don't feel guilty!*"
– Gayle Tritz, Flight Attendant

$10.00
AudioTape
ISBN #0-912559-16-0
ISBN #0-912559-06-3
(Flight Attendant Version)

Now you can play
GREAT GOLF!

By Shelley Stockwell, Ph.D.
and Dr. John Goode

This powerful program of "Great Golf" gets results!
- ★ Improve
- ★ Play focused & relaxed
- ★ Free your mind
- ★ Feel your best
- ★ Build confidence

Daily mental and physical practice truly makes you a perfect golfer. Your success with the Great Golf program is unlimited!

"Great Golf is a game played on a 6 inch course – the space between your ears." – Bobby Jones

$10.00
Audio Tape
ISBN #0-912559-20-9

CB SONG
And The Dating Game Reject

by "Shell Belle"
Alias Shelley Stockwell

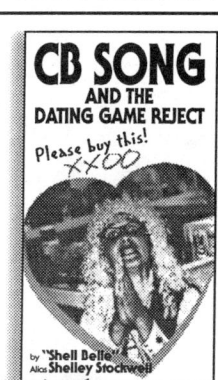

Shell and the Belles star in this hilarious new music video which is also available on audio tape.

"Please buy my video!!!"
– Shell Belle

HILARIOUS NEW MUSIC VIDEO!

$10.00
Audio Tape
ISBN #0-912559-31-4

$10.00
Video Tape
ISBN #0-912559-30-6

MER•KA•BA:
Ascension to the 4th Dimension

By Shelley Stockwell, Ph.D.
Tonal Music by Wayne Perry

14 Breaths to Enlightenment!
Powerful consciousness expansion for your highest good! Learn the ancient Egyptian initiation rite as you expand your consciousness.

"A powerful and mind altering experience not to be missed!"
– Kay Risberg, Hypnotist

$10.00
AudioTape
ISBN #0-912559-26-8

MEET YOUR ANGEL
Closed Eye Meditation

by Shelley Stockwell, Ph.D.
Music & Vocals: Jeannie Fitzsimmons
Trumpet & Flugle Horn: Jim Hale

Cross over into the world of wonder and connect with your higher self, guides and angels.

$10.00
Audio Tape
ISBN #0-912559-35-7

KUNDALINI RISING
The Ancient Rite of Enlightenment

By Ormond McGill, Ph.D.
and Shelley Stockwell, Ph.D.

One of the most remarkable experiences of your life!

$10.00
AudioTape
ISBN #0-912559-38-1

YOGA NIDRA HYPNOYOGA
The Ancient Oriental Method for Advancing to Cosmic Consciousness

by Ormond McGill, Ph.D.
The Dean of American Hypnosis

$10.00
Audio Tape
ISBN #0-912559-34-9

THE WELLNESS TAPE
A Journey of Renewal

By Shelley Stockwell, Ph.D.
and Dr. Lilia Prado, O.D.

Hynotherapist Shelley Stockwell and Medical Doctor Lilia Prado teach you how to feel your very best.

Tap into your body's innate ability to renew, heal and revitalize. Hypnosis is not a miracle, its results just seem that way!

$10.00
AudioTape
ISBN #0-912559-32-2

I LOVE EXERCISE
Motivation is Fun!

By Shelley Stockwell, Ph.D.

Eliminates negative scripts and gets you moving again.

"Thank You Shelley!"

$10.00
Audio Tape

THE VIOLET FLAME
The Most Beautiful Meditation In The World

by Ormond McGill, Ph.D.
The Dean of American Hypnosis

$10.00
Audio Tape
ISBN #0-912559-33-0

MORE SELF-HYPNOSIS AUDIO CASSETTES...

Closed Eye Meditations for Bliss and Wellness.

 KUNDALINI RISING
The ancient rite of enlightenment. A wonderful experience.
ISBN #0-912559-38-1

 THE WELLNESS TAPE
Tap your body's innate ability to renew, heal & revitalize!
ISBN #0-912559-32-2

 MEET YOUR ANGEL
Connect with your higher self, your guides and angels.
ISBN #0-912559-10-1

 YOGA NIDRA/ HYPNOYOGA
The ancient Oriental method for advancing to cosmic consciousness.
ISBN #0-912559-34-9

 THE VIOLET FLAME
The most beautiful meditation in the world.
ISBN #0-912559-33-0

Self-Hypnosis Audio Cassettes - 60 Minutes Each

Best Seller!

Everything
You Ever Wanted to Know About Everything

Ormond McGill, Ph.D.
Shelley Stockwell, Ph.D.
& The Guides

SELF HELP

Everything
You Ever Wanted to Know About...

- God
- Existence
- Death
- Wisdom
- Money
- Love & Sex
- Joy
- Consciousness
- Everything

♥

"Perfume for the soul"

"... a timeless bible for the new millennium."

"Each insight spread through me like rainbow ink. And I remember that I am the gold at that rainbow's end."

CREATIVITY UNLIMITED PRESS

$14.95 US

9 780912 559292   90000>

MORE SELF-HYPNOSIS AUDIO CASSETTES...

 TIME TRAVEL
Access past & future lives with do-it-yourself hypnosis.
ISBN #0-912559-21-7

 MER-KA-BA: *Ascension to the 4th Dimension* Powerful consciousness expansion for highest good. ISBN #0-912559-11-X

 YES, I CAN!
Achieve your personal goals & highest potentials.
ISBN #0-912559-09-8

 PEACE AND CALM
The perfect stress reducer. You need no tranquilizers.
ISBN #0-912559-08-X

 LOSE WEIGHT!
Lose unwanted pounds forever, gaining energy and confidence. ISBN #0-912559-02-0

 NO MORE ALCOHOL
Break free of alcohol. Feel your life again.
ISBN #0-912559-10-1

 I LOVE EXERCISE
Motivation is fun - gets you moving again!

 NO MORE SUGAR JUNKIE
No more sugar blues, feel alive and terrific!
ISBN #0-912559-03-9

 YES, I CAN QUIT SMOKING
Save money, breathe again and feel healthy.
ISBN #0-912559-04-7

 SLEEP, BEAUTIFUL SLEEP
Sleep soundly & feel rested, at home or away. Good stress reduction. ISBN #0-912559-01-2

 THE MONEY TAPE
Create energy that lets money & opportunities appear.
ISBN #0-912559-10-1

 FLIGHT ATTENDANT WELL-BEING A perfect attitude adjuster. Feel happy, positive. ISBN #0-912559-05-5

 GREAT GOLF
Build confidence, play focused, relaxed & improve!
ISBN #0-912559-20-9

 GREAT TENNIS
Improve your game, play focused & have fun!

Self-Hypnosis Audio Cassettes - 60 Minutes Each

ORDER FORM

Treat yourself, your family and friends to mind expanding, life enhancing books and tapes exclusively from Creativity Unlimited

Check the boxes of your choice (if more than one, insert quantity)

BOOKS
- ☐ TIME TRAVEL: PAST LIFE HANDBOOK ....$ 19.95
- ☐ AUTOMATIC WRITING & HIEROSCRIPTING ....$ 9.95
- ☐ EVERYTHING YOU EVER WANTED TO KNOW ABOUT .....$ 14.95
- ☐ HYPNOSIS & CREATIVE WRITING ....$ 9.95
- ☐ HYPNOSIS: Smile On Your Face & Money In Your Pocket ....$ 19.95
- ☐ SEX & OTHER TOUCHY SUBJECTS ....$ 14.95
- ☐ INSIDES OUT ....$ 6.95
- ☐ DENIAL IS NOT A RIVER IN EGYPT: Bust Bizarre Ways ....$ 19.95
- ☐ WEDDING LOVE LETTERS ....$ 9.95
- ☐ CHANNELING: YOU CONDUIT ....$ 11.95

SELF HYPNOSIS AUDIO CASSETTES
- ☐ TIME TRAVEL ....$10 ☐ MEET YOUR ANGEL.............$10
- ☐ MER-KA-BA ....$10 ☐ YOGA NIDRA/HYPNOYOGA $10
- ☐ YES! I CAN ....$10 ☐ THE VIOLET FLAME...............$10
- ☐ PEACE AND CALM ....$10 ☐ SLEEP, BEAUTIFUL SLEEP........$10
- ☐ LOSE WEIGHT ....$10 ☐ FLIGHT ATTENDANT WELL-BEING ...$10
- ☐ NO MORE ALCOHOL....$10 ☐ NO MORE SUGAR JUNKIE.....$10
- ☐ THE MONEY TAPE ....$10 ☐ YES, I CAN QUIT SMOKING $10
- ☐ KUNDALINI RISING........$10 ☐ GREAT GOLF....................$14.95
- ☐ THE WELLNESS TAPE ....$10 ☐ GREAT TENNIS $14.95
- ☐ I LOVE EXERCISE $10

KIDS AUDIO CASSETTES
- ☐ MOMMY BUNNY'S GOING TO WORK $10
- ☐ U R WHAT U EAT $10

MUSIC AND SONG AUDIO CASSETTES
- ☐ DEEP INTO A CALMING OCEAN $10
- ☐ SEX & OTHER TOUCHY SUBJECTS $10

VIDEO
- ☐ TRANCEFORMATIONS: Hypnosis, Channeling & Past Life $19.95
- ☐ HYPNOTICALLY YOURS; Ormond McGill $19.95
- ☐ STATIC GRIT ON MY CD: ☐ Music Video or ☐ Audio Cassette..........$10.00

SUBTOTAL _____

(CA residents add 8.25% tax)
Foreign countries add $3.00 for each item

ADD $2.50 POSTAGE
& HANDLING PER ITEM _____

PLEASE PRINT: **TOTAL** _____

Name _____

Address _____

_____

Phone: (_____) _____

♡ **SEND CHECK OR MONEY ORDER TO:**
CREATIVITY UNLIMITED PRESS®
30819 Casilina Drive, Rancho Palos Verdes, CA 90275 U.S.A.
OR CALL: (310) 541-4844

ORDER FORM

Treat yourself, your family and friends to mind expanding, life enhancing books and tapes exclusively from Creativity Unlimited

Check the boxes of your choice (if more than one, insert quantity)

BOOKS
- ☐ TIME TRAVEL: PAST LIFE HANDBOOK .... $ 19.95
- ☐ AUTOMATIC WRITING & HIEROSCRIPTING .... $ 9.95
- ☐ EVERYTHING YOU EVER WANTED TO KNOW ABOUT .... $ 14.95
- ☐ HYPNOSIS & CREATIVE WRITING .... $ 9.95
- ☐ HYPNOSIS: Smile On Your Face & Money In Your Pocket .... $ 19.95
- ☐ SEX & OTHER TOUCHY SUBJECTS .... $ 14.95
- ☐ INSIDES OUT .... $ 6.95
- ☐ DENIAL IS NOT A RIVER IN EGYPT: Bust Bizarre Ways .... $ 19.95
- ☐ WEDDING LOVE LETTERS .... $ 9.95
- ☐ CHANNELING: YOU CONDUIT .... $ 11.75

SELF HYPNOSIS AUDIO CASSETTES
- ☐ TIME TRAVEL $10
- ☐ MER-KA-BA $10
- ☐ YES! I CAN $10
- ☐ PEACE AND CALM $10
- ☐ LOSE WEIGHT $10
- ☐ NO MORE ALCOHOL $10
- ☐ THE MONEY TAPE $10
- ☐ KUNDALINI RISING $10
- ☐ THE WELLNESS TAPE $10
- ☐ I LOVE EXERCISE $10
- ☐ MEET YOUR ANGEL $10
- ☐ YOGA NIDRA/HYPNOYOGA ... $10
- ☐ THE VIOLET FLAME $10
- ☐ SLEEP, BEAUTIFUL SLEEP $10
- ☐ FLIGHT ATTENDANT WELL-BEING ... $10
- ☐ NO MORE SUGAR JUNKIE $10
- ☐ YES, I CAN QUIT SMOKING ... $10
- ☐ GREAT GOLF $14.95
- ☐ GREAT TENNIS $14.95

KIDS AUDIO CASSETTES
- ☐ MOMMY BUNNY'S GOING TO WORK $10
- ☐ U R WHAT U EAT $10

MUSIC AND SONG AUDIO CASSETTES
- ☐ DEEP INTO A CALMING OCEAN $10
- ☐ SEX & OTHER TOUCHY SUBJECTS $10

VIDEO
- ☐ TRANCEFORMATIONS: Hypnosis, Channeling & Past Life $19.95
- ☐ HYPNOTICALLY YOURS; Ormond McGill $19.95
- ☐ STATIC GRIT ON MY CB: ☐ Music Video or ☐ Audio Cassette $10.00

SUBTOTAL

(CA residents add 8.25% tax)
Foreign countries add $3.00 for each item

ADD $2.50 POSTAGE & HANDLING PER ITEM

TOTAL

PLEASE PRINT:

Name _____

Address _____

_____

Phone: (_____) _____

♡ **SEND CHECK OR MONEY ORDER TO:**
CREATIVITY UNLIMITED PRESS®
30819 Casilina Drive, Rancho Palos Verdes, CA 90275 U.S.A.
OR CALL: (310) 541-4844

ORDER FORM

Treat yourself, your family and friends to mind expanding, life enhancing books and tapes exclusively from Creativity Unlimited

Check the boxes of your choice (if more than one, insert quantity)

BOOKS
- ☐ TIME TRAVEL: PAST LIFE HANDBOOK ....$ 19.95
- ☐ AUTOMATIC WRITING & HIEROSCRIPTING ....$ 9.95
- ☐ EVERYTHING YOU EVER WANTED TO KNOW ABOUT ....$ 14.95
- ☐ HYPNOSIS & CREATIVE WRITING..$ 9.95
- ☐ HYPNOSIS: Smile On Your Face & Money In Your Pocket........$ 19.95
- ☐ SEX & OTHER TOUCHY SUBJECTS ....$ 14.95
- ☐ INSIDES OUT ....$ 6.95
- ☐ DENIAL IS NOT A RIVER IN EGYPT: Bust Bizarre Ways.................$ 19.95
- ☐ WEDDING LOVE LETTERS..$ 9.95
- ☐ CHANNELING: YOU CONDUIT ....$ 11.95

SELF HYPNOSIS AUDIO CASSETTES
- ☐ TIME TRAVEL $10
- ☐ MEET YOUR ANGEL................$10
- ☐ MER-KA-BA $10
- ☐ YOGA NIDRA/HYPNOYOGA $10
- ☐ YES! I CAN......................$10
- ☐ THE VIOLET FLAME.....................$10
- ☐ PEACE AND CALM $10
- ☐ SLEEP, BEAUTIFUL SLEEP...........$10
- ☐ LOSE WEIGHT $10
- ☐ FLIGHT ATTENDANT WELL-BEING $10
- ☐ NO MORE ALCOHOL..........$10
- ☐ NO MORE SUGAR JUNKIE.......$10
- ☐ THE MONEY TAPE $10
- ☐ YES, I CAN QUIT SMOKING $10
- ☐ KUNDALINI RISING.............$10
- ☐ GREAT GOLF....................$14.95
- ☐ THE WELLNESS TAPE $10
- ☐ GREAT TENNIS $14.95
- ☐ I LOVE EXERCISE $10

KIDS AUDIO CASSETTES
- ☐ MOMMY BUNNY'S GOING TO WORK $10
- ☐ U R WHAT U EAT..$10

MUSIC AND SONG AUDIO CASSETTES
- ☐ DEEP INTO A CALMING OCEAN $10
- ☐ SEX & OTHER TOUCHY SUBJECTS $10

VIDEO
- ☐ TRANCEFORMATIONS: Hypnosis, Channeling & Past Life..................$19.95
- ☐ HYPNOTICALLY YOURS; Ormond McGill $19.95
- ☐ STATIC GRIT ON MY CB: ☐ Music Video or ☐ Audio Cassette..........$10.00

SUBTOTAL
(CA residents add 8.25% tax)
Foreign countries add $3.00 for each item

ADD $2.50 POSTAGE
& HANDLING PER ITEM

PLEASE PRINT: TOTAL

Name _____

Address _____

_____

Phone: (_____) _____

SEND CHECK OR MONEY ORDER TO:
CREATIVITY UNLIMITED PRESS®
30819 Casilina Drive, Rancho Palos Verdes, CA 90275 U.S.A.
OR CALL: (310) 541-4844

ORDER FORM

Treat yourself, your family and friends to mind expanding, life enhancing books and tapes exclusively from Creativity Unlimited

Check the boxes of your choice (if more than one, insert quantity)

BOOKS
- ☐ TIME TRAVEL: PAST LIFE HANDBOOK ....$ 19.95
- ☐ AUTOMATIC WRITING & HIEROSCRIPTING................................$ 9.95
- ☐ EVERYTHING YOU EVER WANTED TO KNOW ABOUT ....$ 14.95
- ☐ HYPNOSIS & CREATIVE WRITING..$ 9.95
- ☐ HYPNOSIS: Smile On Your Face & Money In Your Pocket........$ 19.95
- ☐ SEX & OTHER TOUCHY SUBJECTS ....$ 14.95
- ☐ INSIDES OUT ....$ 6.95
- ☐ DENIAL IS NOT A RIVER IN EGYPT: Bust Bizarre Ways.............$ 19.95
- ☐ WEDDING LOVE LETTERS..$ 9.95
- ☐ CHANNELING: YOU CONDUIT ....$ 11.95

SELF HYPNOSIS AUDIO CASSETTES
- ☐ TIME TRAVEL...................$10
- ☐ MER-KA-BA $10
- ☐ YES! I CAN........................$10
- ☐ PEACE AND CALM $10
- ☐ LOSE WEIGHT $10
- ☐ NO MORE ALCOHOL........$10
- ☐ THE MONEY TAPE $10
- ☐ KUNDALINI RISING...........$10
- ☐ THE WELLNESS TAPE $10
- ☐ I LOVE EXERCISE $10
- ☐ MEET YOUR ANGEL..................$10
- ☐ YOGA NIDRA/HYPNOYOGA $10
- ☐ THE VIOLET FLAME.....................$10
- ☐ SLEEP, BEAUTIFUL SLEEP...........$10
- ☐ FLIGHT ATTENDANT WELL-BEING $10
- ☐ NO MORE SUGAR JUNKIE.......$10
- ☐ YES, I CAN QUIT SMOKING $10
- ☐ GREAT GOLF.................$14.95
- ☐ GREAT TENNIS $14.95

KIDS AUDIO CASSETTES
- ☐ MOMMY BUNNY'S GOING TO WORK..$10
- ☐ U R WHAT U EAT..$10

MUSIC AND SONG AUDIO CASSETTES
- ☐ DEEP INTO A CALMING OCEAN $10
- ☐ SEX & OTHER TOUCHY SUBJECTS $10

VIDEO
- ☐ TRANCEFORMATIONS: Hypnosis, Channeling & Past Life...................$19.95
- ☐ HYPNOTICALLY YOURS; Ormond McGill $19.95
- ☐ STATIC GRIT ON MY CB: ☐ Music Video or ☐ Audio Cassette..........$10.00

SUBTOTAL

(CA residents add 8.25% tax)
Foreign countries add $3.00 for each item

ADD $2.50 POSTAGE
& HANDLING PER ITEM

TOTAL

PLEASE PRINT:

Name _____

Address _____

_____

Phone: (_____) _____

SEND CHECK OR MONEY ORDER TO:
CREATIVITY UNLIMITED PRESS®
30819 Casilina Drive, Rancho Palos Verdes, CA 90275 U.S.A.
OR CALL: (310) 541-4844

ORDER FORM

Treat yourself, your family and friends to mind expanding, life enhancing books and tapes exclusively from Creativity Unlimited

Check the boxes of your choice (if more than one, insert quantity)

BOOKS

☐	TIME TRAVEL: PAST LIFE HANDBOOK	$ 19.95
☐	AUTOMATIC WRITING & HIEROSCRIPTING	$ 9.95
☐	EVERYTHING YOU EVER WANTED TO KNOW ABOUT	$ 14.95
☐	HYPNOSIS & CREATIVE WRITING	$ 9.95
☐	HYPNOSIS: Smile On Your Face & Money In Your Pocket	$ 19.95
☐	SEX & OTHER TOUCHY SUBJECTS	$ 14.95
☐	INSIDES OUT	$ 6.95
☐	DENIAL IS NOT A RIVER IN EGYPT: Bust Bizarre Ways	$ 19.95
☐	WEDDING LOVE LETTERS	$ 9.95
☐	CHANNELING: YOU CONDUIT	$ 11.95

SELF HYPNOSIS AUDIO CASSETTES

☐	TIME TRAVEL	$10	☐ MEET YOUR ANGEL		$10
☐	MER-KA-BA	$10	☐ YOGA NIDRA/HYPNOYOGA		$10
☐	YES! I CAN	$10	☐ THE VIOLET FLAME		$10
☐	PEACE AND CALM	$10	☐ SLEEP, BEAUTIFUL SLEEP		$10
☐	LOSE WEIGHT	$10	☐ FLIGHT ATTENDANT WELL-BEING		$10
☐	NO MORE ALCOHOL	$10	☐ NO MORE SUGAR JUNKIE		$10
☐	THE MONEY TAPE	$10	☐ YES, I CAN QUIT SMOKING		$10
☐	KUNDALINI RISING	$10	☐ GREAT GOLF		$14.95
☐	THE WELLNESS TAPE	$10	☐ GREAT TENNIS		$14.95
☐	I LOVE EXERCISE	$10			

KIDS AUDIO CASSETTES

☐ MOMMY BUNNY'S GOING TO WORK $10
☐ U R WHAT U EAT $10

MUSIC AND SONG AUDIO CASSETTES

☐ DEEP INTO A CALMING OCEAN $10
☐ SEX & OTHER TOUCHY SUBJECTS $10

VIDEO

☐ TRANCEFORMATIONS: Hypnosis, Channeling & Past Life $19.95
☐ HYPNOTICALLY YOURS; Ormond McGill $19.95
☐ STATIC GRIT ON MY CB: ☐ Music Video or ☐ Audio Cassette $10.00

SUBTOTAL
(CA residents add 8.25% tax)
Foreign countries add $3.00 for each item
ADD $2.50 POSTAGE
& HANDLING PER ITEM

PLEASE PRINT: **TOTAL**

Name _____

Address _____

_____

Phone: (_____) _____

SEND CHECK OR MONEY ORDER TO:
CREATIVITY UNLIMITED PRESS®
30819 Casilina Drive, Rancho Palos Verdes, CA 90275 U.S.A.
OR CALL: (310) 541-4844